CRADLE OF LIBERTY

NEW AMERICANISTS | A Series Edited by Donald E. Pease

CRADLE OF LIBERTY

Race, the Child, and National Belonging from
Thomas Jefferson to W. E. B. Du Bois

Caroline F. Levander

DUKE UNIVERSITY PRESS
Durham & London 2006

for David Minter

CONTENTS

ACKNOWLEDGMENTS

I have accrued many intellectual debts in the writing of this book. First I thank those institutions whose generous financial support has enabled and enriched this project at every stage: Rice University's Dean of Humanities, the Gilder Lehrman Institute for American History, the Mellon Foundation, and Rutgers University's Center for Childhood Studies. People have been even more important to this book's completion, and I am honored as well as humbled to be able to count such a wealth of individuals as friends. The friends I made at Trinity University have continued to be invaluable to me through the last five years. Jack Kerkering and Heather Sullivan have been infinitely patient, good-humored, and intelligent sounding boards, spirit lifters, and friends through it all, and my thanks to them go beyond words. A number of Rice University friends have been valued, if more recent, interlocutors: Sarah Ellenzweig, Michael Emerson, Alex Lichtenstein, Kirsten Ostherr, Anthony Pinn, and Allison Sneider have enthusiastically talked with me about or read portions of the project. The late Elizabeth Dietz exerted an enduring influence on this work and much else in my life. My thanks to the graduate students in the Mellon Hemispheric Americas Seminar whose smart reading of portions of this project made it stronger: Elizabeth Fenton, Dave Messmer, Cory Ledoux, Molley Robey, Gale Kenny, and Ben Wise. I am tremendously grateful for these local friends and for those sprinkled across the country who, despite distance, have talked, cajoled, listened, suggested, and supported this book. Rachel Adams, Renee Bergland, Eileen Cleere, Teresa Goddu, Barbara Ladd, Robert Levine, Ross Posnock, Shirley Samuels, Xiomara Santamarina, Carol Singley, Rebecca Sterne, Kenneth Warren, Susan Wood, and Elizabeth Young have all reminded me of the value of this project at key moments, and their unquestioning assumption that I would finish made doing anything else unspeakable. The breathtaking wealth of good humor and brain power that all of these individuals put to my use leaves me more thankful than I can say. Family and friends exerted gentle but steady pressure to ensure this book's completion. Thank you Alan Levander, Emmanuel Abaya, Charles and Germaine Field, Mark and Djinni Field, Michele and Steve Vobach, Karen Flack, Tom Killian, Jennifer Slimowitz, Jan and Walker Stewart, and Sue and John Minkoff. Finally, I acknowledge David Minter's enduring and heartfelt belief in my work. It has been my great good fortune to know David. His generosity continues to inspire my thinking.

Parts of this book appeared in different form in *American Literature*, *American Literary History*, *Henry James Review*, and *Prospects*, and I am grateful for permission to reprint. At Duke University Press, the advice of Reynolds Smith and Sharon Torian, and the careful manuscript editing of Molly Robey and Pamela Francis, have been much appreciated.

CRADLE OF LIBERTY

✺

NATAL NATIONALISM:
THE PLACE OF THE CHILD IN AMERICAN
CULTURAL STUDIES

This book begins with a simple assumption that has potentially far-reaching implications for identity-based discourses like feminist and race studies, as well as for liberalist, social-contract, and psychoanalytic theories: While the idea of the child's difference from adults is a fact on which social and civic institutions largely depend and on which a variety of challenges to those same institutions have been premised, the notion of the child's difference from adults has in fact curtailed more far-reaching efforts to rethink the full range of individuals' ethical engagements in a social world. Childhood is now widely regarded as a distinct developmental phase of an individual's life, but as Ian Shapiro points out, "Democratic justice invites us to view such a development with suspicion."[1] At the very least, careful consideration, if not suspicion, of the cultural meanings inhering in child identity is warranted when we consider that the child automatically complicates the very idea of identity that it seems at first to embody. An identity to which all adults can retroactively but no longer actively lay claim, the child refutes the constancy of individual identity even as it represents its most essential premise that each self is stable. In other words, despite — or, more likely, because of — this obvious fact that the child represents the ephemeral and contingent nature of identity, the child, as Adam Phillips has famously observed, remains "our most convincing essentialism."[2]

The trend over the last century to structure ever more social programs

and civic processes around the notion of an essential child identity has codified a conflation of the child with the state that has its origins in the late
eighteenth century. Contending that the child was the index and "thresh-
old of democracy" in the United States,[3] the mental-hygiene movement
that originated at Johns Hopkins University and largely set the terms for
twentieth-century U.S. social-policy debate made explicit the child's primary place within the liberal-democratic state. Believing that the child's
welfare directly contributed to the nation's overall "education . . . social
security, and standards of health" as well as to its international struggles for
"peace and human welfare," the National Committee for Mental Hygiene
and the Commonwealth Fund scientifically documented that the only way
to strengthen the body politic was by emphasizing childhood.[4] Yet if initia-
tives from the 1909 White House Conference on the Care of Dependent
Children to the 1940 White House Conference on Children in Democracy
consistently argued that society could be perfected through the socializa-
tion of the child, surveys by the National Committee for Mental Hygiene
differentiated between kinds of children, noting that "there is more need for
special classes amongst the colored than amongst the white" children if "the
development of citizenship" is to progress.[5] These early-twentieth-century
configurations of the child as a benchmark of the democratic process and its
racial contours reflect the child's longstanding political significance in the
United States. Thus, even as the child became a key structural element in
national conversations about democratic progress, it continued to index the
inadvertent limits and inconsistencies at the heart of U.S. liberal-democratic
processes.

To the extent that the child has been recognized as having larger historical
importance for discussions of U.S. democratic justice, it tends to be understood as reinforcing women's relegation to a private sphere that facilitates,
even as it remains distinct from, public culture. Linda Kerber, for example,
has contended that "in the years of the early Republic a consensus developed
around the ideas that a mother, committed to the service of her family and
to the state, might serve a political purpose. Those who opposed women in
politics had to meet the proposal that women could—and should—play a
political role through the raising of a patriotic child."[6] More recently, Elizabeth Dillon has argued that women's privacy is central, rather than inciden-
tal, to the development of liberalist politics in the United States and thus

that the mother–child relationship pivotal to nineteenth-century American writing works to facilitate the gendered logic sustaining U.S. liberalism.[7] In such models, the child is understood to reinforce and extend women's association with privacy, shoring up an American political culture in which women are dependent and men are autonomous. Such a model, however, ignores how the child challenges as much as stabilizes the distinctions between dependence and autonomy on which the evolution of a liberalist political structure depends. If liberalism proposes that equal political rights inhere in the condition of being human and are thus universal despite differences among individuals, the child functions as a point of origin for the human and thus has occupied a pivotal position in the writing of political philosophers from Locke to Rousseau. Beginning analysis of a U.S. liberal endeavor with the child rather than with the adult subject, therefore, provides a unique opportunity to chart liberalism's inner workings—to see how the child, by simultaneously representing the promise of autonomy and the reality of dependence, both shapes and constantly threatens to disrupt liberalism's two relational antipodes.

Approaching questions of civic representation by way of the child rather than the adult makes explicit the primary, and often unrecognized, importance of racial formations to narratives of U.S. national belonging. Even as political scientists from Ernest Gellner to David Theo Goldberg have long recognized the ethnic and racial origins of nation-states, U.S. political philosophy has consistently failed to acknowledge the role of race in constituting U.S. civic structures, as Cedric Robinson's *Black Marxism* and Charles Mills's *From Class to Race* have made abundantly clear.[8] This oversight has been compounded by the tendency of U.S. cultural scholars to rely on Benedict Anderson's model of nation formation, which tends to obscure the constitutive place of race in a U.S. national imaginary, as Latin American and African American scholars have repeatedly pointed out.[9] When critical commentaries attend to race, they tend to focus on conflicts between different races within the nation rather than on how the nation is imaginatively created and sustained through racial principles. Assuming adult subjects, such studies, in short, have tended to document explicit episodes of racial conflict and thus have overlooked how the child works to establish race as a central shaping element of ostensibly raceless Western ideals. Excavating the child's importance to the development of white supremacy as a social ontology governing liberal democracy is urgently needed, because the ethical understanding of identity for which political philosophers such as K. Anthony Appiah and Martha Nussbaum advocate requires not only reducing overt episodes of racism but also structurally dismantling the racial logic that historically has shaped social encounters in liberal-democratic systems. The following pages uncover this unrecorded history of the child in the hope of opening new possibilities for civic representation by shedding new light on how Enlightenment, liberalist ideals of freedom, equality, and liberty have worked and continue to work in the United States in tandem with their seeming opposites — dependence, exploitation, and subjugation.

The child carries cultural significance in many nations, but the United States offers a particularly rich venue for analyzing the child's importance to the racial premises underpinning liberal democracy because the nation emerges out of a series of racial encounters between Mexican, Native American, Anglo, and African peoples.[10] Yet analysis of the child in an American context illustrates not only how the U.S. nation materializes out of a series of racial conflicts but, more fundamentally, how the nation is imaginatively created and sustained through the logic of racial hierarchy that the child helps to naturalize. In other words, recognizing how the child facilitates a social ontology of white supremacy is certainly an important step in the ongoing scholarly endeavor of charting the centrality of nonwhite peoples to the nation's history — of recognizing, for example, how Hispanic soldiers played crucial roles in eradicating slavery in the South during the Civil War and in charging up San Juan Hill during 1898. But more fundamentally, such analysis suggests that the concepts of marginality and social dependence that are often used to identify those involved in such lost histories are as important a part of a U.S. liberal endeavor as are the concepts of autonomy and independence with which such an endeavor is more commonly associated.

Scholars are increasingly recognizing the child's centrality to American literary culture. While it is indeed the case that the figure of the child often stands opposed to that of the adult in American writing, this book explores the proposition that this opposition is itself crucial to American political thought and the literary cultures that surround and help to produce it. As such, the following pages argue that American literary and political texts do not so much include child subjects as depend on them to represent, naturalize, and, at times, attempt to reconfigure the ground rules of U.S. national belonging. Charting this untold story reconstitutes critical understandings of nineteenth-century American literary as well political cultures, revealing how the rise of the child does not merely coincide with but helps to constitute American writing and the public cultures it produces. Thus, I ask, most broadly, how approaching American writing with a child rather than an adult subject in mind reframes what we think we know about political and literary forms; how the unique convergence of social forces that the child represents for readers and writers affects our understanding of civic representation and identity; and, finally, how excavating a long history of the child's centrality to U.S. writing alters familiar and well-worn ways of conceptualizing the interlocking ideas of self and culture.

We can begin to delineate the child's importance to U.S. culture by turning to the political, literary, and social discourses that set and recalibrated the terms of national belonging. In his 1853 fictional account of Thomas Jefferson's mixed-blood daughter, *Clotel*, William Wells Brown, for example, declares that the founding fathers who "boast that America is 'the cradle of liberty'" have effectively "rocked the child to death" with their commitment to slavery.[11] Fifteen years later, the Southern author and slavery apologist Augusta J. Evans predicted to General Beauregard that slavery's abolition would produce "a mighty convulsion, which will swing this 'cradle of liberty' . . . as it was never rocked before."[12] Brown's and Evans's invocations of a child in danger of being destroyed by the nation's dramatically shifting racial politics draws on a longstanding association of the new nation with a child. Whether it be John Adams's declaration that Great Britain's "child colonies are of the same ancestry" as the "old English folks" and so "won't be their Negroes" or Thomas Paine's argument that "the infant state of the colonies" justifies their "separation from a corrupt parent" country committed to denying their inherited "rights and liberties,"[13] the child is consistently featured in early national political rhetoric to constitute the very national entity it represents. And if the child acts as a founding myth through which the new nation comes into being, writers such as Brown, Paine, and Adams—whether critiquing or upholding the racial logic centering the new nation—consistently recognize the founding importance of race to the national myth the child represents. The modern nation-state emerging in the late eighteenth century with the American Declaration of Independence and the French Revolution, as early national political commentators consistently recognized, conceptually depended not only on "color and race even more than birth"[14] but, more particularly, on the child's capacity to represent the racial contours of the emerging nation to establish its claims to legitimacy.

At the same historical moment that the child operates as an organizing figure around which national memory is retroactively created and retained, the child simultaneously comes to denote an innocent, natural self seemingly unmarked by social categories like race — a self that writers from Ralph Waldo Emerson through W. E. B. Du Bois would seek to reconstitute beyond the nation's convulsive reach. If every society is organized differently, each "with a distinctive orientation to the self," as Diane Margolis points out, the child works to remind each self of an original "infancy" that "conforms to nobody."[15] Thus, either through a return "to the woods," where "a man" can remember that he is "always a child," or through careful contemplation of the child who exists fleetingly beyond the "veil of race," individuals are consistently encouraged to find in the child the seemingly authentic, pre-social self with which the child had become exclusively equated by the late eighteenth century.[16]

Cradle of Liberty assesses the interdependencies of these two coincidentally emerging concepts of self and state that the child represents. Charting the ways in which the child personalizes the nation and, conversely, makes a tacitly racialized nation a constitutive part of the self, the project explores how state and self intermingle through the child — how the child's capacity to align self with state through the racial narrative the child represents creates and maintains the civic selfhood at the center of a U.S. liberal-democratic tradition. The emergence of the modern nation-state and of the modern child in the late eighteenth century and nineteenth century have been subjects of intensive critical inquiry in the last two decades, yet missing from these two rich bodies of work has been an assessment of how these two ideas work in tandem — how the child who is increasingly understood to be separate and in need of protection from civic life has historically helped to constitute and buttress the nation. The project of *Cradle of Liberty* is therefore to explore how the coincident emergence of the distinct category of childhood with the rise of the modern nation-state affects the creation, expansion, contestation, and duration of modern nations like the United States.

Since the nineteenth century, cultural and political commentators have observed the diverse ways in which race marks and orders the modern nation-state, as Ernest Renan notably remarked, but the child's centrality to this process has gone largely unrecognized.[17] Similarly, critical interest in the child that has emerged in the disciplines of anthropology, cultural studies, history, sociology, psychology, and literature in the wake of Philip Ariès's landmark *Centuries of Childhood* has produced rich analyses of children's social place within and conceptual centrality to different nations,[18] but it has yet to analyze how the emergence of the child as a distinct category of identity helps to found and uphold national culture in the first place. Meaning "to be born," the root of nation, "natio," derives from the idea of the child, and the concept of nation continues to be understood within the founding context that the child provides. Alexis de Tocqueville, for example, observed in *Democracy in America* that "the growth of nations" remains most readily observable "in the cradle of the child."[19] More recently Jacques Rancière has reminded us that birth is a founding "principle of sovereignty" in liberal democracy, where nativity is aligned with nationality so powerfully that natural life appears as the source and bearer of rights.[20] Yet the child is central not only to the state that was invented to govern strangers, but also to the idea of the citizen that was invented to people the state. A mother country, fatherland, and "patria" as much as a child, the United States, "like a family," confers a sense of identity and belonging among its members by re-creating accustomed family relations and extending the nation's founding image of the child to transform those diverse individuals within its physical boundaries into a collective entity committed to creating and upholding a shared civic environment. Thus, just as the idea of the United States as an independent nation is naturalized through a racially inscribed child, so, too, does the nation create a shared environment among isolated individuals by extending this founding racial image to create a distinctive idea of civic selfhood among its members. If the emergence of the nation-state depends on the hardening of the modern dichotomy between adult and child, as Sharon Stephens has suggested,[21] the child therefore naturalizes the very nation that it summons into being through its capacity to constitute individual as well as national identity through the racial narrative it tells. Operating as a reference point for the state and for individuals in various stages of affiliation with it, the child, in other words, works to integrate individuals into the state by racially configuring both. Not simply representing the mythical racial purity of the nation-state or the often marginal civic status of racial others living within such a nation, the child, in short, more fundamentally constitutes self as well as state through representing racial identity as a constitutive element of each.[22] The political integration of citizens into a large-scale society is one of the undisputed historical achievements of the nation-state, as Jürgen Habermas has recently pointed out,[23] and as the following pages illustrate, the child brings subjects potentially at odds with an evolving liberal democratic order into alignment with the state by representing race as constituting each at key junctures in the development of both.

While the significance of race to national formations has been long recognized among political theorists, its importance to constituting a modern concept of the self that the child represents has received less critical attention.[24] "Self" in Anglo-Saxon means "same" and thus has long carried with it a notion of identity and likeness, but Saint Augustine was the first to recognize the importance of the child in shaping identity.[25] Of course, the concept of the self has evolved and changed over historical time, as Charles Taylor has persuasively illustrated, and by the Romantic period, depictions of the child were shot through with a racial content, as William Blake's poem "The Little Black Boy" reminds us.[26] Declaring that his "soul is white" though he is "black as if bereaved of light," Blake's child narrator seeks the recognition of the "English child" who is "white as an angel"—recognition that is achievable only once individuals acknowledge the inevitable centrality of race to the social interactions in which they are engaged. Blake's black boy experiences what the speaker of Lunsford Lane's "The Slave Mother's Address to Her Infant Child" recognizes as unavoidable for her child. While her child is able to "fancy in thy dreams but thou are as free as a bird," the mother—just as W. E. B. Du Bois would fifty years later when he contemplated the passing of his first-born child—distinguishes between fancy and fact, foretelling the inevitable drawing around the infant of "the curtain of despair" wrought by race.[27] Refuting the very possibility of freedom from the social order that its "beauty of innocence" and "shining angel infancy" represent for self-declared "child-lovers" like Nathaniel Hawthorne, the child, as Blake's and Lane's lines make clear, does not so much represent a self untouched by social influences "that might embitter or pollute its waters" as function as a vehicle through which these influences are maintained and upheld.[28] As a result of its complex social significance, the child therefore acquires an "underestimated sensibility" that transforms it for many nineteenth-century Americans like Hawthorne from "a holy thing" into its seeming opposite — "a spirit strangely mingled with good and evil" that is "frightening" because of its indeterminate combination of the "elfish" and "angelic."[29] Laced with cultural significance that disrupts the innocence and authenticity with which nineteenth-century Americans desire to imbue it, the child thus reveals the series of maneuvers through which the idea of the "authentically human" becomes part of the machinery of constructing a civic self.

Writers like Walt Whitman recognized how the child increasingly equated with the self emerges out of and remains of necessity embedded within a complex web of social structures. Even as he acknowledges the child's unique role as representative of a pre-social, pure, and innocent self, Whitman pushes against such popular Romantic understandings of the child. It initially might seem counterintuitive to think of Whitman as contemplating the constructed nature of the child's authenticity, given that he is, after all, the U.S. writer arguably most deeply committed to finding and relishing the genuine. And yet precisely because Whitman's writing purportedly searches for the unmediated and celebrates the authentic, he offers a rich commentary on the child who is assuming a privileged position as bearer of authenticity and "true consciousness" in the nineteenth century. We can begin to see how Whitman comments on the child's increasingly overdetermined place in American culture in "There Was a Child Went Forth," which documents the child's irrevocable imbrication in the social processes that are fundamental to American civic life. Never sequestered from public encounter, the child ventures forth every day, and, as Whitman asserts,

> The first object he look'd upon, that object he became,
> And that object became part of him for the day or a certain part of the day,
> Or for many years or stretching cycles of years.[30]

Not distinguishable from those objects that make up public life, the child absorbs into itself as a foundational part of its identity, the objects that it encounters in an essentially social world. Whitman invokes the private, domestic sphere with which the child tends to be exclusively equated when he depicts

> The mother at home quietly placing the dishes on the supper-table,
> The mother with mild words, clean her cap and gown,
> a wholesome odor falling off her person and clothes as she walks by,
> The father, strong, self-sufficient, manly, mean, anger'd, unjust,
> The blow, the quick loud word, the tight bargain, the crafty lure,
> The family usages, the language, the company, the furniture, the
> yearning and swelling heart.[31]

But such affections are constructed as much as genuine, in that they simultaneously create both "the sense of what is real" and "the thought if after all it should prove unreal."[32]

To consider Whitman's interest in the child is, in some ways, to be reminded of the child's longstanding importance to sexuality studies. From Havelock Ellis, Sigmund Freud, and Erik Erikson to recent efforts of queer theorists such as Michael Warner, James Kincaid, Chris Nealon, and Lee Edelman, among many others, the child has been the point of origin from which to rethink narratives of sexual identity and development.[33] Acknowledging the importance of this work, *Cradle of Liberty* nonetheless largely brackets questions of sexuality, not so much because sexuality can be detached from the child's cultural importance, but, instead, because such work has already been capably undertaken, while the racial contours of the child's impact on civic life remain uncharted. Similarly, I am interested in the child not so much because it upholds as transgresses gender difference, and so I attend less to distinctions between boy and girl children (though I would certainly agree that such distinctions exist) and more to the overarching category of the child. The enduring impulse to equate the child with gender divisions of labor, as I suggested at the outset, has delimited the terms of liberalist critique. Therefore, while I am indebted to the work of many who have capably shown the child's importance to maintaining and developing middle-class culture in the nineteenth-century United States,[34] I resist understanding the child as an outgrowth of bourgeois culture precisely because such an alliance is only a portion of—and thus tends to obscure—the longer history of the child's political importance to national development.

Figure 1   Walt Whitman with Jeannette and Nigel Cholmelly-Jones, courtesy
Library of Congress Prints and Photographs Division (LC-USZ62–92196).

My methodological approach to considering the interdependencies that
the child forges between the U.S. nation-state and the self builds on current research in literary and cultural studies that moves beyond a nationalist
approach to American studies. Even as scholars have pointed out that the
"America" around which the field is organized both conflates the Americas
with the United States and obscures the significance of local and regional
subcultures within the nation, we have continued to assume adult subjects
as the starting point for a critical reconsideration of the shape and texture of
a postnationalist American studies. The child offers a unique vantage point
from which to contribute to this important task of rethinking the place,
dimensions, and duration of the national not only because the child has historically been firmly aligned with the nation, but because the child has become a densely overdetermined imaginary location, often associated with
a self understood to precede or be partially free from the more firmly fixed
political identities of individuals residing within the nation's borders. *Cradle
of Liberty* argues that it is not the child's dissociation from but, rather, its

centrality to the key political debates crystallizing national identity that enables the child to act as a persuasive vehicle through which individuals come to affiliate with the nation at pivotal moments in its development, such as the annexation of the Republic of Texas and the "liberation" of Cuba. With its attention to the child as a primary vehicle through which individual representation within a shifting U.S. liberal-democratic society can be both frustrated and made possible, *Cradle of Liberty* charts the child's conceptual centrality to current critical reconsiderations of both the history and enduring political vitality of liberal-democratic citizenship, even as it argues for the child's centrality to current efforts to think beyond what Jonathan Arac has termed "the impoverished choice between liberalism and identity politics."[35]

Although the child has long been understood as a touchstone for an autonomous, independent self, the child has recently emerged, for scholars of liberalism, as the connective tissue through which the state and the self mutually constitute and shape each other in an increasingly postnational, global era.[36] Declaring that "the self whose choices liberalism celebrates is not a pre-social thing—not some authentic inner essence independent of the human world into which we have grown—but rather the product of our interaction from our earliest years with others,"[37] Appiah, for example, invokes the child to argue that liberalism cultivates rather than frustrates an individual identity that is not so much at odds with the state, as many liberalist scholars have tended to assume, as in need of help from the state to achieve its highest potential.[38] Asking readers, "Shouldn't society step in, in the name of individuality and identity, to insist that children be prepared for life as free adults?"[39] Appiah features the child over which the state exerts a unique amount of power, as John Stuart Mill recognized long ago, to advocate for a liberalism that acknowledges the inevitable dependence of the self on a social world.[40] Yet the child as importantly indicates the state's reliance on the idea of a self in whose behalf society must advocate. Masquerading as essential if historically evolving, the state, in other words, requires the self that the child represents in order to maintain the perception of its power. If "the citizen is the foundation of every social world," as John Tomasi has argued, societal success "requires that ordinary people *behave*" and understand their self in particular ways.[41] This dependence of the state on the idea of self extends back to the nation's origin, as John Adams acknowledged when he pointed out that "the Revolution was effected before the war commenced . . . in the minds and hearts of the people" who had undergone a sea change in their conception "of their duties and obligations" to the state. Experiencing what religious leaders termed a "New Birth," early Americans suddenly recognized themselves as "free agents," according to one Philadelphia minister, and this new attitude toward the self produced new understandings of the state.[42]

Attending to the child highlights this founding affiliation between self and state, illustrating that just as there is no self before the state, there is no state before the creation of the self. Such analysis of the child clarifies an enduring if mistaken idea that "still lingers in the minds" of some liberalist thinkers, according to John Dewey, that "there are two different spheres . . . that of political society and that of the individual."[43] Because of the biological facts of a child's physical size and dependence, there is a current tendency in popular political debates to feature the child to advocate for diverse political agendas by invoking ethical and political categories such as abuse and exploitation. When deployed in such ways, the child not only sustains these dual, separable ideas of self and state even as these discussions attempt to alter the relative relation between the two, but, more particularly, the child also works to facilitate a shift of social responsibility from the state onto the self. The idea that liberal democracy is in crisis has long been a staple of American political life and, as Charles Willard illustrates, such "calamity-howling diverts attention from other [urgent social] problems, consequently feeding state power."[44] In other words, the child at the center of "crisis" debates, ranging most recently from the Pledge of Allegiance to obesity, aids the state in relocating essentially social obligations onto the very individuals who are in need of help from the state to sustain its civic principles. Thus, in such contexts the child facilitates what Mill, predicting Dewey, identified as the persistent and mistaken idea plaguing liberalism that there is an endemic "conflict between government and the liberty of individuals" rather than "an entire social order" that might be committed to the "nurture and direct[ion of] the inner as well as the outer life of individuals."[45] Analysis of how the idea of the child mutually constitutes and differentiates self and state is therefore urgently needed if we are to achieve the social justice with which liberalism is primarily concerned.

As we have seen, such debates tend to feature the child as the test case for a diverse range of liberal agendas. However, because they fail to recognize how the child has long maintained the racial hierarchy endemic to the nation and the liberalist thought governing it, such political deployments of the child inevitably retain a social ontology that forecloses liberalism's radical social potential. Race, as William Chafe points out, is "the Achilles heel of the liberal tradition, challenging its capacity to grow and evolve organically in service to democratic values," and it will remain so until "leaders and citizens" recognize "the original sin of American democracy."[46] This "sin" is, of course, slavery and the white-supremacist logic naturalizing it. As Simon Gikandi reminds us, "The moment that has given us immutable liberal values such as freedom and democracy also contains the seeds of the greatest evil of our time." Thus, the question with which liberalists should concern themselves is "how race came to be embedded in what should have been larger forms of identity such as humanism, modernity, and culture" and how "the very institutions that were supposed to will into being universal and cosmopolitan identities were not simply corrupted by racialism but were immanently racialist and racist."[47] It is only by interrogating the deep logic governing liberalist ideals rather than the social programs growing out of such ideals—a logic in which, as Charles Mills reminds us, "race is in no way an afterthought, a deviation from ostensibly raceless Western ideals but rather a central shaping constituent of those ideals"—that liberalism can become more radical.[48]

To the extent that the child represents the liberal-democratic state, it takes on and perpetuates the racial meanings inhering in that social entity. Analysis of the child therefore does not simply index who suffers from racism (and is therefore equated with a child) but, more fundamentally, reveals racial domination to be a system—like patriarchy—that underpins and enables liberal-democratic societies. The following pages are therefore concerned primarily not with tracking episodes of overt racial prejudice but, rather, with charting how racial hierarchy infuses and determines the ground rules governing social encounters between individuals, regardless of their racial identity. Such a focus, I believe, will not only show the extent to which white supremacy has historically governed liberal democracy. It will also suggest avenues to move beyond the conceptual limitations currently encumbering liberalist pursuits. Such an endeavor requires a reframing of our understanding of the child to reshape existing relations between the individual and the state. "What liberalism requires of us," as Martha Nussbaum insists, "is something more chancy and fearful" than what we currently have, "some combination of adulthood and childhood" that redraws the boundaries separating adult from child, self from state, and that forces us to confront the most "alarming thing about equality," which is that "we are . . . children, and the question is, where is father? We know where we are if one of us is the father."[49] This acknowledgement that we are all partial, dependent citizens as much as the autonomous beings that liberalism assumes is the starting point for any sustained effort to move toward a more comprehensive and capacious model of equitable social interaction and acknowledgment.

Cradle of Liberty's story of the mutually enforcing alliance the child forges between self and nation-state begins in the late eighteenth century and extends through the nineteenth century, with a series of defining events — the U.S. Revolutionary War, the U.S.-Mexican War, the U.S. Civil War, the example of German imperialism, and the U.S. expulsion of Spain from the Caribbean and Cuba — that consolidate the nation's boundaries and generate a heightened sense of unity within the nation. My analysis focuses on literary as well as political narratives because both play a formative role in shaping, as well as reflecting, public perceptions of the nation's territorial expansion and alliances. Extended attention to these narratives reveals the nation to be a contingent, hotly contested political entity that features the child in a wide range of dialogues to expand its transnational influence even while competing for dominance with localized communities and other, often overlooked North American nations like the Confederacy, the Republic of Texas, and Mexico. Specifically, I reconsider some of the most significant literary genres and movements (abolitionist fiction, the sentimental novel, regional writing, and anti-imperialist commentary) and political events (the end of slavery, post-Reconstruction national reunification, and the emergence of an American psychological school) from the precise vantage point of the nation's enduring conceptual dependence on the idea of the child. Doing so reveals that the child has been a sustaining force for the nation from its origins to the present time and thus that the child is of crucial, if so far largely unrecognized, significance to American cultural studies.

Developing largely out of women's studies' attention to motherhood, domesticity, and women's socially marginal status, children's studies has recently made important contributions to our knowledge about the lived experiences, material cultures, and social networks of real children.[50] Acknowledging the significance of this new information about childhood, *Cradle of Liberty* nonetheless does not take the lives of real children or children's literature as its subject. Rather, it focuses on the idea of the child as a rich site of cultural meaning and social inscription.[51] I am interested in the child as a series of representative possibilities rather than as a biological category, so I attend less to who can or cannot be a child or where childhood ends than to the child's signifying responsibilities. Approaching the child as not only born but made — as not only a biological fact but a cultural construct that encodes the complex, ever shifting logic of the social worlds that produce it — offers important insight, I suggest, into thus far neglected, hidden processes of cultural signification. From such a vantage point, the child emerges as not just another distinct category of identity along with class, race, gender, and sexuality but, instead, becomes a vehicle through which these elements of individual identity are stabilized and made legible as distinct aspects of the self. By approaching the child as integral rather than ancillary to the conceptual emergence of the idea of the nation-state, we can begin to understand how the child not only reflects the various class, gender, racial, and sexual ideologies prevailing *within* the United States, as many scholars have richly documented,[52] but more fundamentally how the child functions as a primary building block out of which the interlocking concepts of self and state on which ideology depends emerge. As the blank slate on which the self is shaped and scripted, in other words, the child has maintained the conceptual premise of self from Rousseau to Freud to John Rawls, even as that self's relation to social forces has undergone dramatic reconceptualization.

While I remain interested in the child's representational possibilities rather than in its lived reality, I do want to acknowledge that real children can be deployed to strategically challenge, as well as uphold, the racial principles governing U.S. liberal ideals. The actual child's importance to refuting as well as consolidating U.S. democratic principles is nowhere more evident than in important court cases regarding racial desegregation, from *Sarah Roberts v. City of Boston* (1849) and *Plessy v. Ferguson* (1896) to *Brown v. Board of Education* (1954).[53] Charles Sumner begins his 1849 argument for Boston school desegregation by emphasizing that questions of social justice inevitably hinge on the child—that it is "a little child, of a degraded color, . . . still within the period of natural infancy . . . [who] asks at your hands her *personal rights*." The personal rights of this child require the city of Boston to decide nothing less, according to Sumner, than "the fundamental principles of human rights."[54] After collapsing distinctions between the "real" child who has suffered racial prejudice and the ideological child who has historically naturalized such prejudice, Sumner proceeds to extend the founding image of the child to shape the court's role, which he insists is to act as a "parent to all the unfortunate children of the Commonwealth." The court will only "show itself most truly parental, when it reaches down and with the strong arm of the law, elevates, encourages, and protects its colored fellow-citizens.[55] Despite Sumner's masterly deployment of both the biological and ideological child, Massachusetts Supreme Court Chief Justice Lemuel Shaw found that prejudice was fostered rather than ameliorated by compelling colored and white children to associate together in the same schools. He thus found against Sumner's argument to overturn what Sumner coined "separate but equal" education. Not only did state courts from Nevada (in *Stoutmeyer v. Duffy* [1872]) to West Virginia (in *Martin v. Board of Education* [1896]) use Shaw's finding in *Roberts* as a precedent for upholding racial segregation in schools, but the Louisiana Supreme Court turned to Shaw's decision to uphold its findings in *Plessy v. Ferguson* (1896) that an "unreasonable insistence upon thrusting the company of one race upon the other, with no adequate motive, is calculated, as suggested by Chief Justice Shaw, to foster and intensify repulsion between them rather than extinguish it."[56] Yet the child who challenges segregation in *Roberts* not only upholds segregation in *Plessy* but offers a loophole, as well, for *Plessy* specifies that desegregation can and must occur around any white child who has need of black adults.[57] The child proves integral not only to legal reaffirmations of racial prejudice, but also to the final demise of the "separate but equal" policy that Sumner first used the child to challenge. Supreme Court Chief Justice Earl Warren based his 1954 *Brown v. Board of Education* decision on the testimony of the child psychologist Kenneth Clark, whose famous doll experiment on sixteen school-age children served as evidence that black children, "who are subjected to an obviously inferior status in the society in which they live, have been definitely harmed in the development of their personalities."[58] Convinced by Clark's testimony, Warren finally upheld Sumner's 1849 argument that children "nursed in the sentiment of Caste, receiving it with the earliest food of knowledge, . . . are unable to eradicate it from their natures. . . . [T]heir characters are debased, and they become less fit for the magnanimous duties of a good citizen."[59] Basing his findings on the real children on whom Sumner had earlier relied to make his argument, Warren found — in words reminiscent of Sumner's — that separating black children from white "generates a feeling of inferiority as to their status in the community that may affect their hearts and minds in a way unlikely ever to be undone."[60]

As this brief overview of over one hundred years of legal findings on school desegregation suggests, "real" children often took on the complex ideological representations in which the child had long been engaged and, in so doing, provided individuals with rich opportunities to re-script, as well as uphold, the ground rules of civic governance. Therefore, even though this study is not primarily concerned with actual children, I include visual images of children as well as discursive representations of the child to punctuate the full range of the child's complex social meanings. Images such as *Little Ethiopians* (see figure 2), for example, captures the child's multivalent representations in such social and juridical debates as those just outlined. These "little Ethiopian" children, like Sarah Roberts, have a racial identity that precludes their equal civic affiliation. The popular image thus seems to endorse the idea of "separate, but equal" for little Ethiopians, as well as for little Americans. However, precisely because they must remain little Ethiopians rather than becoming little Americans, the image suggests that the black children represent a constituency of potentially autonomous black selves capable of demanding social and political representation and thus able to reconstitute social space along the lines laid out by social contract theorists such as Locke.

One aim of *Cradle of Liberty* is to rethink the enduring tension that exists between social-contract and psychoanalytic theorists' accounts of the self and the social, even among those who attempt to bridge the conceptual gaps between the two lines of inquiry. John Rawls, for example, recently considered the importance of psychological accounts of the self and the desire with which they are primarily concerned to realizing a politically liberalist

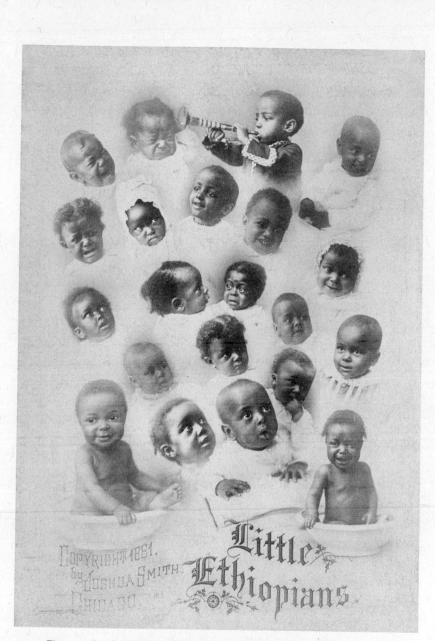

Figure 2 "Little Ethiopians." Courtesy New-York Historical Society (7731d).

model of social justice. Illustrating how individuals' desire inevitably works in the interest of a political ideal of citizenship, Rawls concludes that citizens are not only "normal and fully cooperating members of society, but further [that] they want to be," and want "to realize in their person, and have it recognized that they realize, that ideal of citizens."[61] Pointing out psychoanalysis's often overlooked political utility, Christopher Lane takes issue with such reductions "of desire to basic assumptions about volition and need."[62] Arguing that individuals are not simply an imprint of their national structures, he contends that it is a grave mistake to assume that desire operates according to "conscious and rational precepts," particularly in light of the enduring, acute social injustices that exist within liberal-democratic societies.[63] Even as they seek to bridge the divide separating their respective practices, Rawls's and Lane's accounts actually work to reinforce, rather than refute, the differences that have long existed between the two. Yet even as social-contract theorists' attempts at synthesis continue to subordinate the idea of self to the state and psychoanalytic accounts of identity subordinate the state's historical evolution to a transhistorical self, attention to the child that grounds both lines of inquiry reveals their shared origins, assumptions, and conceptual limitations. Charting the historical unfolding of the child who, for Locke, represented irrationality and thus the limits of consensual governance and who, for Freud, represented the point of origin for theories of individual desire therefore reveals the shared origins and history of these seemingly divergent practices — origins and history that have been subsequently obscured in the twentieth century as a direct result of the child's success in constituting self and state as discrete, at times diametrically opposed, concepts.[64] Further, analysis of the child that has historically constituted an essentially expansionist United States offers important correctives to the oft-cited inattention of both lines of inquiry to the international dimensions of justice, selfhood, desire, and the human.[65]

Throughout the book at large, I approach the idea of nation as historically evolving, yet conceptually fluid, and as integrally engaged in expansionism from its earliest genesis.[66] This project remains attentive throughout to the fact that even though imperialism only began to acquire an invidious meaning at the end of the nineteenth century during the Spanish–American War of 1898 and the Boer War of 1899–1902 (a fact that many critical commentaries of imperial cultures reproduce), the emergence of imperialism coincided with and irrevocably shaped the creation of nation-states like the United States, a fact that Adam Smith's magisterial *Wealth of Nations* (1776) makes abundantly clear by arguing, at the very same moment that the American colonies are creating a separate nation, that the idea of nation is outmoded, parochial, and in the process of being replaced by an international free-market capitalism more profitable to all developed nations than colonialism and nationalism.[67] Choosing such geographic sites of engagement to map the racial contours of the U.S. nation-state as the nation-founding conflict between the colonies and Britain, the U.S.-Mexican border disputes of the antebellum era, and the transnational alliance between the United States and Germany from 1776 on but peaking in the post-Bismarck period beginning in 1891, the six chapters that make up *Cradle of Liberty* offer a representative rather than a comprehensive view of the operations of U.S. racialized nationalism over the course of more than a century. However, such encounters collectively suggest the range, shape, and texture of the nation's reliance on the idea of the child. Realizing that I just as easily might have chosen other productive sites to explore the dynamics of U.S. nation building—Hawaii and the Philippines being just two of many examples— I have selected those particular episodes which highlight the flexibility and capaciousness of the nation and the child that represents it. Even so, because the project attends to U.S. engagements with other nations, it opens itself to the charge of exceptionalism. Yet I suggest that the following chapters do not so much engage in as delineate the contours of the United States' exceptionalist history. By stabilizing the individual within a firmly fixed national imaginary, the child keeps the United States at the narcissistic center of political debate. We can see the workings of the national absorption that the child stimulates in an immensely popular image that circulated widely after September 11, 2001 (figure 3). Translating a complex, violent expression of geopolitical tension into a centralizing narrative of U.S. victimhood, the image circulated nationally to unify the racially diverse U.S. populace it depicts behind the Bush administration's aggressive policy of dominating demonized racial others. If 1989 signaled the triumph of the Western ideal of liberal democracy, as Francis Fukuyama has observed, then such images reveal the child's role in authenticating that triumph even as the United States engages in a global war on terror. Yet as Frederick Douglass reminds us in "What to the Slave Is the Fourth of July?" the child with which

Figure 3 "Girl with Flag." Courtesy Ethan Miller/Reuters.

the nation has long been equated has the potential to impede as well as to perpetuate the deep logic of race structuring U.S. culture: Douglass suggests that "fellow-citizens" are capable of "tearing away . . . the hideous monster" that is "nursing at the tender breast of [our] youthful republic," even after the Civil War.[68] This book charts a history of the child's role in liberal-democratic processes in the hope of contributing to those processes' present and future vitality. Thus, the following chapters ask, most generally, how acknowledging the racial meanings inhering in child identity might reconstitute critical understandings of American political as well as literary culture. But they collectively encourage a rethinking of the child as a cultural ideal to which we are committed.

Like my approach to nation, I conceive of the idea of self not as a static structure but as a process, as did major late-nineteenth-century psychologists like William James, Pierre Janet, and James Mark Baldwin—prominent psychologists who pioneered what Russell Meares has identified as the "school of self" that was eclipsed during the last half century of positivism and behaviorism but that has recently begun to be rediscovered and reintegrated into psychological and psychoanalytic discourse.[69] Psychoanalytic, anthropological, philosophical, sociological, and cultural-history accounts of the self have tended to assume a certain equivalency between the child and the self. Yet this impulse to identify the child as the point of origin for the self has its own history—a history as recent and contested as that of the nation-state, for all we tend to think of both as permanent, rather than transitory, features of the human landscape. The project, in other words, excavates the historical evolution of what the philosopher Joseph Margolis has described as certain cultures' impulse to invoke "its own offspring" as a way of "forming encultured selves," and it does so by mapping the child's circulation through dominant discourses of self, such as American psychology and the novel.[70] Encouraging individuals to foster a civic self—to give themselves over to a collective that requires isolated individuals to consent to creating a shared environment—the discourses of self that the novel and American psychology promoted feature the child not so much to foster and privilege a private or pre-social self as to inculcate the specifically civic self that, as Hobbes noted, predominates in modern democracies and is characterized by a love of order, country, and social betterment.[71] Such a self Charles Taylor has recently identified as essential to "civic humanism," or the belief that humans, when properly motivated, can maintain a new structure of social relations in which, with a sense of oneness with others, individuals engage in the modern experiment of creating a liberal-democratic world defined by order, security, and peace.

The book's six chapters chart the child's representations of self and state from the early national period to the child's crystallization of the self through the rise of American psychology and the state through the rise of imperialism. Beginning with the acknowledgment that literary production, social theory, and political culture were integrally blended in the pre-twentieth-century United States, each chapter considers the dual questions of American literature's political impact and American political culture's literary effects. To bring literary and political texts into the most richly productive play, the chapters span a diverse range of archival as well as literary sources to explore the child's obscured links to the racial politics governing U.S. national culture and to show how political representation in the United States emerges and continues to be shaped by the "fact" of racial identity. Thus, the first chapter illustrates how the child featured in a wide range of literary, political, and social texts organizes the new nation through a logic of white supremacy so powerfully that subsequent abolitionist writing depends on the enduring association the child creates between race and nation to argue for slavery's abolition. By featuring child protagonists as the linchpin of their abolitionist argument, popular periodicals and stories like *The Slave's Friend* (1836) and *Tales of Peter Parley about Africa* (1830) argue for slavery's abolition by reinforcing the idea that such unbridgeable differences distinguish black from white individuals that slavery can be abolished without jeopardizing the racial logic on which the nation was founded. I am interested in this chapter in showing that the child featured in a wide range of early national texts represents a foundational, and increasingly urgent, national question of where freedom ends and slavery begins as a drama of racialized bodies that might have various desired outcomes but nonetheless is unimaginable in terms other than those of essential racial difference.

The second chapter illustrates how pro-slavery as well as antislavery political rhetoric depends on the child's alignment of race with nation. Recognizing the South as a product of and response to a diverse range of regional, and national, constituencies fighting for dominance along the Mexican border in the antebellum era, this chapter illustrates how the child that is featured in political rhetoric to justify the creation of the Republic of Texas in 1836 and the U.S.-Mexican War in 1848 in turn operates as a cornerstone for Southern writers like Augusta J. Evans to argue for the creation of yet another nation—a separate Southern nation that would uphold the white supremacy the United States was forgetting in its increasing commitment to freeing its slaves. By situating North–South relations within a broader set of geographic struggles that reveal the U.S. imperial contest to be ongoing inside as well as outside of the nation's expanding boundaries, chapter 2 illustrates not only how the child organizes the United States around white supremacy so powerfully that slavery can be abolished without undermining the nation's racial principles, but conversely how the child constitutes race as an organizing principle of oppositional, if ephemeral, Anglo nations that temporarily challenge the United States by retaining slavery as a logical corollary to white superiority.

The third chapter illustrates how popular nineteenth-century novels that do not interest themselves with slavery or race relations nonetheless feature child protagonists to encourage readers to align themselves with these competing, often contested national interests. In an effort to argue for the importance of popular novels, feminist scholars have approached the protagonists of sentimental novels as "little women" rather than the children they in fact are. Once we recognize these characters as children, we can begin to recognize how such protagonists — precisely because they are children — operate as part of a more extended textual machinery devoted to resolving the particular social and contractual problem that children represented for the nation since its inception. Sentimental novels, chapter 3 suggests, not only utilize the child's unique capacity to represent the nation but also help to resolve the particular problem that children as a class of people inherently incapable of consent pose to the Lockean consensual model of liberal-democratic community around which the nation was constructed. By featuring children as stand-ins for complicated sets of anxieties about national unity, popular novels, in short, present children as agents of national interpellation — as powerful vehicles for soliciting readerly consent to national affiliation and governance precisely because of children's uniquely contested relation to the national body.

Taking U.S.-German transnational relations as its focus, chapter 4 explores the child's role in creating and critiquing late-century U.S. expansionism. The conviction that the United States was a white nation certainly facilitated its expansionist era, but white supremacy continued to function as an imperfect crusading ideology, shot through with more contradiction than is often recognized. Taking the transnational dimensions of the child's ideological significance as its focus, chapter 4 explores how the child protagonists that Mark Twain features in his early 1890s transatlantic writing represent race as complicating rather than sustaining national progress. After charting how the "universal history" perspective propounded by contemporary nineteenth-century social scientists like John Fiske, James Nourse, Theodore Poesche, and Robert Knox aligns the United States and Germany because of the two countries' shared Aryan ancestry, this chapter illustrates how the child protagonists in Twain's little-known 1891 translation of the popular German children's story *Der Struwwelpeter* and in his 1894 *Pudd'nhead Wilson* and *Those Extraordinary Twins* challenge this idea that racial purity explains national supremacy. Illustrating that the purity of "the Anglo-Saxon race" is "an illusion," the child protagonists in Twain's German translation in turn offer an important, and thus far overlooked, context for understanding Twain's critique of U.S. race relations in *Pudd'nhead Wilson* and *Those Extraordinary Twins*. From the perspective the preceding German stories provide, in other words, we can see how Twain's insistence on the conjoined twins' prior history as an attraction in "a cheap museum in Berlin" operates as a pivotal context for analyzing his 1894 commentary on U.S. racial politics. We can see, in short, how instrumental the racial purity the child represents is to an evolving U.S. international, as well as national, project.

Chapter 5 explores how late-nineteenth-century American psychological models of the self that take the child as their interrogatory subject in turn depend on the child's longer history as a representative of the nation's racial contours. In his 1919 "A Child Is Being Beaten," Freud acknowledges how foundational the history of U.S. racial logic is to the psychological self the child comes to represent when he writes that it is "almost always the same books" —books "such as . . . *Uncle Tom's Cabin* . . . whose contents give a new stimulus to the beating phantasies" of his patients. Chapter 5 illustrates, first, how pivotal American psychological models that posit the child as a special site for understanding the self in fact emerge out of a longer conceptual dependence on the child as a representative of an explicitly racialized nation, and second, how writers like Henry James and Pauline Hopkins refute the racialist psychological self the child comes to represent. The distinctly American school of psychology being developed at institutions like Harvard and Clark University in the 1890s and represented by such texts as William James's *Principles of Psychology* (1890), James Mark Baldwin's *Social and Ethical Interpretations in Mental Development* (1897), and G. Stanley Hall's *Adolescence* (1904) therefore not only ensure that the child continues to represent race as an essential, increasingly fixed element of the self well into the twentieth century, but also enable the critique of such a concept of self by writers ranging from James to Hopkins.

The concluding chapter of *Cradle of Liberty* brings the child's longstanding alliance with both self and state together through analysis of Cuba's enduring conceptual importance to the innovative models of nation developed by advocates of an alternative nationalism like W. E. B. Du Bois. Exploring the child's enduring legacy as an image through which the foundational place of race within the state continues to be contested and consolidated over the course of the late nineteenth century and early twentieth century, this chapter analyzes how early-twentieth-century black intellectuals like Du Bois developed the earlier thinking of writers like Twain, James, and Hopkins to explore the full range of possibilities for individual representation within the racial state. Fascinated with Cubans' struggle for independence, as well as with the psychological theories of self in which he was trained under William James, Du Bois features the child through which insurgent Cubans justified their pursuit of an antiracist independent republic to explore the possibility of renegotiating the increasingly fixed place of race in U.S. political culture. Placing Cuban political rhetoric that featured the child and the children's stories of the Cuban political commentator José Martí in *Le Edad de Oro* in conversation with Du Bois's depictions of the child in such texts as *Dark Princess*, *The Souls of Black Folk*, and *Darkwater* and with the wealth of commentary on Cuba in popular African American periodicals, this concluding chapter suggests that with their "Immortal Child" and "children of our America," Du Bois and Martí, respectively, complicate the liberal-democratic nationalism the child long represented. In so doing, they offer provocative opportunities for rethinking American literary and political history from the vantage point that analysis of the child makes available.

Covering wide-ranging texts, movements, and national formations from the late eighteenth century through the twentieth century, *Cradle of Liberty* illustrates that the child operates as a rich vehicle for constituting U.S. national identity through the idea of racial purity; for scripting competing, alternative nations into being in relation and opposition to the United States; for rethinking the relation between race and nation; and for representing racial identity as a prerequisite for incorporation into the national body. By exploring how diverse imaginings of the nation result from the child's capacity to represent race, this book excavates a long, vital history of cultural and political interaction between these two concepts of nationhood and childhood. It argues for the political necessity of taking seriously the child that these diverse literary and political cultures produce, because this child tells an important story not only about how the United States emerged as a global force, but also about how it continues to endure in an increasingly postnational, global era.

one

THE CHILD AND THE RACIAL POLITICS OF NATION MAKING IN THE SLAVERY ERA

I n his famous critique of slavery, *Considerations on the Keeping of Negroes* (1754), John Woolman emphasizes how arbitrary, if well entrenched, the association of slavery with "colour" has become in the Colonies by asking his reader to consider the plight of a child. The suppositional child to whom Woolman draws his reader's attention is a "white child" who, abandoned by the death of its parents, comes under the power "of a person, who endeavours to keep him a slave." The sense of outrage this image of an enslaved white child provokes in individuals otherwise untroubled by the idea of the "many black [who] are enslaved" is, according to Woolman, the direct result of the generally accepted, if "false," idea in the Colonies "of slavery being connected with the black colour, and liberty with the white." Woolman uses a child to explain how "colour," and the ideas of essential racial difference that have become associated with it "through the force of long custom" may justify slavery, but in so doing he hopes to convince his readers that these "false ideas [that] twis[t] into our minds" finally undermine the Colonies' abiding commitment to liberty.[1] Over a hundred years later, as the nation goes to war to determine the fate of slavery within its borders, the popular *carte de visite* of "Rosa, Charley, and Rebecca: Slave Children from New Orleans" (figure 4) uses the child to ask its viewers the same question: how can a nation that is, as Lincoln asserts in the Gettysburg Address, "conceived in Liberty, and dedicated to the proposition that all men are created equal"

OUR PROTECTION,

ROSA, CHARLEY, REBECCA.

Slave Children from New Orleans.

Figure 4 "Our Protection: Rosa, Charley, and Rebecca" (ca. 1861–65).
Courtesy Gilder Lehrman Institute of American History (GLC 5111.02/1052).

condone slavery?[2] Not so much protecting the three seemingly white children it cloaks as indicating their vulnerability to the slave institution the nation continues to countenance, the American flag comes to symbolize the contingency, rather than the unprecedented ascendancy, of freedom in the new nation, and the disjunction between the children's racial identity and the surface color of their skin makes palpable the final inadequacy of race to justify slavery in a nation that is founded on principles of freedom.

As these exemplary representations suggest, the child that is consistently featured in a wide range of political tracts and popular narratives from the Revolutionary era to the Civil War operates as an important ideological site for representing the shifting conceptual place of race within the new United States. While Russ Castronovo, Jay Fliegelman, and Ronald Takaki, among others, have documented how the Colonies' political separation from Great Britain was compared to a child's inevitable separation from its parent, and thus how the child operates as a powerful icon of a new nation in U.S. political rhetoric, such repeated representations of the child not only help to create a cohesive national identity but also, as Woolman's account and the image of Rosa, Charley, and Rebecca make clear, more particularly register the extent to which this national identity has been shot through with a racial subtext that constantly threatens to undermine, even as it enables, a unified account of U.S. nation formation.[3] The white child featured in political texts therefore not only represents a coherent narrative of the nation's political origin that is subsequently challenged in the antebellum era by black as well as by white social commentators, as scholars like Castronovo have importantly pointed out, but also registers in its representation of race the inherently fractured and contradictory nature of the nation it exemplifies.[4] In so doing, the child functions as a particularly rich discursive site that both authorizes a distinct national identity and, in its depiction of the integral, complicating place of "colour" in that identity, reveals the conceptual instabilities that have been embedded within the nation since its inception.

The child's capacity to represent race as both constituting and complicating U.S. national identity deserves particular attention at the current critical moment, when a wealth of scholarship has, on the one hand, identified the centrality of race to national formations and, on the other hand, undertaken to theorize the child's ideological significance to U.S. public cultures. While "race and nation are never very far apart," as Etienne Balibar has pointed out, they exist in particularly close proximity in the case of the United States.[5] There, as Stephen Jay Gould has noted, the nation's founding document, Jefferson's Declaration of Independence, and the widespread publication of Johann Friedrich Blumenbach's *De Generis Humani Varietate Nativa*, a treatise on racial classification and taxonomy that would provide much of the foundation for contemporary racial categorization, appear at precisely the same historical moment.[6] Such a convergence points to the ways in which the genesis of the United States, like that of many modern nations, depends on what Charles Mills has described as an obscured racial, as well as sexual, contract that partitions "human populations into 'white' and 'nonwhite' " individuals and that transforms a citizenship of "we the people" into one of "we the white people."[7] Yet the wealth of recent studies that have assessed the child's political significance to a wide range of U.S. public cultures thus far has not assessed how the child's capacity to forge founding alliances between race and the new nation may prove crucial to the political work it subsequently accomplishes in public life. The recent work of Lauren Berlant, Gillian Brown, James Kincaid, and Michael Warner, for example, has tended to overlook how the racial meanings historically inhering in the child they take as their subject may in fact help to shape the numerous political cultures to which they show that the child richly contributes.[8] However, charting the crucial role the child has historically played in transforming nonwhites into racial others from the early national period through the nineteenth century creates an important cultural context for understanding the child's ongoing significance to these wide-ranging U.S. social formations. Excavating the child's conceptual centrality to the constitution of a tacitly racialized infant nation explains, for example, why the ideal type of "patriotic personhood in America," as Berlant has noted, continues to be the "infantile citizen."[9] Therefore, if the comparison of racial others to children is widely recognized, analysis of the child's role in instantiating race as an integral, enduring, and complicating element of U.S. national identity creates a crucial context for understanding its enduring cultural power.[10]

The following pages will explore how these repeated discursive representations of the child work initially to install and then to reinforce race as a founding, unstable element of the new nation. Indeed, the depictions of the child consistently featured in various popular narrative forms in the roughly hundred-year period between the wars represent a primary, and increasingly urgent, national question of where freedom ends and slavery begins as a drama of racialized bodies that might have various desired outcomes but is nonetheless unimaginable in terms other than those of essential racial difference. Thus, regardless of which side of the slavery debate it is representing, the child operates as a powerful vehicle for establishing a logic of racial difference that links slavery to black bodies and liberty to white ones in order to found the nation and then reinforce its organizing racial ideals as it eradicates slavery. By representing national identity in explicitly racialized terms, the child featured in a wide range of texts helps to consolidate one of the largest shifts in thinking about identity in the history of the United States. Indeed, the success of this project appears so total that by 1857 U.S. Supreme Court Justice Roger B. Taney can argue for the majority in the case of *Dred Scott v. Sanford* that African Americans are "so far inferior, that they ha[ve] no rights which the white man [is] bound to respect."[11] Yet if this juridical declaration seems to suggest that ideas of essential racial difference have been firmly established as part of the natural order by mid-century, in what follows I chart how the figure of the child proves so integral to the process through which such ideas come to be perceived as natural in the first place that, even after slavery is abolished, color continues to operate as a powerful organizing principle of U.S. national identity. Consistently overlooked in Judge Taney's oft-quoted and infamous answer to the question of the individual's place in a racial state is the conceptual importance of the child—the fact that Scott's case hinged on his two children, Eliza and Lizzie. Born on board the steamboat *Gipsey*, north of the line of the State of Missouri, Eliza, like her sister Lizzie, who was born in the State of Missouri, posed the greatest challenge to Taney's question about race and citizenship—in short, about whether "a negro whose ancestors were imported into this country" but who is "born of parents who become free before [her] birth" can be a "citize[n] of a State, in the sense in which the word citizen is used in the Constitution."[12]

"A CHILD BLENDS IN HIS FACE THE FACES OF BOTH PARENTS"

By the time that Ralph Waldo Emerson made this claim in 1856, ideas about racial identity and concerns about the social cost of obscuring clearly defined racial differences were well-established topics of popular discussion and were widely acknowledged to have national significance for the future of U.S. political culture. If the child is literally a composite of its parents' bloodlines, as Emerson suggests, the characteristics associated with particular bloodlines made questions of blending them finally questions of prime significance to the present and future political well-being of the nation. When Emerson states that the very "fortunes of nations" depend on "the deep traits of race" inhering in their inhabitants, he summarizes a longstanding popular view that a nation's success is a direct result of the characteristics of the race that inhabits it. Happily for the United States, the nation's "Fair Saxon" people have historically ensured its "democratic principle" with the "decision and nerve" that are as unique to their racial makeup as their "fair complexion, blue eyes, and open and florid aspect." With their "fair hair, blue eyes, and . . . fine complexion," these Anglo-Saxons are "the only race which truly comprehends the meaning of the word liberty," and they therefore use the incomparable "resources of mental and moral power that the traits of the blonde race betoken," according to social commentators like Robert Knox, to "hit on that capital invention of freedom."[13] Given the mission, according to James D. Nourse, "of reconciling order and liberty, and teaching mankind the science of government," the Anglo-Saxon founders of the nation create "a government that has been formed so entirely for the good of the people," according to Francis Lieber, that "never in the history of the world has so much wisdom and humanity been shown in . . . civilization."[14] Thus, the child featured in figure 5—a child who, as George Bancroft reminds readers of *Literary and Historical Miscellanies* (1855), "inherits" not only "the physical" but the "moral characteristics of the race to which it belongs" and thus its "true instinct for liberty"[15]—epitomizes an explicitly Anglo-Saxon commitment to, and expression of, liberty in the new nation. The "unquestionably . . . distinguished . . . aptitude for free institutions" and "unconquerable love of liberty" that the child featured in the carte de visite represents for its viewers therefore forms the very foundation of, as well as the justification for, "our American liberty," as Nourse writes in *Remarks of the Past and Its Legacies to American Society*.[16]

Such popular nineteenth-century commentaries on the racial origins of the nation are a direct outgrowth and extension of early national political discourse, which consistently likens the Colonies to a child wrongfully enslaved because of its Saxon, freedom-loving blood. Indeed, in a wide range

Figure 5 "Boy Dressed as Drummer." Courtesy New-York Historical Society (75784d).

of political narratives, the nation's founders use the image of a child to advocate for the establishment of an autonomous political entity that is based on, and fully realizes, the Anglo-Saxon love of freedom inhering in its inhabitants. By persistently imagining the Colonies to be a child that is wrongfully enslaved because of its racial identity, the nation's founders describe the emergence of an autonomous political entity as the logical result of the race of its inhabitants. As the "common children" of their "brethren of Great Britain," the Colonists, according to James Otis, should exist in "a state of equality and perfect freedom" with their parent country.[17] "Descended from the same common ancestors" as the people of Great Britain—"great and glorious Ancestors" who, according to the conveners of the First Continental Congress, "participated in all the rights [and] liberties" of free government and not only "maintained their Independence" but also transmitted "the blessings of Liberty" to all their offspring—the colonists have a biologically inherited predisposition to pursue liberty and protect freedom.[18] Indeed, it was because of this biological imperative that their "forefathers . . . left their native land, to seek on these shores a residence for freedom" and thereby extended the Anglo-Saxon love of liberty to new parts of the world. Ever "born the heirs of freedom," according to Congress, these early colonists "retain[ed] the strongest love of liberty" shown only by the "pre-eminent rank of English Freemen" as they built a new colony in America.[19] As Congress declares in 1775, it is this illustrious Anglo-Saxon "ancestry," and none other, "from which we derive our descent."[20]

Yet even as this shared racial heritage does not stop Great Britain from planning to "enslav[e]" rather than encourage the freedom of its "fellow subjects in America," the racial characteristics of the Colonists ensure that they will pursue freedom even if they must finally break from the parent country. After asking the people of Great Britain if "the descendants of Britons [shall] tamely submit" to "nothing less than "a ruinous system of colony administration" that is expressly calculated for "enslaving these Colonies," the Continental Congress asserts that their shared Saxon "spirit of freedom," as well as "the memory of our gallant and virtuous ancestors," makes "surrender[ing] those glorious privileges for which they fought, bled, and conquered" unthinkable.[21] Able to imagine because of this racial heritage "nothing so dreadful as voluntary slavery," the Colonists are therefore able to do nothing less, according to "A Declaration by the Representa-

tives Setting Forth the Causes and Necessity of Their Taking Up Arms,"
than resolve "to die Freemen rather than to live Slaves."[22] Moving from
the desire for the "Peace, Harmony, and mutual Confidence, which once
happily subsisted between the Parent Country and her Colonies" to an un-
wavering commitment to "disarm[ing] the parricide which points the dag-
ger [of slavery] to our Bosoms," Congress uses the image of the child on the
verge of enslavement to insist that the Anglo-Saxon identity of the Colonies'
inhabitants justifies their conclusion that "our attachment to no Nation on
Earth should supplant our Attachment to Liberty."[23]

The racial characteristics of the enslaved child Colonies require that they
not only break from Great Britain but continue to distinguish the inchoate
nation the Colonists create from all others. Indeed, the founding fathers
emphasize the extent to which racial characteristics operate as an organizing principle of nationhood when they try to convince other nations that, by
not permitting the Colonies to enjoy in quiet "the inheritance left us by our
forefathers"[24] but "forging Chains for her Children" in America, Great Britain has relinquished all right to govern the Colonies. In its July 1775 "Speech
to the Six Confederate Nations, Mohawks, Oneidas, Tuscaroras, Onondagas, Cayugas, Senekas, from the Twelve United Colonies," for example,
Congress uses the story of a child who "carries a little pack" for its parent
to emphasize the new nation's loyalty to the racial tradition that its father
fails to keep.[25] After telling the six Indian nations that the king of England
assured "our fathers" that the "covenant chain which united" them would
ensure that "their children should be his children," the Congress describes
how such a father forgets the racial ties that should bind him to this child.
Convinced by a jealous group of servants that the child walks too easily, the
father enlarges the child's pack, heedless of its request that "the pack might
be lightened." The child "takes it up again" obediently, but when he finds
himself staggering under its weight and asks once more for relief to no avail,
he throws off the pack instead of allowing it to "crush him down and kill
him." In so doing, this child representative of the Colonies is not so much
disobeying as pleading for justice and defending "the old covenant-chain
of the fathers" that bound them in a racial tie the parent has disregarded.
Therefore, when this "child" representative of "America" finally takes up
the "hatchet" against its father, it does so, according to the Congress, not
for "conquest" but, instead, to protect and assert the love of liberty that is in

the blood it shares with the stubborn parent who ignores the dictates of its racial heritage.[26] So racially dissolute as to be able to destroy those who are "of the same blood as themselves"—indeed, capable of a "black and horrid design" against liberty that calls into question its own racial purity— Great Britain will treat non Anglo-Saxons even more cruelly, Congress tells its nonwhite audience to persuade them to support the Colonies.[27]

The racial logic that the child represents generates the new nation, but it also, in turn, enables slavery to exist within it. As cultural historians have pointed out, ideas about essential racial difference proved crucial to resolving the founding contradiction between slavery and liberty that initially threatened the early United States.[28] Indeed, because blacks "are inferior to the whites in the endowments both of body and mind," as Thomas Jefferson writes, slavery becomes justifiable and necessary in a country founded on the concept of freedom.[29] Fellow Virginian St. George Tucker concurs with Jefferson when he asserts that, because "Africans are really an inferior race of mankind," they should be "exclu[ded] from a society in which they have not yet been admitted to participate in civil rights," particularly if the nation's leaders want to avoid "depreciat[ing] the whole national character."[30] When Jedidiah Morse defines the American people in his 1789 *American Geography* as only those who "are descended from the English," he is insisting on the racial purity of this "national character," regardless of the numerous racially diverse individuals inhabiting America.[31] Thus, as Kenneth Warren has noted, while slavery when used as a synonym for tyranny may "not always carry with it the full social and historical weight of African-American enslavement," the image of the enslaved child that is repeatedly deployed by Anglo-American Colonists to justify their separation from Great Britain works to establish and maintain not only Anglo-American freedom but also African American slavery as a practice consistent with the new nation's racial heritage.[32]

However, the child featured in early national political rhetoric not only represents freedom as the exclusive right of Anglo-Americans and slavery as the natural condition of racial others. It also consistently registers the conceptual inconsistencies underpinning these particular associations between race and nation. Therefore, even as it represents white supremacy as a conceptual point of origin for the nation, the child registers the contradictions inhering in the exclusive alignment of whiteness with U.S. identity. James

Otis challenges the predominant impulse to premise national identity on racial attributes when he insists, in *The Rights of British Colonies Asserted and Proved* (1765), that the Colonists both "black and white" are "free born" and therefore are "entitled to all the essential civil rights" for which the Colonies are preparing to fight.[33] Abigail Adams, like Otis, insists that the nation's ideal of liberty should be of more importance to the nation's founders than the racial distinctions on which it supposedly rests when she declares that the "passion for liberty cannot be equally strong in the breasts of those who have been accustomed to deprive their fellow creatures of theirs."[34] But it is Thomas Jefferson who uses the popular political image of a child to represent how the racial logic justifying the new United States may finally undermine its defining ideological commitment to freedom. Invoking the child to chart how the nation's racial logic can be at odds with the slavery that it seems initially to justify, Jefferson describes the influence that a slaveowner's "boisterous passions" and "unremitting despotism" have on the white child who "looks on [as] the parent storms. . . . Nursed, educated, and daily exercised in tyranny," such a child, regardless of the liberty-loving impulses coursing through its veins, must inevitably "catch the lineaments" of its parent's "wrath" and "imitate it" on a "circle of smaller slaves."[35] By teaching the child to be a despot, such training, to Jefferson's mind, effectively undermines the racial characteristics the new nation is supposed to exemplify and is therefore catastrophic for American independence as well as for the child who represents and protects it. Operating as a complex, shifting signifier of both the nation's racialized love of liberty and the challenge that its commitment to slavery finally poses to its defining ideals, the child becomes a rich vehicle for expressing the discrepancies, as well as the political possibilities, of race as a cornerstone and an engine of national identity. At once representing the nation's defining commitment to freedom and what Samuel Hopkins terms "the inconsistence [*sic*] of promoting the slavery of the Africans, at the same time [as] we are asserting our own civil liberty," the child featured in political narratives, in other words, simultaneously represents Anglo-Americans' love of liberty and the ways in which the racial logic on which the nation is founded finally undermines its identity—the ways in which, as Otis writes, "those who every day barter away other men's liberty will soon care little for their own."[36]

Black petitioners for liberty appropriate the child's multivalent political meanings in an attempt to upset the prevailing alliance of racial with national identity and thereby advocate for their own freedom in the new United States. Developing Hopkins's notion that "maintaining this struggle for our children's liberty" while "holding so many blacks in slavery" will "weaken the claim [of] the natural Rights of our American Brethren to Liberty," such petitioners consistently used the image of a wrongfully enslaved child as a centerpiece in their attempts to challenge a racial logic that claimed freedom as an exclusive characteristic of Anglo-Saxon citizens.[37] By equating themselves with the wrongfully enslaved child because they were "stolen from the bosoms of tender parents and brought hither to be enslaved," the Massachusetts slaves advocating for freedom in 1773, for example, exploited the child's complex representation of race's role in nation making to insist that their liberty be recognized by the men who are themselves fighting "against the designs of their fellow men to enslave them."[38] After invoking both their own condition and "the miserable Condition of Our Children," who remain unjustly in a "State of Bondage and Servitude," Connecticut slaves in 1779 ask their "good mistress, the free State of Connecticut" to recognize their "freedom and independence" in their own ongoing "war with tyranny."[39] Just as political petitioners draw on Colonists' reliance on the image of a wrongfully enslaved child to advocate for freedom, so, too, does Phillis Wheatley famously use the child, in *Poems on Various Subjects, Religious and Moral* (1773), to argue that her "love of freedom" depends not on her racial identity but on the experience, acquired "young in life," of being "snatch'd" from Africa. While this "seeming cruel fate" enslaves her as a child, it finally teaches her to resist "tyrannic sway" and, in so doing, readies her to be a free citizen of the new liberty-loving nation, not in spite but because of her racial identity.[40] It is this unique capacity to love liberty not because it has been long enjoyed but rather because it has been withheld that leads Massachusetts slave petitioners to ask that "their Children who wher Born in the Land of Liberty not be heald as Slaves" but, rather, fulfill the destiny of what they in fact are — "a freeborn Pepel."[41]

Important as it is that both blacks and whites use the image of the child to advocate for freedom, my point is not so much that the child was available to multiracial constituencies as that the image itself helps to fix race as an integral, founding, if initially unstable element of the new nation's identity. As a linchpin in the formation of U.S. national identity, the child, as we have seen, represents the new nation as essentially racial—as a direct outgrowth and product of Anglo-Saxon characteristics that in turn distinguish the emergent nation from all others and work to justify slavery within it. Yet even as the child featured in early national political rhetoric helps to organize national identity around the idea of white supremacy—even as it helps to transform "we the people" into "we the white people" in the United States—it registers the conceptual limitations endemic to this association of race with nation. However, as the slave question becomes an urgent national concern in the antebellum period—as, according to Abraham Lincoln, the question of whether this nation is a slave nation is the question indisputably before the American people—the child increasingly represents whiteness not as a variable but as an unequivocally preeminent cornerstone of the nation's political identity to ensure that race will continue to organize national identity after slavery is abolished. In other words, if the child featured in early national political writing registers the ideological incongruities of white supremacy as a premise of national identity even as it aligns the two, the child at the center of abolitionist rhetoric increasingly insists that whiteness is an essential element of the nation's structure and identity, as racial others are on the verge of joining its citizenry. Thus, while abolitionist political rhetoric "force[d] the practitioners of racial oppression to develop a theory" of essential racial difference, as George Fredrickson has shown, abolitionists conversely depended on the idea of white supremacy, and the child who represents it, to argue for slavery's abolition.[42]

We can see clearly how the child works in abolitionist rhetoric to reinforce the founding association of white superiority with national identity in arguably the most famous U.S. antislavery novel ever written, Harriet Beecher Stowe's *Uncle Tom's Cabin*, and in its child protagonists, who, as Stowe reiterates, function as "representatives of the two extremes of society." After placing "the fair, high-bred child, with her golden head . . . and her black, keen, subtle, cringing, yet acute neighbor" side by side as "representatives of their races," Stowe insists that insurmountable, essential racial differences will continue to differentiate the two even as she uses the child to bridge enduring distinctions between slave and citizen. The comparison that Stowe draws between "the Saxon, born of ages of cultivation, command, education, physical and moral eminence; [and] the Afric, born of ages of oppression" illustrates how abolitionist rhetoric strategically uses the child to insist that the white superiority that has historically structured the nation will continue to unequivocally and forcefully organize it, once freedom is granted to all.[43] No matter how appealing, the black child, according to the Reverend R. R. Raymond, cannot function as an equally compelling imaginative catalyst for conceptualizing the nation's ideals of liberty, because such a child is not of the race whose love of liberty initially birthed the nation.[44] Overlooking what Charles Chesnutt and others would later insist on—that both the changing definitions of race in the South and the racial amalgamation that the child often represented work to blur the strict color line separating blacks from whites—Stowe's argument for freeing slaves depends on a logic of essential racial difference in which the "all-pervading, all-conquering Anglo-Saxon race" is destined to remain superior to and separate from all other races, regardless of their status as slave or free.[45] Therefore, by using the child to insist on the ongoing, inevitable cultural power of whiteness, Stowe, in the tradition of much abolitionist political rhetoric, successfully persuades her audience that ending slavery will affirm, rather than undermine, the nation's Anglo-Saxon identity—will affirm, rather than jeopardize, race as the nation's constitutive and enduring ideological element.

The success of Stowe's insistence that white supremacy remain a necessary and sufficient precondition of national identification and affiliation is evident in the commentary of many who fought to free the slaves. As Abraham Lincoln declares, "All *feel* and *understand*" intuitively that slavery is wrong, "even down to the brutes and creeping insects" who hold a proslavery position. "So plain that no one, high or low, ever mistake[s] it," the correct feelings about slavery are intuitively shared both by "the man who wishes to take the good" of slavery and by "the most dumb and stupid slave that ever toiled for a master."[46] Indeed, it is only those individuals, according to Henry David Thoreau, who show such "a universal woodenness of both head and heart" as to be in danger of having "livers in the place of hearts" who can mistake "that moral sentiment" that makes all men free. Challenging all citizens to develop "heart room" for those "more deeply oppressed" than themselves, slavery offers a unique opportunity for individuals to reaffirm their collective commitment to a nation defined by liberty. Exciting in the populace "the activity of a common principle," slavery, in other words, does not impede as much as ensure that "all men shall feel as brethren, and mingle their hearts in anthems of gratitude and love" as they undertake to uphold and protect national governance. As a result, "the nation" will experience "a new birth" — "its heart [will be] opened" and true, abiding "sentiment [will be] awakened in America."[47] Binding individuals to the nation-state ever more powerfully, Wilson Armistad concludes, the collective task of freeing slaves within the nation will thereby ensure that the nation's "liberty" will continue to "be [an] expansive" and vital part of the nation's identity.[48]

Yet even as individuals increasingly consent to the project of eradicating slavery, they do not consent to eliminating the racial logic that the child upheld as a cornerstone of the nation. As James Russell Lowell declares in "The Prejudice of Color," the "colored people of the so-called free states are still held in slavery by something stronger than a Constitution": they are held in slavery by nothing less than "the force of a depraved and unchristian public opinion."[49] More visceral than attitudes about slavery, ideas about racial difference are subsequently much more difficult to dislodge. Reinforcing collective consent to the idea that nonwhite individuals warrant less consideration, Lowell describes how, just as "newspapers . . . say the *Honorable* Member of Congress . . . to excite our favorable sympathies" in their readers, they inevitably "say a *colored* man or woman to indicate that there is no need of our troubling our sympathies at all" about the black man, slave or free.[50] Abraham Lincoln highlights this sharp divergence in thinking about slavery and race when he declares in 1858 that he is adamantly opposed to slavery but has never "been in favor of bringing about in any way, the social and political equality of the white and black races." Convinced that the "physical difference between the white and black races . . . will forever forbid the two races living together on terms of social and political equality" and therefore that "blacks must remain inferior," Lincoln represents prevailing public ideas about race held even by those actively fighting to free the slaves.[51] The antislavery-leaning Union soldier John Jones, for example, asserts in an October 3, 1862, letter to his family that he expresses the general sentiments of soldiers when he insists that he does not "want to fight for the nigger"; rather, he wants to erase "the black stain of human slavery" from "the fair escutcheon [of] America, the boasted 'land of the free.'"[52] Making a crucial distinction between the black race and the "black stain" that slavery leaves on the national character, Jones insists that many soldiers' "prejudice of color" does not allow them to fight for "the negro."[53] Thomas Draper concurs, asserting that he cannot fight to promote the emancipation of "the Negro," because the black race "is an inferior grade."[54] Even those few soldiers, like Oliver Edwards of the 37th Massachusetts Regiment, who insist that "the term abolitionist is the proudest name one can bear," declare that they fight primarily because they want to "leave the blessing of freedom to our children and our children's children as we received it from our Sires of the Revolution but without the foul blot of slavery."[55] Thus, regardless of whether they have any "sympathy with *the abolition* plan" or fight "simply to save the Union and put down rebellion," many soldiers, according to George Tillotson of the 89th New York Volunteers, believe that even if "the negro is a *human* being and as such has a right" to freedom like the "white man," the "farther he gets from" whites, "the better it please me."[56] Consenting both to abolishing slavery and to retaining white supremacy as a defining characteristic of the postbellum nation, these correspondences suggest the enduring importance of racial hierarchy to nineteenth-century constructions of individual as well as national identity.

Analysis of such abolitionist rhetoric in general, and of the slave-ship stories that are its centerpiece in particular, reveals the specific process through which the child installs whiteness in the national imaginary so completely that race operates as one of its ongoing organizing principles even after slavery is abolished. As Herbert Klein has recently shown, abolitionist slave-ship stories captured "the popular imagination" of American writers and readers alike with unprecedented force in the antebellum era, and they did so in large part because they reread the dominant narrative of nation formation explicitly within the context of the nation's involvement in the slave trade.[57] In these stories, the child operates as a "key cultural and political artefact," representing, as Paul Gilroy has suggested slave-ship artifacts inevitably do, a rich, diverse range of associations between racial and national traditions.[58] Insisting that the nation's genesis and resulting identity depend as much on African American slaves' labor as on Anglo-Americans' struggle for liberty, the child featured in slave-ship stories seems, at first glance, to reclaim a suppressed national history of racial difference to challenge the nation's conceptual reliance on white supremacy. It is precisely such an alternative, suppressed, and hybrid history with which Nathaniel Hawthorne seems to be interested in "Chiefly about War-Matters," his popular 1862

Atlantic Monthly essay. Hawthorne declares that the "children of the Puritans" are connected with those of the "Africans" through a "historical circumstance, known to few" that indelibly binds "the character of our sacred ship," the *Mayflower*, to that of the slave ship.[59] By suggesting that the African, as well as the Anglo-Saxon, race is indispensable to, and generative of, the national story, Hawthorne seems to challenge the idea that the nation was founded exclusively on the Anglo-Saxon love of freedom inhering in its citizens.[60] Indeed, in Hawthorne's account, the often overlooked fact that the nation's genesis and development depends on blacks as well as whites because of the history of the slave trade explains the "instinctive sense of kindred" that nineteenth-century Anglo-Americans subsequently feel for African American slaves and their "irresistible impulse to attend [to] their rescue, even at the cost of blood and ruin."[61] However, while Hawthorne is willing to revise American history and identity in light of its often unrecognized dependence on Africans—while, in other words, he is willing to script into the official national story the "monstrous birth" that causes the nation's "white progeny" to "spring from an identical source" as her "dark one"—he does not question that essential racial differences distinguish the ships' white children from her dark children, despite their altered proximity to each other.[62] Revising the nation's identity in light of an altered history of its racial origins, in short, may put blacks inhabiting the United States because of the slave trade at the center of the national story, but it does not so much call into question as reinforce the racial logic that makes the altered, and increased, proximity of black child bodies to white ones in some way "monstrous." It is this mutually reinforcing relationship between abolishing slavery and reinforcing essential racial difference—a relationship that ensures that white superiority will continue to drive the nation after slavery is abolished—that the child at the center of slave-ship stories describes for readers. Thus, while its predecessor registered the intricate and often unstable alliance between race and nation in the early national period, the child featured in abolitionist slave-ship stories reinforces the preeminence of whiteness in the postbellum United States so successfully that, as W. E. B. Du Bois predicts, the "problem of the twentieth century" will be nothing less than "the problem of the color-line."[63]

THE CHARACTER OF OUR SACRED SHIP

To advocate for the abolition of slavery, the numerous slave-ship stories written in the antebellum period make the slave trade central to the nation's history, but, as we will see, through the child at their center, they do not so much challenge as codify the ideas of racial difference that the child has long represented and on which the nation has been dependent since its inception. Indeed, firmly fixed ideas about race and its central place in the nation operate in these narratives as necessary preconditions for successfully making the case that, as Samuel Goodrich's famous child hero Peter Parley tells his readers, "Slavery is a bad system."[64] In her *Evenings in New England* (1824), Lydia Maria Child begins this process of reminding readers of the strict alliances between particular national and racial identities when she asks her readers to identify different nations with different images. The "dark-looking" figure "casting a terrified look on the vessel which he sees off the coast," the narrator tells her child companion, is "Africa" and is "frightened at the sight of a ship" because of the "large number of vessels [that] go there for the express purpose of stealing the negroes for slaves."[65] By identifying Africa as a black body that is in constant fear of losing its national identity because of the slave trade, Child firmly aligns race with African, as well as U.S., national identity even as she insists that this particular alliance is always already under threat because of the slave trade. Just as the Anglo-Saxon's love of liberty gives birth to the United States, so, too, do Africans' racial characteristics—their docility and timidity—create a nation in which its black inhabitants are particularly susceptible to being preyed on by the slave trade. Thus, the author of *Watch and Wait*, writing at the end of the slave-ship story's era, summarizes how one of its primary goals—to "increase [readers'] love of liberty and their hatred of tyranny" by scripting a "story of exciting adventure—"depends on a strict affiliation of racial with national identity—an affiliation that equates "negro blood" with "patience and submission" and "white blood" with true "Anglo-Saxon inspiration" and "resistance" to tyranny. This unequivocal alignment of racial with national identity ensures that the "Anglo-Saxon blood coursing" in the American child hero's veins will naturally "boil" at the "indignity" of being whipped and will thereby ensure that he resists being enslaved on African, as well as U.S., soil.[66]

After exclusively aligning white with American and black with African identity, slave-ship narratives proceed to represent the numerous ways in which the nation's slave trade can capture the "wrong" racial bodies—the ways in which it is flawed because it cannot always operate according to the precise logic of racial identity that differentiates black from white, African from American. *The Slave's Friend*, a periodical, repeatedly refers to this possibility of wrongfully enslaving child representatives of U.S. freedom when, for example, it describes the plight of a "white child" who was kidnapped, and "sold for a SLAVE," because her kidnappers were able to successfully "stai[n her] black." While it may be a common thing for "colored children to be stolen" and sold for slaves, the *Slave's Friend* shows how the slave trade can be extended to absorb the white child, whose skin testifies to its love of freedom but can also be made to look black. Slave traders thus have as much motive for stealing the white child who represents the nation's love of liberty as the black child who cannot, because even if children contain the distinguishing characteristics of their respective races and the nations with which those races are equated, "the only difference" between them is color, and "the black color" can be added to, as well as finally "rubbed off," the white child's skin.[67]

This potential for the slave trade to disregard racial difference can alter not only the surface color of the white child's skin, but also the racial characteristics that define the nation it represents and to which it belongs. *The Boy Slaves* (1849), for example, represents to its "proud Caucasian" readers how "thousands of their own color, . . . despite [their] boasted superiority of intellect [and] the whiteness of [their] skin," can become the slaves "not only of their oppressors" but "of th[eir] slaves," as well.[68] After charting the process through which three white, initially free children on board a slaver become slaves by falling victim to slave traders who alter the surface color of their skin, *The Boy Slaves* describes how their enslavement gradually transforms the character of the newly enslaved white child. "Kept awake by the memory of the sufferings they had endured in slavery" as much as by "the anticipation of liberty," the boys chart for readers the dangers that a slave trade that does not always respect racial difference poses to Anglo-Saxon identity and the nation it has created.[69] It is the personal recognition, through the experience of being enslaved, of how the slave system's quiet practice of trading in whites as well as blacks, Americans as well as Africans, compromises rather than enhances U.S. national identity that causes the child hero of *The Little Robinson Crusoe* (1855), for example, to resolve no longer to "sail to the coast of Africa, to purchase poor negroes to work in the plantations" but, instead, to retake possession of "the ship" where he was enslaved to free all Africans.⁷⁰

However, it is by convincing readers that slavery not only transgresses but also produces racial difference that Samuel Goodrich's famous story of the slave trade, *Tales of Peter Parley about Africa* (1830), and its child hero argue successfully for slavery's end in the United States. By showing that slavery exacerbates rather than contains the threat that racial others pose to the nation's ideal of liberty, Peter convinces readers that the slave trade cannot be in the best interest of a nation committed to the racialized ideal of freedom. Selling more than 7 million copies before the Civil War, books within Goodrich's Peter Parley series were often ghostwritten by other authors, including Nathaniel Hawthorne, and exerted immense influence over American audiences, who, as Goodrich claimed, read his books to learn "the first ideas of Geography and History."⁷¹ However, Goodrich uses the child to reveal that slavery can often produce the very racial others it seeks to control and therefore runs counter to American ideological interests. Goodrich immediately reverses the causal relation between slavery and racial otherness by introducing into his shipboard story a different kind of vessel "more dreadful" to the sight of those aboard Captain Riley's slave ship than "the troubled sea" on which they find themselves. Manned by a dark-skinned crew and "sent out to rob and plunder other vessels," the corsair complicates the crew's mission to buy African slaves by capturing Captain Riley's ship, along with "several American vessels," and "reduc[ing]" the Anglo-American crew, as it has already done the "many poor Americans [who remain] still in slavery" along the Barbary Coast, to a state of abject slavery. At the mercy of the "barbarous and cruel race" Captain Riley's crew had planned to enslave, Peter, unlike the other crew members, learns the racial logic that drives the slave trade in Africa. While Africa consists "chiefly of two races of men, Arabs and Negroes," they in turn have "mixed and produced others" of "dark" skin, whom they randomly enslave as opportunity allows. All of "very dark complexions" and collectively "cruel, vicious, and unprincipled," these races nonetheless create important racial distinctions only after they enslave each other and come to perceive their captives as essentially different—as "very much worse than themselves." Not preceding and explaining but, rather, following slavery, this racial otherness subsequently designates the captives as essentially different, inferior, and "fit only to be made slaves of." With the knowledge that slavery does not contain but, rather, produces and perpetuates the threat that racial others pose, Peter Parley is able not only to free the wrongfully enslaved Captain Riley and his crew but to reconsider the impact of the slave trade on U.S. national identity. Declaring that "every good person should condemn" slavery and "hasten the time when there shall be no slavery in the land" because blacks in the United States will always be "degraded . . . outcasts and always despised" regardless of the slave trade, Peter makes clear that eradicating slavery reaffirms rather than undermines the racial order on which the nation is based, furthering its defining racialized ideals of liberty and freedom.

By repeatedly tracking how the black child can achieve freedom in the United States without acquiring the Anglo-Saxon racial characteristics of its founders, slave-ship stories finally reassure readers that abolishing slavery will not alter the racial logic that has long organized the nation. While they posit the black child's first sight of the slave ship as a crucial moment of coming into consciousness of its new condition as a slave, slave-ship stories nonetheless insist that the black child's racial identity precedes such a moment and subsequently remains intact despite any and all changes to the child's social status. In *The Recaptured Negro* (1821), for example, the child hero, Dazee, is described as suddenly "amid this vast solitude" having "his attention" arrested by "one object. . . . [I]t was a ship which lay at anchor at a little distance, and which he well understood was brought there to convey himself . . . to the land of slavery."[72] *The Life and Adventures of Olaudah Equiano* (1829) likewise describes the moment that Equiano sees "a SLAVE SHIP riding at anchor, waiting for her cargo" as a moment of altered consciousness, produced by the recognition that he is going "to the country of these white people to work for them."[73] While both Dazee and Equiano end up free—Dazee through the unexpected intervention of a missionary ship that relocates him to Sierra Leone and Equiano through the "indulgence" of his shipboard master and his "own indefatigable industry," which enables him to obtain "the sum required for . . . liberty"[74]—both find their liberty subsequently circumscribed. Mrs. Farrar's *Adventures of Congo in Search of His Master* (1825) describes in detail how the black child's liberty must necessarily remain delimited by the racial characteristics that, as much as its skin color, define its racial identity. Though her black child protagonist, Congo, shows a love of liberty that should make him an equal citizen in the United States, when he declares to a white man named King that "though you are a King, you have no power over me," his capacity to conceptualize "his liberty" is undercut by the racial identity that caused his enslavement in the first place.[75] Because Congo is unable to see any of the white race, even a band of Irish beggars, as other than his "master," he escapes "out of the clutches of *the master*" but cannot "claim his liberty and become equal, or a *"whiteboy*," because his racial identity, rather than his slave status, determines his social and civic status in the United States.[76]

WHITE INFANT NATION

By illustrating how slavery runs counter to the racial ideals of the nation, the child featured in antebellum political rhetoric simultaneously works to eradicate slavery and to reinforce the enduring power of white supremacy to an audience anxious about the impact of emancipation on the nation and the racial order that has historically defined it. The child, in short, works as a pivotal vehicle through which the United States becomes a racial polity that is tacitly governed by a racial contract "between civilized whites, producing a white republic" that effectively excludes racial others even as it frees them.[77] While the child in the early national period challenged this emerging association of white supremacy with national identity, even as it aligned the two, the child featured in slave-ship stories establishes white superiority as an unequivocal and enduring cornerstone of a nation that, in freeing its slaves, nonetheless seeks to reinforce their inferiority. The long-term success of this political rhetoric becomes apparent in the postbellum era when, as Arthur Mann has shown, an explicitly Anglo-Saxon national identity flourished.[78] Yet if the Anglo-Saxonists that emerged in the half-century after 1880 were committed to reinforcing the idea that "some groups were less capable than others of becoming part of the American people," we can clearly see the accelerating explanatory power of this racial logic in the commentary of one immensely popular national organization in the postwar period: the Daughters of the American Revolution (DAR).[79] When the DAR first convened on October 11, 1890, it immediately identified a pure, white, Anglo-Saxon child body as the point of origin for all "true" offspring of Revolutionary forebears. Making DAR membership contingent on "the blood which flowed in the Revolutionary hero"—blood that the organization declares "is still coursing in us"—*American Monthly* magazine, the DAR's official publication, explicitly clarifies that its criteria for membership in the national body inheres in the racial body of the nation's Anglo-Saxon forebears, in "this bone and sinew and nerve and muscle [that] are but the outcome of our Revolutionary hero" and that are "ours by direct inheritance."[80] This undeviating racial inheritance and the racial characteristics it transmits precede all other criteria for membership in the national corpus and therefore preclude all female offspring of color, regardless of their ability to prove that their Anglo-American or African American ancestors had been of "material aid to the cause of independence," from claiming affiliation with the original national body.[81] By fixing white supremacy within the nation so firmly that slavery can be abolished without jeopardizing the racial logic on which the nation was built, the child ensures that if, as *The Child's Anti-Slavery Book* declares, "every negro child that is born is as free before God as the white child, having precisely the same right to life, liberty, and the pursuit of happiness," race will continue to create crucial distinctions between the two free but differently raced children, finally determining their relative social, political, and civic positions within the national body.[82] Therefore, by representing racial identity as such an integral component of the nation and its inhabitants that emancipation does not so much alter as extend the racial logic that has undergirded the nation since its inception, the child consistently featured in popular political narratives from the early national period through the Civil War illustrates with increasing urgency that, if Abraham Lincoln's 1857 question of "whether this nation shall be an entire slave nation" has been settled, the question of when it will no longer organize itself around white supremacy has not.[83]

two

SOUTHERN FICTIONS AND THE "RACE" OF NATIONS ALONG THE MEXICAN BORDER

William Gilmore Simms uses his position as spokesperson and advocate for the antebellum South to remind Southerners that the founding fathers' creation of "the man-child Liberty" out of the "noblest rac[e] of mankind"—the Anglo-Saxon race—goes far toward explaining Southerners' increasing resistance to "the people of Massachusetts Bay."[1] By rejecting the annexation of the slaveholding Republic of Texas in 1844—by flinging "from our possession a vast and noble territory, acquired by our kindred, and essential to the natural expansion of our race"—the people of Massachusetts Bay, Simms declares in his "Oration on the Sixty-Ninth Anniversary of American Independence" (1844), "trespa[ss]" on the "Independence" that the nation's founders nurtured "in the cradle." That is, by rejecting the inclusion of additional slaveholding territory within the national body, the United States subordinates the "Anglo-Saxon origin of [George] Washington" to the idea of liberty for all that his racial purity helps to create. In so doing, the United States denies the racial heritage that produced "the fiery accents of Patrick Henry" and the "stern propriety of Daniel Webster" and that, fifty years later, enabled a small number of Anglo-American Texans to conquer "the slavish and timorous race" led by "Santa Anna."[2] However, Simms contends that the same "independence which prompted our ancestors to enter the field in 1776" and their offspring to create the independent Republic of Texas in 1836 will now embolden the nation's true "noble progeny" to defend this "birth-right of the free souls" from those who would undermine the racial hierarchy that has historically defined the United States.[3]

As Simms's 1844 commentary makes clear, the alternative, increasingly oppositional Southern identity emerging in the twenty years before the Civil War not only depends on the same racial logic, as we saw in the preceding chapter, through which the child organized the nation. It also takes imaginative shape and energy from another, albeit short-lived, infant republic. Springing from the same Anglo-Saxon origins as the United States and upholding those founding racial ideals by retaining slavery, the Republic of Texas comes by 1844 to exemplify the magnitude of the conflict within the United States between the foundational concepts of white supremacy and freedom for all. Taking seriously Houston Baker's request that we "turn South again" to rethink the enduring national significance of race,[4] the following pages suggest that recognizing the U.S. South as a product of and response to the diverse range of regional, and national, constituencies fighting for dominance in the antebellum era is crucial to excavating the full range of territorial disputes and expansionist struggles that characterize antebellum North America. As Jon Smith and Deborah Cohn have observed, it is all too easy to forget how the very factors that allegedly make the South unusual within the United States make it acutely familiar within broader categories that a hemispheric approach makes available.[5] While I agree with Smith and Cohn that positioning the U.S. South within the larger geographic context of the Americas opens up important new vantage points from which to understand regional relations throughout the hemisphere, I would further suggest that these often overlooked histories of the U.S. South's connections with Latin America and the Caribbean shed important light on ongoing territorial disputes within the United States. Therefore, by situating North–South relations within a broader set of geographic struggles that reveal the U.S. imperial contest to be going on inside as well as outside the nation's expanding boundaries, we can see how the child at the center of "the official stories through which a nation — 'a people' — speaks itself into existence," as Priscilla Wald remarks, can also work to create alternative national narratives that enable, even as they threaten to rupture, the "official story of America."[6] By analyzing the child's conceptual centrality both to U.S. efforts to acquire Mexican territory and to the creation of alternative nations that lay claim to the same territory (like the Republic of Texas and the Confederacy), we can see not only how the child organizes the United States around white supremacy so powerfully that slavery can be abolished without undermining the nation's racial principles, but, conversely, how the child constitutes race as an organizing principle of oppositional, if ephemeral, Anglo nations that temporarily challenge the United States by retaining slavery as a logical corollary to white superiority.

With its contested, ever shifting, and provisional borders, the U.S.-Mexico frontier during the nineteenth century offers a particularly rich site for charting how alternative white nations are created in relation, and in opposition, to a United States that is increasingly committed both to abolishing slavery and to expanding its borders to include racial others. "Very few places have been subjected to as much [criticism] as the border between the United States and Mexico," as Rolando Romero points out.[7] Yet if the U.S.-Mexico border is, as James Clifford contends, a "place of hybridity and struggle, policing and transgression" that subverts "binarisms" with the "powerful political visions" it creates,[8] critical studies committed to the exploration of what Ella Shohat has identified as the "conflictual hybrid interplay of communities within and across borders" tend to overlook the full significance of the short-lived Anglo nations created within this contested geopolitical terrain in challenging the emergent narrative of U.S. exceptionalism that finally shores up the boundary between Mexico and the United States.[9] Amy Kaplan, for example, begins her landmark analysis of how nineteenth-century domestic fiction facilitates U.S. expansionism with a consideration of the 1847 *Godey's Ladies Book* article "Life on the Rio Grande."[10] However, her exclusive focus on how Northern writers like Sarah Josepha Hale and Catherine Beecher contribute to a program of U.S. manifest destiny overlooks, first, how competing white nations are conceived in response and in opposition to such U.S. political programs; and second, how the domestic fiction produced within these particular geopolitical spaces facilitates the creation of opposing national identities that lay claim to the idea of manifest destiny to establish and extend their borders.

The term "manifest destiny" was used, as Oliver Morton recalls, to describe not only U.S. westward expansion but also Southern leaders' "daring ambition" to "found a gigantic tropical slave empire" that would outstrip and finally conquer the "free republic" to the North.[11] Preceding and precipitating the creation of this separate Southern empire, the Republic of Texas, during its nine-year life, similarly had the potential to become, in the words of General Hamilton, "a powerful separate empire" that, by uniting "the ambition of Rome and the avarice of Carthage," could, John Calhoun feared, easily become "the real Empire . . . of the country."[12] Just "emerging from its cradle with a population of less than 100,000 souls" and "without a dollar in its Treasury, nor a regular soldier belonging to it," this "young nation," according to Joseph Eve, American minister to Texas in 1842, "successfully makes offensive war upon a nation containing a population of eight millions."[13] In so doing, feared the unnamed author of *How to Conquer Texas, before Texas Conquers Us* (1845), Texas showed its capacity to "become the real Empire" of the continent.[14] Such an empire threatened not only to expand its slaveholding influence to the North but also to incorporate into itself Southern regions like Cuba, where slavery already existed, albeit in modified form. In so doing, the Republic of Texas provided during its short life as an independent nation a powerful model of alternative imperial aspiration to an increasingly separatist South. As the prominent nineteenth-century political economist J. E. Cairnes argued in his 1862 lecture "The Slave Power," the "Southern party since 1820 had as its leading idea, its paramount aim, almost its single purpose . . . to extend slavery, and to achieve power by extending it." He therefore contended that "the Seminole War, the annexation of Texas, the war with Mexico, and the filibustering attempts on Cuba and Central America over the previous half-century were all about Southern aggression."[15] John Stuart Mill agreed with Cairnes that the South's increasing dual commitments to separatism and expansionism were the direct result of "American slavery [which] depended on a perpetual extension of its field and must go on barbarizing the world more and more" if it were to survive.[16] "Set[ting] themselves up, in defiance of the rest of the world, to do the devil's work," the South needed to expand if it wanted to flourish as an independent, agricultural entity and so it would necessarily "propagate [its] national faith at the rifle's mouth in Mexico, Central America, Cuba," were it to succeed in forming a separate nation.[17] Modeled on Texas's territorial aggression, this essentially expansionist South in the minds of political philosophers from Mill to Cairnes and Olmsted was therefore led by Southern slave owners who, as Olmsted contended explicitly, "wished to expand their holdings." "Moved by romantic

excitements and enthusiasm" and "inflamed by senseless appeals to their
patriotism and their combativeness," these Southern slave owners specifically targeted slaveholding territories outside their sphere, such as Cuba,
because in "annexing Cuba they might secure larger estates and make use
of much cheaper [Cuban] land and labor."[18] As these accounts of the rival
nations along the U.S.-Mexico border remind us, the idea of manifest destiny was a hotly contested right, facilitating not only the expansion of the
United States but the creation of other young nations that threatened, many
Americans feared, to absorb the nation to the North and to encompass
South America.[19] By temporarily laying successful claim to the expansionist
agenda too often associated exclusively with the United States, competing
albeit short-lived nations like the Republic of Texas and the Confederacy in
turn require that we not only consider how domestic fiction facilitates a U.S.
expansionist agenda, but also how it might just as importantly, as Elizabeth
Moss suggests, further a wide range of competing sectional, regional, and,
I would add, national interests.[20]

By turning to the work of Augusta J. Evans, a domestic writer who structured her argument for a separate Southern nation out of the political rhetoric her firsthand experience of the U.S.-Mexican War (1846–48) and the
Republic of Texas (1836–45) made available to her, we can begin to see
how domestic fiction features the child to help script diverse and alternative Anglo nations into being in relation and in opposition to a United
States committed to westward expansion. While stories of the Mexican
border written in the North, like "Life on the Rio Grande," facilitate U.S.
manifest destiny by erasing the "violent political context" in which female
protagonists exert their domestic influence,[21] Augusta J. Evans identifies
that very political context — Texas nationhood, Texas annexation, the U.S.-
Mexican War, and the accelerating conflict over slavery — as the impetus
for her career as a domestic writer and makes such political conflict the
focal point of her fictional vision of alternative Southern nationhood. It
was "rambl[ing] about the crumbling walls of the Alamo, . . . recalling all
[the] bloody tragedy" out of which the infant Republic of Texas was born,
Evans later recalled, that inspired her to "write about it for those who had
never looked upon" such an evocative site of national struggle.[22] Evans's
first novel, *Inez: A Tale of the Alamo* (1855), identifies the Republic of Texas
as an important precursor to and model for the creation of a "sovereign,

independent nation" at the South that, as her subsequent novels *Beulah* (1859) and *Macaria; or, Altars of Sacrifice* (1864) illustrate, can distinguish itself from the "vast populous empire" at the North by upholding and protecting the racial principles that originally founded the United States but are, in her opinion, being compromised by abolition.[23] Written when Evans was fifteen years old, *Inez* went through at least three British publications in addition to dozens of U.S. ones, and *Godey's Lady's Book* predicted that Evans's novel would "doubtless have a good run during the present excited state of the public mind."[24] Her subsequent novels were all bestsellers, with *St. Elmo* selling more copies than any other nineteenth-century novel except *Uncle Tom's Cabin*. And yet despite the remarkable success of her fiction—illustrated by the fact that steamboats, hotels, two villages, and a cigar were named for *St. Elmo*—and despite her long-term correspondence with powerful political figures such as Confederate General P. G. T. Beauregard and the Confederate Congressman J. L. M. Curry, Evans remains relatively unknown. One reason for this lack of interest, not surprisingly, is her unapologetic championing of the Confederacy and slaveholding. As Susan Ryan has recently commented, nineteenth-century domestic writing has "come to represent for Euro-American women in the academy the earnest, middle-class, white activism" that Harriet Beecher Stowe most clearly exemplifies.[25] Yet, as we saw in the preceding chapter, the antislavery logic of *Uncle Tom's Cabin* did not so much refute as reinforce the racial hierarchy that had long governed the United States. From the new vantage point that such an analysis makes available, popular pro-slavery novels like Evans's *Beulah* or Caroline Lee Hentz's *The Planter's Northern Bride* are not so much refutations as extensions of their Northern abolitionist counterparts and therefore become important documents for rethinking familiar literary histories of the U.S. South's difference from the North. Recognizing that pro-slavery and antislavery literature throughout the Northern and Southern regions of the United States shared the racial logic that the child represented thus reshapes familiar narratives of American literary history.

Southern novels such as *The Planter's Northern Bride*, for example, feature the child not to advocate for slavery's end, as the child does in abolitionist fiction and in such popular Northern images as "The Secession Bubble" (figure 6), but to further the idea that slavery is a natural and healthy expression of the nation's founding principles. If certain bodies become particu-

THE SECESSION BUBBLE.

"IT MUST BURST"

Published by J.H. BUFFORD 313 Wash.t St. Boston.

Figure 6 "The Secession Bubble. It Must Burst." Courtesy Library of Congress, Prints and Photographs Division (LC-USZ62–89744).

larly romanticized or filled with meaning in the South, as Houston Baker and Dana Nelson have observed, the child's body offers a uniquely rich site of national contestation and confirmation, given its longer history in U.S. nation formation. Because the child uniquely represents the "conflicts that erupt when individuals strongly disagree," as Gillian Brown has observed, the child becomes a rich site for charting the overlapping and contested national ideologies vying for dominance in the antebellum era.[26] Hentz's 1854 response to *Uncle Toms' Cabin*, for example, rewrites Stowe's comparison of little Eva and Topsy to persuade readers that slavery binds rather than ruptures the nation. Sitting "side by side . . . beautiful representatives of the North and the South, hand linked with hand and heart meeting heart," the dark-haired Effie and blonde Dora, according to Evans, represent "that harmony which ought to exist between the two regions."[27] Not only is the child powerful enough to heal sectional friction, but the child is capable of maintaining "natural: racial hierarchies between master and slave, even when slave insurrection threatens. After demanding that a slave carry his child "in triumph over the wooly heads" to him, the slaveholding protagonist of Hentz's novel raises his infant above his head for all his slaves to see. "The admiration, love, and devotion" that the infant immediately evokes among the slaves, according to Hentz, sustains slavery precisely by reminding the slaves that "father and child are beings of a superior world," and thus that their "future master," though a child, will become, like their current master, a "father" who should be "welcomed by his children," rather than a tyrant who should be resisted and defied. By strategically deploying the child who has functioned as a focal point around which slaves and master "feel right," Hentz asks her readers to recommit to the nation by recognizing "North and South [as] branches of the same parent tree."[28]

While Hentz deploys the child to advocate for national unification under the institutional sign of white supremacy, Evans looks South and West to the alternative nations formed along the U.S.-Mexico border to advocate for the creation of yet another nation—a separate Southern nation that would uphold the white supremacy that Evans and other separatists feared the United States was forgetting in its increasing commitment to freeing its slaves. Just as Hentz featured the child that "blends in its veins" the "blood of the North and South" as a "representative of the reunion of these now two divided parties,"[29] so, too, does Evans feature the child that justified the creation of the Republic of Texas to justify the creation of a separate Southern, slaveholding nation. Because political writers along the U.S.-Mexican border appropriated the founding U.S. image of the child to imagine alternative nationalisms to the one the United States represents, the child became a powerful vehicle through which writers like Evans authenticated a Southern nation that realizes the political mission of such alternative nations as the Republic of Texas.

"BIRTHING LIBERTY"

The Anglo-Americans leaders who settled the Texas-Coahuila province of the new State of Mexico in the 1820s consistently featured the child in order to constitute a second Republic of North America around the same racial logic that founded the United States. In their argument that Texas should separate from its corrupt parent country of Mexico, early leaders like J. D. B. Debow, Stephen F. Austin, Sam Houston, and Noah Smithwick imagined the new, infant Republic to be expressing and upholding the racial principles on which its "true" parent country—the United States—was originally created. It is their "Anglo-American character and training," according to William Kennedy's *Texas: The Rise, Progress, and Prospects of the Republic of Texas* (1841), that cause early settlers quickly to resist "the loose and anarchical rule which Mexico inherited from her European parent."[30] As James Galt asks readers of *Political Essays* (1844), "How could a population coming . . . from the United States, thoroughly imbued with all the sentiments and opinions of the fatherland be willing to submit to the tyranny of Santa Anna or any other despot?"[31] The answer, of course, is that they cannot and so must struggle to constitute a new nation that reproduces and extends the racial legacy bequeathed to them as the offspring of this fatherland. With an "Anglo-Saxon population as the majority of its citizens," Texas's success over Mexican "oppression" is a foregone conclusion, according to many social commentators like Galt.[32] It is the "wisdom, prudence, and energy of character" that "the Anglo-Americans, who formed the principal strength of the Texan colony, possessed in a high degree," Orceneth Fisher contends, that ensure that they will be able, despite their insignificant resources, to succeed "in establishing their independence" from "the mixed population which, under the general name of Mexican, lay scattered within and adjacent to the Tropic."[33] Understanding the struggle for separate Texas nationhood as reenacting and upholding what D. G. Burnet, provisional president of the Republic, describes in his inaugural address as the "gallantry which we derive from the illustrious conquerors of 1776,"[34] those who fought for Texas independence construed the "present situation of Texas [to be], in many respects, analogous to that in which American colonists were placed."[35] Therefore, when Branch T. Archer rallies "Texians" to arms on November 3, 1835, by asking that they "give evidence that we are the true descendants of that band of heroes, who sustained an eight year's war against tyranny and oppression and gave liberty to the world"—just as when Travis repeats to his men at the Alamo the words of John Adams or when its writers model the Texas Declaration of Independence on the 1776 Declaration—founders use U.S. nation formation and the racial logic the child at its center represents to justify the creation of a separate Republic of Texas.[36] This "inchoate nation" is, in turn, repeatedly likened to the child whose racial narrative helped to constitute it, and the "young nation just emerging from its cradle" is described by Stephen F. Austin and Noah Smithwick, among many others, as being "baptized with the Alamo and Goliad.[37] Founded by "sons of freedom" and "descendants of Anglo-Saxons, . . . this infant country," according to J. D. B. Debow, even "in its swaddling clothes" will "soon swallo[w] up" its opponents, because "in point of character for intelligence, vigor, and enterprise, the Mexicans are far inferior to the Anglo-Texans."[38]

The white supremacy that the child represents not only ensures the child nation's successful creation but, in turn, guarantees that the new infant Republic of Texas will be able to expand its territories and extend Anglo-Texan rule over the very Mexican population that attempted to conquer it. If the inchoate nation, according to Stephen F. Austin, "has been in labor since 1810," the "small but prolific stock" who "give birth to liberty" by founding the Republic of Texas twenty-six years later show all "the power, influence and language of our Anglo-Saxon ancestors" and therefore will easily be able to "establish a form of government upon the most perfect model the world has ever seen," as William Allen's *Texas in 1840, or the Emigrant's Guide to the New Republic* (1840) reminds readers.[39] Giving "character and complexion to the whole nation," these "descendants of Anglo-Saxons," Allen continues, will easily be able to establish a "government of laws, a system of human rights, and security against the exercise of lawless power."[40] Yet this superior

Anglo-Texan government, as Republic of Texas Secretary of State Asbhel Smith predicts, must also inevitably subdue racial others, because the unavoidable outcome of bringing "the two races, the American distinctively so called, and the Spanish Americans or Mexicans, . . . into inseparable contact" through war, is that "the inferior must give way before the superior race."[41] It is "part of the destiny allotted to the Anglo-Saxon race to civilize . . . this continent," and so Smith foresees that the "energy, industry, and talents of the American populace" will quickly supplant the government, tradition, and culture of their enemy wherever that enemy is found.[42] Understanding "the young empire" they helped to create to be "the most remarkable monument to human energy and industry ever raised," those who founded the infant republic firmly believed that, as Sam Houston declared, nothing less than "the Pacific will bound the mighty march of our race and empire."[43] Thus, "should Mexico not make peace with Texas," the *Telegraph and Texas Register* tells readers, "the army of the Republic will plant its banner west of the Rio Grande and march on till the roar of the Texian rifles shall mingle in unison with the thunders of the Pacific."[44] In short, believing that the racial superiority that the child represents as successfully founding the infant nation against great odds will easily enable the Republic of Texas to "embrace the shores of the Pacific as well as those of the Gulf of Mexico," those who undertook the Mier Expedition sought to enforce President Lamar's 1840 declaration that the people of New Mexico "must finally be compelled to unite with us under the same constitution and laws and share our destiny as an undivided nation."[45] Believing as Frédéric Leclerc contended in *Texas and Its Revolution* (1838), that Mexicans would "readily s[ee] that they were dealing with a race of men completely different from themselves" to whom they were "far inferior,"[46] Colonel Thomas Jefferson Green refused to let his capture and forced march with other Mier Expedition prisoners dampen his enthusiastic belief that the Rio Grande, "once settled with the enterprise and intelligence of the English race," would transform Texas into the premiere empire in the world. Thus, with "an empire and a history of her own," the infant nation boasted a racial superiority that must inevitably, as *The Texas Almanac* declares, "secure independence, freedom and happiness under the glorious Lone Star Flag."[47]

Yet even as the white supremacy that the child represents functions as such a powerful organizing principle of the infant Republic that it under-

takes to subdue Mexican territory in what Edward Hale, British agent to
Texas, describes as "quite the Anglo-Saxon-American style,"[48] the child
operates as a central device through which the United States insists that
Texas has failed to uphold and protect the ideals of the parent country, not
reflecting "glory on the Anglo-Saxon race," as President Houston contends,
but rather desecrating its ideals by condoning slaveholding.[49] Despite the
protestations of founders like Smithwick, Lamar, and North that the Republic of Texas is the loyal "offspring of the United States" and retains a
"strong attachment to the parent land" because it gave the infant nation
"birth, and nursed us," the "question . . . of importance to the United States,"
according to the author of *How to Settle the Texas Question* (1845), is not
whether the people of Texas are "independent, but whether they are to
consist of slaves and slaveholders"—whether the people of Texas "rejoice
under the plough of free labor, or groan under the unwilling and unblessed
toil of slaves."[50] By choosing the latter, Texas transforms itself from "an infant nationality toddling along" uncertainly but nonetheless representing
"the great Hope of the American Union" into an "abomination" of the principles of liberty and freedom that the Union holds dear.[51] In "raising the
black flag of slavery," this infant government, says Cassius Clay, actively "resists that liberty which has made" the United States "forever memorable in
the annals of the world" and therefore should be aborted rather than nurtured.[52] Though "of Anglo Saxon blood, bone of our bone and flesh of our
flesh," these "recreant Saxons of Texas, the descendants of Washington and
Jefferson and Adams and Franklin," says Clay, have created an infant nation
that desecrates rather than upholds the racial principles the child represents
as foundational to Anglo-American national identity.[53] By "propagat[ing]
slavery" rather than promoting liberty, Texas, in other words, becomes a
"renegade from the land and religion of its fathers" and thereby forfeits any
protection that "its adopted and fostering country" might provide.[54] Thus,
if Texas "establish[es] the Anglo-American race one remove farther to the
South and West" and is therefore "auspicious to the interest of humanity,"
the "extension of liberty, of knowledge, and of liberal principles" that the
"birth of a Republic" in Texas promises remains unrealized, according to
many U.S. political leaders.[55] As a result, its nationhood, though conceptually dependent on the white supremacy the child represents, destroys what
Galt describes as the United States' fondly held hope that parent and child

nations will combine to realize the ideals of liberty and freedom for all that the child has long represented in the Anglo-American political tradition — to create, in other words, "without slavery, with union, with . . . peace and liberty" a national family "reaching from the Atlantic to the Pacific" and presenting "a glorious example to the world" of Anglo-Saxon principles.[56] Given Texas's slaveholding, it is only by transforming the infant, independent nation into "a star in our constellation" that the people of the United States can hope to uphold "the freedom for which our fathers toiled and shed their blood."[57] Refuting Noah Smithwick's contention that the Texans' 1835 fight at Gonzales is nothing less than "our Lexington," Elizur Wright, secretary of the Anti-Texas Committee, and Cassius Clay argue that the inception of the infant independent nation of Texas "violat[es] the principles of the Declaration of American Independence" and the precept that "no person shall be deprived of life, liberty or property."[58] In so doing, Texas has the potential to fatally undermine "the existence of real liberty among our own freeborn people."[59] As "the most momentous [challenge] which has ever been brought before the nation since the Declaration of Independence," this second independent Republic of North America, according to the Massachusetts Friends of Free Institutions, requires that "every lover of freedom concentrate his energies to save the nation from the great impending calamity" posed by Texas's perversion of the racial principles the child represents.[60]

By successfully annexing the Republic of Texas and the Mexican territory that Texas was unable to obtain, the United States asserts dominance over its corrupt offspring and reestablishes the United States as the one nation that upholds the Anglo-Saxon love of liberty and freedom for all that the child has long represented. Some agreed with Ohio Representative D. R. Tilden that the annexation of Texas had put "the Union at the mercy of a few desperate men in Texas" — "Spaniards or Mexicans by birth and education" — who "deny the self evident truths upon which we base our hopes of a free government" and therefore "will force us into a war with Mexico," but most concurred with Lewis Cass of Michigan that "Mexico has attacked the United States" in occupying Texas and therefore has created "a most important crisis in the history of this country."[61] With a "Mexican army . . . past our boundary, and now upon the soil of the Republic," the people of the United States must recognize that the nation faces a "crisis

which will affect our character and our destiny for a long series of years."
Should the nation meet the challenge that a "hostile army in our country" and "a foreign banner float[ing] over the soil of the Republic" clearly
represent "promptly, vigorously, [and] energetically as becomes the representatives of a great and spirited people," the United States will "furnish a
lesson to the world." Calling on the unique "spirit in our country" and the
"instinct which never fails us in all questions of national honor" but produces "one spontaneous exhibition of patriotism," Cass asks his constituency not to let Mexico "check our onward march and prevent the extension of our principles, and the powerful operation of our example" as the
"seat of rational liberty" for the whole world. With nothing less at stake
than the nation's indisputable position as "a landmark . . . [and] haven of
liberty" — "a beacon, pointing out the shoals of Democracy" for all mankind — Cass invokes the Puritan legacy of John Winthrop by telling listeners
that "the eyes of all Christendom are upon us," watching and "scrutinizing"
the nation's response to Mexico's act of aggression.[62] "Just, honorable, and
necessary," this war with Mexico, Representative R. M. McLane of Maryland concludes, requires that all Americans fight to uphold and extend the
racial ideals that the child represents as having long governed the country by "driving the Mexican armies beyond the Rio Grande.[63] In his *Life of
Franklin Pierce* (1852), Nathaniel Hawthorne reinforces that these ideals —
ideals that, as we have seen, are claimed by alternative nations like the Republic of Texas in their struggle for dominance along the Mexican border — nonetheless, remain the exclusive attribute of the United States, as
its valiant invasion of Mexico proves. Demonstrating in his involvement
in the Mexican war "patriotism such as it had been in revolutionary days,"
Hawthorne's young protagonist embodies the very racial principles that the
child historically represents as constituting the nation. "A youth with principles of democratic institutions" that are epitomized by his "blue eyes and
light curling hair," Pierce epitomizes "the old type of Revolutionary" feeling that long typified the "best blood in America" and that elicits in his men
the "sentiment of patriotism for the whole land" enabling them successfully to wage "the Mexican war."[64] In so doing, Hawthorne's Pierce successfully ensures that, as William Hale asserts, "killing a Mexican" during
the U.S.-Mexican War becomes exactly "like killing an enemy in the independence war."[65]

"A JUMBLE OF RACES"

As we have seen, the child helps to constitute alternative and opposing national identities along the antebellum Mexican border by representing the racial principles that originally created the United States but that are, according to some, being compromised by its increasing commitment to abolition. The challenge that the infant Republic of Texas posed to the United States in the 1840s signaled the "beginning of an irreparable split between North and South," as Norman Tutorow, Gilbert Barnes, and Louis Filler have shown, and Texas, as Democrat James Buchanan predicted in 1844, became the "Trojan Horse" that precipitated the rise of sectional democracy.[66] However, the child's capacity to script diverse, flexible national identities out of the racial principles it embodies facilitates this split by helping to create not only the Republic of Texas but a third "white" nation that encompasses land along the Mexican border and that, like Texas, aims to uphold the white supremacy the United States is forgetting by desiring to abolish slavery. Integral to the imagining of this third nation is the writing of Augusta Evans. Crafting an argument for a Confederate nation out of the political logic she encountered while growing up in San Antonio as "the war between the United States and Mexico was in full swing; and soldiers were stationed there, waiting to be sent to reinforce General Zachary Taylor,"[67] Evans used the rationale for one infant nation to advocate for the creation of another. Recognizing how the racial narrative the child represents could act as a powerful catalyst in creating and sustaining alternative national identities, Evans featured the child in her fiction to help Southerners imagine a separate Southern nation based on the strict racial hierarchy that originally organized the United States but was being undermined, in many Southerners' estimation, by abolition. Convinced, according to her biographer, "of the essential similarity between 1836 and 1850"—between Texas's creation of an independent nation in response to oppressive Mexican rule and the South's increasing national alienation in the face of what Evans herself describes as the "Northern fanaticism" that creates "waves of Abolitionism, which . . . pollute the sacred precincts of the 'White House'"—Evans placed the child at the center of her writing to advocate for the emergence of a Southern nation that successfully opposed the "deadly poison" through which Northern abolitionists destroy the very "vitals of the nation they claim to represent."[68] If, as Evans comments in one of her many advisory letters to General Beauregard, "the cause of our beloved, struggling Confederacy may yet be advanced through the agency of its daughters," the depiction of independent nationhood that the child protagonists of *Inez: A Tale of the Alamo* (1855) enable precedes and offers an important road map for charting her contribution, as one such daughter, to the formation of a separate Southern nation.[69]

Elizabeth Moss calls *Inez: A Tale of the Alamo* one of the most "creative and ambitious interpretations of the causes of northern and southern hostilities" ever written,[70] but key to Evans's interpretation is the alternative national identity that the child represents. Evans said that it was "recalling all [the Alamo's] bloody horrors" while watching, from the top of the "moldering, melancholy pile" of the Alamo, U.S. troops led by General Taylor preparing to invade Mexico that caused her "heart to throb" with a desire to write *Inez*.[71] She used the novel's child protagonists to show that the racial narrative embedded in these overlapping expressions of national identity is foundational to the creation of an independent South that would successfully uphold the racial purity to which both nations desire to lay claim. Featuring San Antonio's racially diverse populace as a backdrop, Evans uses her child protagonists to depict the possibilities, as well as the dangers, involved in founding a new Anglo nation amid racial mixture. It is precisely the threat that indigenous racial others pose to a new nation based on the idea of white supremacy that the child protagonists of *Inez* confront and overcome. The novel tracks the fate of two children from "one of the Southern States" who are forced to leave their private school and move to Texas because of the suddenly reduced circumstances of their parent and guardian. Modeled on the Evans's family history, the "very unfortunate . . . speculations" that lead Mr. Hamilton "to sell our plantation and negroes" force Florence's father to "the worst" extremity of all—moving "to Texas"—where he hopes, as did many from both the North and South during the economic downturn of the 1840s, to remake his lost fortune and evade his creditors.[72] While this relocation to San Antonio does finally enable Florence, by novel's end, to reclaim her "old home" in the South (both "the plantation" and the slaves that "were sold with it"), crucial to this reclamation of land and authority is Florence's education in the importance of racial hierarchy to national order—an education that ensures that she will protect and uphold the white supremacy on which slaveholding society depends.[73] Indeed, Florence's special need to learn the importance of racial hierarchy to national vitality is evident in the physical differences that immediately distinguish one cousin from the other. The "striking [physical] difference[s]," on which the narrator insists, between Florence's "brilliant black" hair and eyes and Mary's "soft blue eyes and golden curls" foreshadow the sharp ideological divisions that will soon become apparent in their new home — that "far off town, in a far off state" that has a "loveliness" reminiscent of "a tropical town of the far east."[74]

San Antonio provides a particularly powerful backdrop for the commentary on race and nation that Evans's child protagonists represent, because, as Frederick Law Olmsted, among many other nineteenth-century social commentators, argues in his 1854 *A Journey through Texas*, San Antonio is a city unlike any other — a city characterized by an "odd and antiquated foreignness" that is evident in "its jumble of races, costumes, languages and buildings."[75] As "the first of a new class of conquered cities into whose decaying streets our rattling life is to be infused," San Antonio provides a "contrast of nationalities," and of races, that remains its "chief interest" for Olmsted,[76] as well as its chief challenge for Anglo leaders. Fearing "Anglo-Saxon rule . . . after the Revolution" that treats the "conquered people" of Mexico "as vermin to be exterminated" rather than as citizens to be consulted, the few Mexican residents who remain nonetheless display a "variety of feature and color" that derives from "the old Spanish, the Creole Mexican, and the Indian, with sometimes a suspicion of Anglo-Saxon or Teuton."[77] The "racial character of the town is palpable at the [city's] entrance," where "the triple nationalities" of Mexicans, Germans, and Americans offer the viewer a kind of racial palimpsest in which the "sauntering Mexicans [who] prevail on the pavements" are nonetheless subordinate to the "bearded Germans and sallow Yankees," who provide a powerful daily reminder of "the intruding race who have caused all this progress."[78] Such a racially hybridized mixture successfully impedes "Anglo-Saxon rule," and as the Northeastern journalist Richard Harding Davis argues a number of years later, Texas remains "America's only in its possession, [but] Mexican in its people, language, and mode of life."[79] The *Harper's Weekly* writer Jonathon Speed concurs, asserting, "Though they have been American citizens for more than forty years," those who inhabit the territory "overlapping between Mexico in the U.S." are almost as much an alien race as the Chinese, and have shown no disposition to amalgamate with the other Americans."[80] Composed of "whites, negroes, and Indians," as well as Mexicans, the population of San Antonio, according to Philip Paxton, a resident in the 1850s, represented a real social danger to the order of whatever white nation of which it was compelled to be a part.[81]

Confronted with the social challenge that San Antonio's racially hybrid population represents to white nationhood, the two child cousins in Evans's novel quickly confront, through their involvement with Father Mazzolin, the racial "influences" that "contaminate" a young nation's integrity.[82] Father Mazzolin immediately confirms the suspicions his "crisp black hair, swarthy complexion, and never-to-be-mistaken eyes . . . [that] blen[d] . . . cunning, malignity, and fierceness" are meant to raise by delighting in secret correspondence that alerts him that Stephen F. Austin is "in the Calaboose" as "no friend to our nation" and that "Santa Anna is blood-thirsty enough" to kill all the "cursed heretics" that Austin has encouraged to settle in Texas.[83] While "noble Washington," according to the narrator, stands "alone on the pedestal of greatness [as a] bright beacon to warn every ruler, civil or military, of the thundering whirlpool" that imperils liberty, the Catholic rule that Mexican priests like Father Mazzolin maintain over residents threatens to undo those heroic exertions of independent nationhood occurring at the Alamo.[84] Thus, even as the "small, but intrepid band" of "brave-hearted Texans" defying "the tyrant who had subverted the liberties of [their] country" struggle to realize Washington's ideals under "the new-born banner" of freedom that they raise "majestically over the sunny prairies of their western home," another system of governance imperils this infant, Anglo-American nation.[85]

Yet in Evans's novel, the primary site of engagement in this explicitly racialized struggle for freedom is not the "garrisoned" Alamo, where "dark bodies of Mexican troops move heavily to and fro," but, rather, the home, where the child bodies of Anglo-Americans become the target of Father Mazzolin's attempts to install the "system of ignorance, superstition, and crime" that will "crush the liberties" of its residents and, finally, of the whole "glorious Republic."[86] Seeing a "dark form glid[e] to the bed side" where Mr. Hamilton is dying, Mary learns of the priest's successful attempt to conquer Florence's father's soul and, finally, of his plan either to make all Anglo residents "submit" to the Catholic rule of Mexico by secretly converting their children or to drive every "last American child . . . to the far bank of the Sabine."[87] Alerted to the fact that Florence has been targeted by Mazzolin and secretly "wears a crucifix about her neck, and kneels in the confessional," Mary—her "face colorless as marble"—confronts and reconverts Florence from the despotic "iron rule" of Rome by proving to her that the "Papacy [is] the sworn foe to liberty."[88] Just as the "noble band" at the Alamo raise their "eyes to the blackened sky" before their "final sacrifice" for freedom (242), so, too, does the child Mary "lift her eyes" to the "brilliant hues of the setting sun . . . once more" before she dies.[89] Willing to "yield up" her life "as the price of independence" and "common liberty," Mary, like the "intrepid Texans," upholds the racial ideals on which independent nationhood, according to Evans, depends.[90] Recommitted to these notions of independence and self-governance because of Mary's intervention, Florence returns to the South to reclaim her plantation and to run it as "every lover of liberty" and "patriot" should.[91] With San Antonio as a cautionary example of how "a fai[r] spot," rich in all resources and full of beauty, can nonetheless be riddled with "sloth" and "degradation" because of the oppressive and unenlightened rule of racial others who illicitly assume power, Florence declares that, as mistress, she now has "higher aims" for her authority.[92] Admitting after she settles into the "parlor of her old and dearly loved home" that she "shudders to think what I should now have been" had Mary not "saved" her, Florence predicts "happiness on earth" for herself, her slaves, and the South if they can live according to the lessons in racialized nationalism that the infant nation of Texas—and the child Mary who upholds white supremacy as a cornerstone of its emerging national identity—provides.[93]

By rejecting the Catholic law of Mexican inhabitants, the child that Evans's first novel features not only protects the racial ideals for which the founders of the infant Republic of Texas fight but, in turn, becomes a primary vehicle through which Evans begins to advocate for a separate Southern nation that, through its slaveholding, maintains the white supremacy essential for national order. Construing "the South as the bastion of national virtue" in her nonfiction prose, Evans featured the child that installs white supremacy as a cornerstone of alternative nations like Texas in her domestic fiction to advocate for a separate Southern nation that would uphold the racial logic that originally organized the United States but that was being forgotten by "Northern fanatics."[94] By "dragging . . . the low sensual African . . . up from his normal position and violently thrust[ing] him into an importance which the Creator has denied him," Northerners, according to Evans, destroy "national harmony" by "delug[ing] the world" with "monstrous trash" that "seeks to render all classes of society dissatisfied with their normal condition."[95] Responding to this tendency of antebellum Northern literature to advocate for racial equality, Evans contended that "the civilized world gazes in amazement at the unblushing and fanatical sacrilege" committed by "the depraved and unprincipled politicians at the North," who successfully effect "the mutilation of the American Constitution" with their attacks on slavery.[96]

Hoping to do for her own cause "what Thomas Paine had done for the Patriot position in the Revolution,"[97] Evans energetically argued in multiple public venues that the South was forced into the role of "bodyguard for the liberty of [a] Republic" jeopardized by the "total lack of intellectual culture now pervading national politics."[98] As the "most enlightened of any [class of citizens] in the country," Southerners are the only constituency who can "attend properly to the interests of the country," because they alone have managed to retain the "talents, learning and statesmanship" on which the early United States was founded. As "the *only free* people left upon the American continent," according to Evans, the South "asks but her *sacred constitutional rights*" be respected. Yet because these rights have "been grossly and persistently violated," the South, after "iron[ing] down our just indignation . . . because of our devotion to the 'Union,'" is forced to act. While it initially "shuddered and shrank from laying hands on the magnificent Temple which our forefathers reared in proud triumph," the South is finally forced—like "the thirteen States [that] cut the chains of Great Britain to regain their birthright, Freedom"—to "sever the galling links that bind us to" such an oppressive people.[99] Thus, it is "the Demon of Fanaticism" shown by Northerners—not the secession of the Southern states—that has "insanely destroyed the noblest government which the accumulated wisdom of centuries has ever erected." Acting on the love of liberty that defines their Anglo-Saxon forebears and justifies their separation from Great Britain, according to Evans, the South, like these forebears, must resolve to "defend her constitutional rights at *all hazards*" and thus to accept as inevitable the "Revolution" that results from her fight to protect her "Independence."[100]

While she likened the political plight of the South to that of the child Colonies in her correspondence and articles, Evans's second novel, *Beulah* (1859), advanced the cause of an oppositional Southern nation by featuring the child as a representative of the racial principles on which the United States was founded. Evans read John Stuart Mills's *Principles of Political Economy* while she managed an orphan asylum, and this diverse education proved productive for her subsequent novel, *Beulah*. Telling the story of a young orphan child whose struggles become analogous to the "struggles of the southern people," as Elizabeth Fox-Genovese has pointed out, Evans's novel uses the child to encourage readers to support the creation of an alternative, independent nation that resists and finally overcomes the "despotic" rule of a parent country wrongly committed to destroying the racial hierarchy that has historically ensured the nation's well-being.[101] Evans takes her child protagonist's name from Isaiah 62:4: "Thou shalt no more be Forsaken; neither shall thy land any more be termed Desolate: but thou shalt be called Hephzibah and thy land Beulah: for the Lord delighteth in thee, and thy land shall be married." While critics have focused on Beulah's perpetually deferred adoption through marriage, as Fox-Genovese notes, they have tended to overlook the ways in which her name signifies Southern land. Yet Beulah functions as a powerful and immensely popular representative of both the plight and future of the South precisely because of the racial narrative she successfully upholds in the face of her own isolation as a "young child separated from its mother, and wailing in some starless desert."[102]

Beulah's physical placement at the novel's opening between two other children — her sister Lillian, a six-year-old with "large, soft blue eyes, set in a frame of short, clustering golden curls," and Claudia, whose "fierce Italian blood" is evident in her "brilliant black eyes" and "long, dark ringlets" — highlights her own "marble-like whiteness" and the power of that whiteness to explain as well as generate her repeated declarations of independence and insistence that she is "too proud to be adopted" by those who do not share her ideals.[103] The "fierce, proud spirit" that makes Beulah inassimilable into the families that visit the orphan asylum ensures her separation not only from adoptive families but from the "little blue eyed angel" sister who she loves as fiercely as her own autonomy but who agrees to affiliate with those unlike her.[104] Told that she is "all fire and tow" and therefore, despite her physical similarity to her sister, "horribly ugly," Beulah must recommit to the fierce independence that offends her would-be Northern parents and "nerve" her "brave spirit" to hold true to her ideals, even when they require giving up her fair sister.[105] Like the South she represents, Beulah may appear "horribly ugly" to those who reject her, but the "brave endurance" and love of liberty to which her color attests ensures that she will triumph over her enforced isolation—that she will not be "like dumb, driven cattle," but will instead be "a hero in the strife."[106] Doing so requires that she refuse all social affiliations that compromise the ideals that her "proud little spirit" represents and that all who associate with her agree to "sign [her] treaty" of independence.[107]

As an icon of an emergent Southern nationhood, Evans's child protagonist not only explained the Confederacy's emergence but encouraged many Southerners to create living representatives of such distinctly Southern ideals. Beulah became a popular girl's name in the South, where "hundreds of living Beulahs," according to the *Guadalupe County Gazette*, "do homage" to the novelist's ideal of Southern nationhood.[108] *Beulah* was not only a popular novel that sold 22,000 copies in the first nine months of its publication; it was also subsequently made into a six-act play by Harry G. Horton, and then a movie in 1915 starring Henry B. Walthal, who had played the male lead in *The Birth of a Nation*. Evans's *Beulah* continued to circulate as a powerful narrative of Southern nationhood after Reconstruction and well into the twentieth century. And as we have seen, *Beulah* won widespread acclaim for Evans in no small measure because, as the national confrontation over states' rights and the slave question mounted, readers found in her fictional child a powerful model for imagining a separate Southern nation based on the racial ideals the child had long represented.

The child that Evans features in the two novels that preceded *Macaria; or, Altars of Sacrifice* (1864) makes possible her third narrative's outspoken commentary on secession and the formation of a Southern nation that, in realizing the racial ideals of its forebears, is capable of becoming what the United States no longer can be—a "vast populous empire, rich in every resource" and the "guardian of peaceful liberty."[109] Claiming in *Macaria* that all "just governments rest on the consent of the governed," Evans redirects the Lockean political rhetoric that constitutes the United States into her rationale for separation from it.[110] As *Macaria*'s female protagonist, Irene, declares, secession is "the only door of escape from [the] political bondage"

into which "the diabolical hate and fiendishness" of "the spirit which actu-
ates the North" desires to place the South.[111] Declaring that "national, like
individual life, which is not noble, free, and honorable is not worth living,"
Irene concludes that the South is not "a people who can survive their liberty"
and become subject to "the despotic government at Washington." Rather,
Southerners are a people who, "deprived of liberty, can not exist."[112] As such,
they not only resemble their forebears, but they uphold, by forming a separate nation, the principles that "once constituted American freedom, and
rendered the republic in earlier years" exemplary.[113] Declaring that "Freedom — Independence" lie beyond the "long dark vista stretch[ing] before
the Confederacy" if the South continues to act wisely, Irene outlines the
necessary steps that will "crown the South a sovereign, independent nation"
and encourage it to become, once "purified from all connection with the
North" — particularly from its "mischievous element of New England Puritanism" — "a prosperous and noble" nation.[114] By declaring "free trade" and
opening "our ports . . . to all the markets of the world, except Lincolndom,"
the South will establish itself as a far-reaching new republic that will flourish through upholding "the institution of slavery."[115] Furthermore, once the
new nation selects "our Presidents . . . solely for their intrinsic ability and
nobility of soul," discourages "home manufactories," and supports "iron
currency," Evans predicts, it will quickly become a dominant economic influence in "trans-Atlantic nations" as well as in those "anarchical pseudo-
republics" of "South America and Mexico."[116] Written during the Civil War,
Macaria clearly construes an expansionist South as attempting, in the formation of a "sovereign, independent nation," to redeem the failed promise
of the American Revolution.[117] Yet crucial to Evans's creation of this final
account of imperial Confederate nationhood, as we have seen, is the child
that helps to generate multiple national formations out of the concept of
racial purity that it represents.[118]

"FAIREST CHILD OF SOUTHERN WATERS"

The "vast populous empire" that Evans predicts the South will establish
in "South America and Mexico" becomes the joint project of a number of
Southern writers, adventurers, and filibusters before, during, and after the
war, who, like Evans, rely on the child as an icon of a racially pure sepa-

rate South to argue for such expansionist undertakings as creating the 1854 Republic of Sonora, founding a "Universal Republic" with the Confederacy as capitol, and invading Cuba.[119] In short, by deploying the child as a racial icon, the Confederacy — just as the Republic of Texas had done — not only founded a separate nation that conceptually depended on even as it distinguished itself from the United States, but also attempted to prove its racial superiority by undertaking a series of expansionist projects aimed at conquering racial others. A minority of Southerners, such as Simms, believed that "bringing the State of Cuba" under the control of "the people of our Southern States" while separating from the United States was a mistake, and that there would be "time enough to think of adding Cuba to our domain when we ourselves are rendered secure . . . from the perpetual annoyance of abolition."[120] However, most Southerners believed that Cuba offered enticing opportunity for wealth.[121] Even as Evans argued for Cuban incorporation into the Confederacy, for example, she relied on the *Denhigh*, a famous blockade runner that went between Mobile and Cuba, to keep her supplied with fineries such as gold pens, stockings, handkerchiefs, and champagne. Southern novelists like Lucy Holcombe Pickens contributed to the South's imperial ambitions to acquire Cuba by featuring the child as the linchpin in her pro-filibustering 1854 *The Free Flag of Cuba*. Because Cuba is "the fairest child of southern waters," Pickens asserts, all true "sons of Washington" are obligated to liberate the "degraded children of tyranny" from Cuba's "despotic oppressor," Spain.[122] Declaring that the goal of Narciso López's filibustering expedition to Cuba was "not to conquer the Spaniard" but, rather, to give "the bright child of the waves" the liberty that only the South could truly represent and defend, Pickens, like those from Louisiana, Mississippi, Texas, and Florida who created the Order of the Lone Star and mounted a "Lone Star Expedition" to invade Cuba, relied on the alternative Anglo nationhood that Texas had represented to advocate for an imperial South. "Free[ing] the beauteous child" from the "dark oppressors" who make "so many *slaves*" of their subjects, according to Pickens, would bestow "the greatest amount of good to our race" and to the young Southern nation that supposedly embodied and upheld it.[123]

Fifty years later, as the United States finally took control of Cuba in the Spanish–American War, U.S. political commentators would return to the South's expansionist projects in Cuba — and their reliance on the child —

to deny U.S. imperialist designs on Spanish territory. Murat Halstead's *The Story of Cuba* (1898), for example, asserted that "the ill-fated López expedition . . . was of course in the interest of the formation of more Slave States in the United States" and stated conclusively that the "Cuban filibustering expeditions of a former generation . . . were distinctly to provide for the admission of more Slave States in the American Union."[124] Precisely because they were associated with the South, such imperialist interests had no relation to "the true feelings of the American people and the real state of affairs in the American Union" when war with Spain finally did occur.[125] Because "the general condition of things in the United States [is] very different from what it had been at the time of the expeditions of López and during the period which immediately followed it," Italo Canini asserts, "the sympathy which the people of the American Union . . . feel for the cause of Cuban liberty [is] purified from suspicious motives and influences."[126] If Cuba had initially been "an object of dread" for the United States because of slavery, "it became at a later period an object of vehement desire," because the United States supposedly could no longer "be accused of having gone into this war for want of more territory."[127] Purified of the self-interested motives that characterized Southern efforts to acquire Cuba—efforts that, as Pickens's novel illustrates, rely on political rhetoric featuring the child—U.S. political commentators invoke the same political discourse to declare that the United States is not engaged in "a war of conquest." Instead, it merely recognizes in Cuba's fight against Spain "the same genius which prompted the thirteen infant colonies to declare themselves free from the mother country."[128] Such a recognition of Cuba's similarity to the United States, however, works not toward parity but toward conquest, and "the lone star of Cuba," according to Canini, will soon "find its place by the side of what was once the lone star of Texas [in] our national emblem."[129] As we will see in the final chapter of this book, the United States assumed control over Cuba, as it did over Texas, through reappropriating the representations of the child that helped to script diverse racial states into being.

Despite the final failure of both Texas and the South as imperial nations, the child continued to enable dissenting visions of the South's affiliation with and interpellation into the United States well into the twentieth century. We can see the child's enduring centrality to Southerners' reimaginings of the South's place in the national body by turning to D. W. Griffith's *The Birth of a Nation* (1905), where the answer to the social chaos that emancipation creates—a chaos in which Southern states are "treated as conquered provinces" rather than as equal participants in the national project, according to the film's opening caption—is offered by a child. Frightening black children by pursuing them while covered with white hoods, white children are the origin and "inspiration" for "the new revolution" that will reunite the nation—that will align "former enemies in the North and the South" in the joint project of "resisting the Carpetbaggers' political folly."[130] By drawing on their prior racial heritage as "the unconquered race of men from old Scotland," these new patriots form a Klan that, by mimicking child's play, reasserts the white supremacy that has long organized the nation. Gillian Brown has suggested the powerful sway that child's play generally has in shoring up a U.S. national imaginary,[131] but, as the preceding pages have suggested, the racial meanings represented by the child and the play in which it engages are crucial to the creation of a number of alternative, opposing national formations that threaten to rupture as well as to reinforce that U.S. national identity. Representing the complex range of emergent national stories competing for dominance in the antebellum era, the child therefore offers important clues about the uneven developments of Anglo nationhood in the nineteenth century. In the next chapter, I will show how the complex set of competing national histories that the child authenticates through pro-slavery as well as antislavery political debate structures an American popular literary tradition that was not concerned with slavery. I will show, in other words, how the child's political meanings from the early national period through the Civil War transform familiar understandings of American literary as well as political cultures.

⤜⤛

three

CONSENTING FICTIONS, FICTIONS OF CONSENT: THE CHILD AND THE NINETEENTH-CENTURY SENTIMENTAL NOVEL

The preceding chapters have charted how the child at the center of a wide range of pro-slavery and antislavery writing consistently upholds racial hierarchy as a sign of national identity. With the child's foundational importance to three white-supremacist nations within the American hemisphere as a context, this chapter tracks popular American sentimental writing that, while not interested in slavery or race relations, nonetheless features the child to uphold the idea of a racial state. "The debut of the child as a central figure of popular and literary culture is one of the most striking aspects of sentimental discourse," Elizabeth Dillon notes.[1] Ala Alryyes concurs that the rise of the novel was indelibly "intertwined with the child's story," observing that, "whereas children are virtually absent from eighteenth-century fiction, they populate every manner of sentimental text in the nineteenth century."[2] Literary critics have tended to understand these child protagonists as part of what Phil Fisher identifies as "the political content of sentimentalism," which, he asserts, "is democratic in that it experiments with the extension of full and complete humanity to classes or figures from whom it has been socially withheld."[3] Thus, as Andrew Delbanco and Joan Hedrick have argued regarding *Uncle Tom's Cabin*, it is the image of the child that inspires Stowe to extend the sentimental novel's framework to include the plight of racial others.[4] While I do not dispute the child's importance to sentiment's pluralist aims, I would rather observe that the child not only targets disadvantaged others as objects of sentimental outreach but, conversely, shores up the very essential racial hierarchies the novel and the child at its center seek at times to transcend. As we will see, the child's complex, contested relation to the concept of consent that is at the heart of liberal-democratic governance transforms the child at the center of sentimental fiction into a particularly effective vehicle through which to encourage readers to develop a possessive investment in whiteness and thereby to affiliate themselves with a racial state. Regardless of the sentimental novel's subject matter, then, and regardless of whether the sentimental novel engages with questions of race or slavery, the following pages illustrate how the child featured in sentimental novels represents a racial logic that privileges whiteness to persuade individuals in various stages of civic affiliation — be they black or white, slave or citizen — to consent to collective, communal governance.

The child has long played a crucial role in the ongoing process of soliciting individuals' consent to national authority, as many scholars of U.S. political culture have shown.[5] Even as the child justified the Colonies' break from the "corrupt" parent country of Great Britain and helped to create a new people who, as Ian Shapiro, among others, has noted, based their national identity on an abstract Lockean philosophy of universal rights, the child signified both the promise of the inchoate nation and the ongoing, endemic conceptual threats to its successful continuance.[6] In *Some Thoughts Concerning Education*, John Locke recognized the particular problem that children as a class of people inherently incapable of consent, pose to his consensual model of liberal-democratic community. Children, according to Locke, "*when little, should look upon their Parents as their Lords, their absolute Governors*" precisely because they are incapable of the unconditional requirement for elective inclusion within the Lockean consensual body politic: "reason."[7] Locke's concern that "the Characters of [the child's] Mind" are not and cannot be trained to be consistent with the consent necessary for civil society registered powerfully with a new nation that required the loyalty of the next generation for its successful continuation.[8] Operating as a focal point around which Locke and early U.S. citizens considered the conceptual limits as well as possibilities of consent, the child therefore contested even as it helped to constitute the new nation's Lockean liberal-democratic tradition. The child, in other words, epitomized the difficulty as well as the necessity of gaining and retaining consent in a new liberal-democratic society like the United States that was based on racial hierarchy.

Responding to the threat as well as promise that the child posed to the new nation, an extensive textual machinery consequently developed that was devoted to resolving the particular social, and contractual, problem that the child had represented to the nation since its inception. Legal and advice manuals considered, and attempted to settle, the problem that the child potentially posed to the civic order and longevity of the new republic. William Story's *A Treatise on the Law of Contracts* (1844), for example, catalogued children generally as "persons incompetent to contract" because of their incapacity to consent, but the work's description of the particular conditions under which the child might lawfully enter into a contract reproduces the consensual requirements of citizenship.[9] Those few contracts that could be initiated before the age of consent — "fourteen years in a male, and twelve in a female" — must be "made voluntarily and freely, and with a knowledge on the part of the infant" about his or her right to choose.[10] If late-eighteenth-century and nineteenth-century Americans repeatedly revised their social contracts in an attempt to realize at every level of governance the consent to the larger social contract that the U.S. Constitution codified, the child became a primary site for gauging the success of this national project. Not only were courts increasingly interested in determining as well as directing children's power of choice, but the popular child-rearing books that proliferated beginning in the 1820s offered parents advice on how to ensure that their offspring grew up to uphold, rather than undermine, the nation's ideals. While the single most important parental duty, according to Benjamin Rush, is fitting children "for uniform and peacable government" in a country unique for its "peculiar form of government," books like Lydia Maria Child's *The Mother's Book* (1835), H. W. Bulkeley's *A Word to Parents* (1858), and Heman Humphrey's *Domestic Education* (1840) enjoyed wide sales because they provided parents with helpful strategies for teaching the child "that he does not belong to himself but is public property" and that he must "watch for the state, as if its liberties depended upon his vigilance alone."[11]

By featuring the child who most acutely represented the challenges as well as possibilities of gaining individual consent, novels engaged in this ongoing textual project of soliciting individuals' consent to collective governance.[12] By using the child's story to encourage individuals to affiliate with and reaffirm their consent to national governance at critical moments of the nation's collective life, nineteenth-century novels, as Jean Franco observes, not only offered important "blueprints of national formation" but continued to contribute to the nation by providing "imaginary solutions" to the threat that "racial heterogeneity" and other dangers posed to the nation's order and longevity.[13] Popular fiction written in both the North and the South during the Civil War, for example, encouraged adults and children alike to align themselves with national interests by inviting all readers to imagine themselves as child protagonists engaged in the war effort — as active participants in upholding national interests, albeit diversely construed, rather than as bystanders in the national struggle. As Alice Fahs has recently shown, this fiction so effectively depicted war as "a splendid adventure facilitated by the embryonic national state" that Theodore Roosevelt recalled in his autobiography the importance of such tales to infusing his Civil War boyhood with a sense of national purpose.[14] Whether or not they addressed threats to national integrity explicitly, popular fiction tended to feature child protagonists as stand-ins for complicated sets of anxieties about national identity. Nineteenth-century fiction, in short, featured children as agents of national interpellation, as powerful vehicles for soliciting readerly consent to affiliation and governance, precisely because of their uniquely contested relation to the national body.

However, by representing whiteness as a founding element of individual as well as national identity, the child at the center of nineteenth-century U.S. domestic novels most powerfully worked to resolve the conceptual challenge to consensual government that the child had historically embodied. By teaching readers to understand whiteness as a cornerstone of individual civic identity — to develop, regardless of their own racial identity, what George Lipsitz has termed a "possessive investment in whiteness" as an indisputable and authenticating sign of social affiliation[15] — the child featured in sentimental novels therefore extended the racial representations defining the nation to individual members of a collective body, encouraging individuals to shape their selves in accordance with the precepts of a racial state. Not only a textual vehicle through which racial others like Harriet Wilson, Harriet Jacobs, and Frederick Douglass represent their condition as non-citizens, as Karen Sánchez-Eppler has richly illustrated, the child more fundamentally represents race as a precondition of civic selfhood and incorporation into the national body.[16] If the child "serves as a term of universal social reference," the child featured in the nineteenth-century novel, in other words, not only models "how reading might shape identity and character," but more particularly aligns that "identity and character" with the state through illustrating that whiteness is at the center of the civic self the state recognizes and values.[17]

To argue for the importance of the popular novels written by women that Nathaniel Hawthorne descried, feminist scholars have tended both to approach protagonists as "little women" rather than as the children they are and to focus on the bonds that sentimental novels forge "between predominantly white women and their racial, class, and nation others" rather than on how such novels help to create and maintain these essential racial, class, and national differences in the first place.[18] The assumption that child protagonists of sentimental fiction are women in training has led critics to focus exclusively on girl protagonists and to thus overlook the wealth of boy children peppering the pages of sentimental fiction. Louisa May Alcott's most popular little woman, Jo March, has long been an overdetermined site of feminist critics' identification, with Catherine Stimpson and Carolyn Heilbrun, among many others, identifying her as an important early role model.[19] Yet even as such important scholars indicate Jo March's significance, her lifelong project of raising "little men" has received scant attention. Thus, scholars have failed to recognize how the boy protagonists as well as the girl protagonists of such novels—precisely because they *are* children as much as they are little men or little women—represent and offer various resolutions to the challenge of gaining consent that the child has long embodied.[20] Just as the child protagonist of *The Scarlet Letter* is able to exert social control over her "dissenting" parent precisely because of her status as a child,[21] the child protagonists at the center of popular novels such as Alcott's *Little Men*, Maria Cummins's *The Lamplighter*, and Frances Hodgson Burnett's *Little Lord Fauntleroy* solicit the consent of individuals to collective governance by representing whiteness as an essential element of the civic self.[22] Reinforcing racial hierarchy as a conceptual mainstay not only of the nation but of those individuals who desire recognition by and affiliation with it, popular boy protagonists as well as girl protagonists operated as vehicles through which characters and readers came to recognize whiteness as a founding ideological attribute of the civic self. "Dangerous," according to Laura Wexler, "not because it was *feminine* but because it was *racist*, just like the culture of the men," the nineteenth-century U.S. sentimental novel therefore features the child that represented both the promise and contingency of the nation to transform those who might dissent from collective governance by a white nation into individual upholders of its racial logic.[23]

CONSENT AND SENTIMENT

Gaining and retaining the consent of individuals residing within the United States was absolutely essential for the political vitality and longevity of the nation, as Abraham Lincoln was acutely aware. Asserting that "in this age, and this country, public sentiment is everything. *With* it, nothing can fail; *against* it, nothing can succeed. Whoever molds public sentiment, goes deeper than he who enacts statutes, or pronounces judicial decisions," Lincoln insists on the importance of attaining the collective consent of the individuals within the nation to direct its most fundamental political processes, to guide its decisions, and to protect its national integrity.[24] Going "deeper" than the juridical procedures and laws that govern how its people behave, consent, according to J. H. Raymond, emerges from "the great heart of the nation," which beats "true alike to freedom and the constitution," even as it is not reducible to either.[25] Not simply encouraging the nation's people to "cultivate peace with all nations and form entangling alliances with none," consent more fundamentally reflects the nation's defining characteristics — consent is, in short, the "immortal sentiment" that by remaining vital, according to Raymond, will ensure that "this nation endures," even as it addresses internal conflict and contradiction.[26] Producing "the Constitutions and laws" that, according to William Seward, cannot "rise above the virtue of the people," consent embodies and preserves within each individual "the love of freedom and the sacredness of the rights of man" that keep the nation's identity alive and well.[27] Therefore, once consent is successfully achieved, according to the nineteenth-century social commentator John Thomas, the nation can transform its laws not as a refutation but as an assertion of the "large patriotism of Washington" and can continue to direct the nation "as Washington [had] probably intended it."[28] Because the "noble sentiment" of individuals within the nation ensures that the high ideals that produced the nation "will always carry the field" against the lower ones that threaten it, existing laws that are based on the "erroneous sentiments of the American people" will inevitably be overturned in favor of legislation that reflects "the genuine instincts of the people."[29] Working in tandem, then, consent and sentiment operated as a system of checks and balances that maintained an authentic, genuine national identity.

Able to represent this interlocking relation between sentiment and consent with distinctive force because of its unique relation to both, the child not only forged bonds between individuals regardless of racial difference but more fundamentally established whiteness as the most natural and therefore desirable identity for all citizens, regardless of their race.[30] With cartes de visites and daguerrotypes popular commodities by the 1850s, photographs of children, for example, testified to the ongoing importance of whiteness not only to a nation that was increasingly committed to freeing its slaves, but also to the identity of the individuals residing within it.[31] Serving as important "scientific 'evidence' of the dominant influence [that] pure blood over mongrel" had in founding the nation, Francis Galton argued that photographs of children documented the importance of race to social progress. Advocating that Anglo-American families take annual pictures of their children to record the superior development that Anglo-Saxon blood ensured, Galton helped to transform the child into a powerful barometer of an individual family member's civic identity and status. The child portraits that W. E. B. Du Bois included in his 1900 international "Types of American Negroes" exhibit, like the one in figure 7, attest to the father of the Black Power Movement's awareness of the child's importance to the project of locating race within the self as part of the larger project of locating the self within the state.

Popular nineteenth-century scientific accounts similarly turned to the child to determine the racial origins and evolution of the individuals making up a distinct national people. Once Charles Darwin's *On the Origins of the Species* and *The Descent of Man* indisputably located human origins in the animal kingdom, scientists began to focus on the child as the key to unlocking the mystery of human evolution.[32] As John Fiske asserted in *The Meaning of Infancy*, "the theory of evolution" reveals childhood to be the most powerful key to understanding man's "superiority" and thus has "given to childhood a vast biological importance."[33] Believing that the child represented "a still closer kinship to the natural world" than anyone had imagined humankind

Figure 7 "African American Girl," head and shoulders portrait. Courtesy Library of
Congress, Prints and Photographs Division (LC-USZ62-124807).

possessed, scientists, as James Sulley argued in *Studies of Childhood*, needed to cast an "inquisitive eye on the infant" to determine the racial influences shaping individual and national identity.[34] The American child held particular interest for evolutionary theorists who saw the "wonderful progress of the United States" as a clear indicator of the powerful "results of natural selection."[35] While many natural scientists, including Sir Charles Lyell, turned to the "New World" as a rich source of data because of the "originally grander scale" of its "ancient strata . . . plentifully charged with fossils," the American child offered the richest field for scientific observation.[36] Because this child, according to Sulley's *Studies of Childhood*, functioned not only as a "product" of his country, but also as "a monument of his race, and . . . a key to its history," scientists made the American child the subject of extensive evolutionary inquiry in order to understand the remarkable success of the United States in "convert[ing its] forefathers from brute creatures into human creatures." It is the unshakable conviction that "nature is more thoroughly heeded . . . in our country than in any other community known to history" that caused American scientists like John Fiske to assert that the individuals who inhabit the U.S., more than those of any other nation, are capable of "boundless progressiveness."[37]

This unique capacity for progressiveness is both represented by and depends on the nation's children, who "recapitulate" America's unique evolution.[38] Because the child is "the real bearer of evolution," all of "man's progressiveness" depends on "his infancy."[39] While scientists like Chamberlain posit that the child's uniquely prolonged period of postnatal "helplessness" brings about "the helpfulness of mankind" and thereby provides the door "through which the capacity for progress can enter," it is more particularly each child's repetition of "the chief [physical and mental] stages which the race passed through before him" that determines the nation's progress.[40] According to this popular nineteenth-century scientific view, each child "recapitulates" its nation's particular evolutionary history and, in so doing, is afforded the opportunity to "suppress" its nation's "useless past" and to "purify" its ancestors' "animal nature."[41] Because many scientists believed that "the child is a little compressed, synthetic picture of all the stages of man's evolution," the opportunity that a nation provides for its children to develop is, according to W. F. Crafts, "one of the best thermometers of [its] progress."[42] Therefore "prolonged infancy and childhood" become, according to Thomas Atkins in *Out of the Cradle into the World* (1895), the best guarantees of "man's power over nature" and form "the foundation of all his progressiveness."[43]

In such a model, the unique progress of which the United States is hypothetically capable depends on American children's successfully shrugging off what scientists term their "savage" origins and developing into completely civilized citizens. In short, each child's development should help to strengthen an American national identity that defines itself in opposition to, and as the "natural" evolutionary outcome of, the nation's savage origins. William Dean Howells, for example, comments in *A Boy's Town* (1890) that, although "a savage is a grown-up child," it is "even more true that a child is a savage," but Alexander Chamberlain actually itemizes the numerous characteristics that reflect the savage origins with which each American child must struggle: "the child and the savage" both "have a quick eye for the natural world," a remarkable "resistance to physical pain," and a "morbid ambition."[44] Because they so closely resemble one another, Chamberlain finds it as "hard to know [savages] as it is to know children." However, scientists can overcome the obstacles their child subjects pose by using the same strategies that enable them to "enter into the realities of primitive man's thought."[45]

Such study is imperative to stimulate national progress because too many adult citizens continue to show the savage traits that attest to the nation's incomplete evolution. While numerous nineteenth-century social commentators identify American children with "savages," and thus with the nation's "savage" origins, they are keenly aware that this stage is all too often unsuccessfully repressed in adult citizens who subsequently fail to fulfill the nation's evolutionary promise. According to the child-study expert Stanley Hall, "We have only to go among the most refined American homes and schools to find" indisputable evidence that "the old savage traits" still exist.[46] The prevalence of such characteristics causes Chamberlain to admit that, because American citizens retain "much of the savage," whether "the child is more savage than the adult is often quite a relative matter." Many scientists argue that American society has "not yet learned that art of developing the individual from infancy" and is therefore responsible for this failure "to fulfill perfectly the rich promise with which childhood begins."[47]

To help American children develop more successfully and thereby ensure the nation's optimal evolutionary progress, many scientists turn their attention to the special "problem" of civilizing the American boy, who, they argue, is particularly troubled by "the primal, vigorous instincts and impulses of the . . . savage."[48] Howells, among others, contends that "the world of boys" remains completely "outside of the laws that govern grown-up communities" and rather resembles the rituals and customs of "far-off savages."[49] It is this very characteristic, however, that makes communities of boys such a compelling source of information for social scientists. One such community was established in the 1870s by the philanthropist John McDonogh, who gave 800 acres of land near Baltimore for the education of poor boys. In his 1884 study of the McDonogh boys, *Rudimentary Society among Boys*, John Johnson asserts that while his analysis of "juvenile society may appear trivial" initially, "a nearer view of the customs of the McDonogh Boys . . . reveals that they are worthy of scientific observation."[50] Because boys, according to Johnson, "repeat the history of their ancestors and of the race itself," and in so doing "represent the evolution of a primitive savage into a civilized being," the sociologist may discover through careful analysis of a "company of lads" both "the rudiments of primitive society" and "the germs of its development." Johnson shows how the boys' community, like "many savage societies," feels a bond "of a very striking intensity," but he also records how the boys "naturally" evolve "beyond" this rudimentary developmental stage to acquire the racialized identity that signifies the nation's uniquely successful evolution. For example, as disputes arise, the boys institute "custom and law, and a system of property" and even set up inheritance laws that enable departing boys to will their property to their friends. Rules governing property acquisition become increasingly sophisticated, and the boy who violates them is "universally regarded as dishonest."[51] Through this seemingly natural process of conquering their savage impulses, cast-off boys earn the right to reenter and uphold the society that initially rejected them.

Basing their models on such findings, reformers argue that if the nation wants to maximize each child's supposedly "natural" development from "savage" to "citizen" and thereby maintain national superiority, education needs to be reconceptualized so that it mirrors the developmental process itself. Rather than "stifling and crushing" children's natural interests in the world, Thomas Atkins contends in *Out of the Cradle* (1895), those interests should be "assisted and guided" to produce the "habits of industry, order, and morality" that characterize the nation's successful citizens.[52] In his immensely popular *Education: Intellectual, Moral, and Physical* (1860), Herbert Spencer bemoans the tendency of American parents to "dress their children's minds as they do their bodies, in the prevailing fashion." Comparing the American parent to the "Orinoco Indian" who "puts on his paint before leaving his hut," Spencer argues that the American boy's "drilling" reflects his parents' "social position" rather than "facts in which [he] is interested."[53] To engage children's interest in education and thereby ensure optimal social evolution, Spencer suggests that educators "carry each child's mind through a process like that which the mind of humanity at large has gone through" and let the child learn important facts "as the race learnt them." Doing so will transform the pupil from a "mere passive recipient of others' ideas" into "an active inquirer" of lived experience.[54] By "playing amidst trees and plants," for example, the child becomes acquainted with botany, just as rambling "among rocks gives him many lessons in geology."[55] Such active learning "productively" channels the "savage," antisocial energy of youth — what Atkins identifies as the inevitable "fidgets, riotousness" and tendency to "break things" — and ensures that even the most resistant student will grow into an upstanding and informed adult.[56] The social effects of such educational reforms on the nation would be profound. Not only would more children develop into the citizens who reflect the nation's remarkable evolutionary success, but such changes would ensure that "individuals left out of the old scheme of education" because of physical or psychological defect — in short, "the blind, the deaf, the slow of mind, and the restless of spirit" — could now, according to Fiske's *The Meaning of Infancy* (1883), be "reverently educated by the new democratic order in spite of all their defects." Thus, as a result of "the school becom[ing] more flexible and variable in its method," even "unselected" Americans can be reclaimed by and, in turn, help to develop the nation.[57]

Like these scientific and visual accounts, nineteenth-century novels turn to the child to uphold the idea that national superiority depends on each individual's learning those racial traits that will ensure the success of the new democratic order and, in so doing, insist on the importance of whiteness to individual identity. Teaching readers to value whiteness as a signature trait of selfhood, child protagonists, in other words, make social affiliation contingent on the acquisition of the nation's requisite racial characteristics. While scholars have identified the various strategies that nineteenth-century domestic novelists used to encourage readers to identify with racial others, they have not considered how such novels, regardless of whether they address the slave question or include racial others, feature the child that has long represented race as an organizing principle of the nation in order to encourage individuals to understand whiteness as a founding element of a socially legible self.[58] By representing as central elements of their plots the process through which their indigent child protagonists either gradually "become" white or use their whiteness to bring initially resistant individuals into the national order, these novels teach readers to desire — and illustrate how they might acquire — whiteness, regardless of their racial identity, as a signature trait of national incorporation and affiliation.

Scholars have tended to distinguish sentimental fiction from contemporary scientific discourses, equating the "Darwinian world of struggle in which it was assumed most Americans functioned" exclusively with a realism and naturalism that rejected "the romantic material and formulas of earlier fiction" and demanded that the author act "like a scientist" who depicts "objectively" all subjects, no matter how "unliterary."[59] David Shi summarizes the prevailing view when he states, in his recent survey of American literature, that late-nineteenth-century writers "seized upon cultural realism as an antidote to syrupy sentimentalism."[60] And yet, as Fiske, the most influential advocate for evolutionary theory in the United States, remarks in *The Destiny of Man* (1884), "the sympathetic emotions" are produced by "the very same causes . . . which developed science."[61] In so doing, he voices a general view held by nineteenth-century men of science that sympathy — a primary component of sentiment — plays a crucial, if unexplained, role in the natural world and therefore requires extended scientific analysis.[62] Darwin's *The Expression of the Emotions in Man and Animals* (1897), for example, states conclusively from extensive research that "sympathy is innate" in the animal kingdom.[63] In *The Order of Things*, Michel Foucault reminds us of the pivotal role that sympathy plays in nature and early scientific studies of it.[64] Thus, although current scientific discourse tends to minimize the significance of sympathy, nineteenth-century natural scientists determined that it was an essential component of animal experience.

We can begin to see these all too easily forgotten interconnections between sentiment and science by turning to the writing of Louisa May Alcott, whose novel of child development analyzes the relation between human beings and the natural world to posit an effective schema of social regeneration.[65] While *Little Men* (1871) initially seems to offer an unrealistic, even highly improbable, account of the social redemption available to indigent and homeless children, closer inspection reveals that Alcott also depicts at-risk boys as inevitably shaped by the new scientific laws that are radically redefining how individuals perceive the natural world.[66] As it carefully tracks the process through which indigent, antisocial children are transformed into upstanding middle-class American citizens—a process that requires children to shed the "savage" impulses that, for evolutionary theorists, indicate a lack of civilization and to adopt the "civilized" behaviors coincident with national ideals—*Little Men* illustrates how this developmental model requires the erasure of other "less evolved" and therefore undesirable selves. Reading Alcott's sentimental text from the vantage point of the contemporary scientific accounts of social regeneration just outlined makes explicit what is implicit in sentimental fiction from its genesis in the early 1850s to its demise in the late 1880s: that its child protagonists extend what we have seen to be the child's longstanding work of maintaining the racial premises of national identity and perpetuating racialized narratives of civic affiliation. Attending to the boy protagonists of *Little Men*, therefore, provides an important framework for approaching immensely popular sentimental novels like *The Lamplighter* and *Little Lord Fauntleroy* that bracket the era of the sentimental novel.[67] Each featuring a girl and boy protagonist, these two novels chart the emergence and logical conclusions of sentimental fiction's interest in the child as an icon of racialized nationalism. But Alcott's explicit depiction of the child protagonist's role in upholding a racial state is necessary to trace the implicit investment of writers like Cummins and Burnett in the child.

FROM SAVAGE TO CITIZEN

At the end of *Little Men*, Jo Bhaer admits that she likes to think of her Plumfield "family as a small world." But as the novel makes clear, this world —and, by extension, the family that represents it—has been radically redefined by emerging scientific theories of evolution and natural selection.[68] Nowhere is this more apparent than in Alcott's descriptions of the children who live and learn under the Bhaers' care, for if the goal of their small boarding school is to make boys productive members of society, the Bhaers must first acknowledge the animal impulses each child inherits and with which he must contend. The novel insistently equates the boys who attend Plumfield with animals to reveal their "true" nature. During bath time, for example, the boys collectively resemble "a school of young whales at play."[69] While individual boys are equated variously with "colts," "owls," "squirrels," "wild hawks," "beavers," and "robins," the essential animal nature of all boys is most apparent in the novel's "scientific" recounting of a particular creature—the brop—that the boys create and pretend to be. The brop, according to the narrator, is an "interesting animal not to be found in any Zoological Garden, unless [a scientist] has recently brought one from the wilds of Africa." Its "peculiar habits and traits," which include "grunt[ing], "giv[ing] a shrill hoot," and "talk[ing] good English," are carefully recounted "for the benefit of inquiring minds." This new, mysterious animal requires scientific analysis because it epitomizes the boys' chaotic blend of civilized and uncivilized impulses. Its animal body, incorporating such household items as shawls and lampshades, indicates the latent conflicts between its domestic and animal natures. Determined by "the few privileged persons who have studied them" to be "a remarkable mixture" of wild and civilized impulses, the brop represents the particular challenge that misfit boys pose to traditional educational systems that fail to acknowledge the power of their animal nature.[70]

The instructional home that Jo offers these at-risk boys acknowledges their innate animalism, but the first and most important step in Plumfield's alternative-educational system is to encourage each boy to claim the particular animal impulse he exhibits. Jo repeatedly figures her boys as animals—as "robins who stray into her nest" in need of the "cast-off feathers" with which she clothes them.[71] The newly established scientific fact that "boys are animals" appears to restructure every aspect of domestic life.[72] As the novel opens the "house seem[s to be] swarming with boys," who wreak domestic havoc by jumping over desks, sliding down banisters, and dripping on furniture.[73] Yet if Plumfield's initial permissiveness to the boys' animal nature seems to preclude its educational mission, as the newly arrived Nat assumes when he says that Plumfield reminds him more of "a great family than a school," its more flexible domesticity always works to reinforce its educational goals of "self-knowledge, self-help, and self-control."[74] These goals require first and foremost that every boy acknowledge his animal nature. By accepting that he acts like a pig, Stuffy, for example, internalizes that sloth and gluttony need to be counterbalanced with restraint and industry. Likewise, admitting that he resembles a wild horse in need of taming helps Dan to understand as problematic his hostility to restraint of any kind.[75] Domesticity plays an important role in helping the boys to identify their animal impulses and thereby understand their different developmental goals, as when, for example, each boy receives a sugary cookie from Jo in the shape of the "beast or bird" that most closely characterizes him.

Acknowledging their animalistic impulses helps the boys to feel sympathy for others' weaknesses, thereby transforming Plumfield into "a little ecosystem where everyone can help each other."[76] As Foucault suggests, sympathetic identification plays an important role in the natural world, and Jo encourages her boys "to treat other people as they like to be treated themselves." Though "sympathy is a sweet thing" that "works wonders for each boy," the true "science of teaching" is knowing which children "to mix" in order to maximize the power of sympathetic feeling. Jo, for example, teaches her "wilderness of boys" to "feel great sympathy for Nan," an unruly tomboy she brings to Plumfield, because she not only will help Jo "make little gentlemen" out of the boys but also "needs help" in learning "good manners."[77] When Nan temporarily reverts to her antisocial ways, Jo treats her like the animal she resembles to instill the sympathetic regard on which Plumfield's order depends. Although she admits that she does not "like to tie [Nan] up like a naughty little dog," Jo nevertheless straps Nan to a bed frame because she believes that she "must be treated like a dog" if she does not "remember any better than one."[78] By enabling Nan's temporary regression to her canine origins — her "growl[ing] and grovel[ing] on the floor" — Jo finally instills the sympathy and self-regulation essential to domestic order.[79]

Despite Alcott's careful depiction of how children's sympathetic feelings can work to create a harmonious world, *Little Men* registers a strong concern that nature, as it is being newly described in evolutionary theory, may be powerful enough to destroy the family and the mutual sympathy it teaches. This concern is most evident in the fate of the crab family that Dan, the boy most interested in natural science and most "untameable," brings back to Plumfield. Though the boys provide a cage for the crabs and they seem to be "settled in their new house," their home does not remain harmonious for long. Rather, the boys return to find "two little crabs scuttling about the floor" and "a third clinging to the top of the cage evidently in terror of his life," while below him the big crab sits "eating one of his relations in the coolest way." Alcott insists on the familial relations of the crabs as she describes in minute detail the following scene of slaughter. However, her inability to determine whether the bizarre image is "sad" or "funny" indicates its indecipherability within the emotional register of domestic culture:

> All the claws of the poor victim were pulled off, and he was turned upside down, his upper shell held in one claw close under the mouth of the big crab like a dish, while he leisurely ate out of it with the other claw, pausing now and then to turn his queer bulging eyes from side to side, and to put out a slender tongue and lick them in a way that made the children scream with laughter.[80]

The conflation of screaming and laughter—of horror and humor—registers the potential failure of affective bonds to keep family members in the natural world from being "dismembered" and subsequently transformed from relatives into food and the dish on which it is served.

To illustrate how the family finally exerts control over these socially seditious impulses, Alcott first represents the children at Plumfield as having the savage nature that, according to scientists, indicates their (and, by extension, the nation's) most rudimentary and therefore animalistic developmental stage. Nan, for example, proves her "wildness" by transforming a doll that should train her in nurture into a "savage." After painting Poppydilla "brick red" and dressing her "up with feathers, and scarlet flannel, and one of Ned's leaden hatchets," Nan lets her "Indian chief" loose to "tomahawk the other dolls" in the nursery, which runs "red with imaginary gore."[81] Such savage impulses cause the younger children at Plumfield to conduct sacrificial rituals in the spirit of early peoples who "had altars and things" on which they put "live creatures to sackerryfice."[82] One such sacrifice is made to the awful, imaginary Kitty Mouse, who demands the ritualistic incineration of all of the human images with which the children play. After

Demi tosses all of his soldiers on the funeral pyre, Daisy, "with a face full of maternal woe," commits her "dear dollies" to the coals. However, the Kitty Mouse proves insatiable, compelling the children to offer an entire play village to appease its "awful voice." The children, "cheering and dancing like wild Indians" as each cottage burns, seize in their frenzy the "one lady who had escaped to the suburbs" and cast her mercilessly "into the very heart of the fire." The final offering of Teddy's toy kid lamb, Annabella, most powerfully conflates the children's imaginary play with their natural origins. Because she is made of animal skin, Annabella expresses her "anguish and resentment" in a "very awful and lifelike manner": after curling up her legs to avoid the flames, "she [flings] her arms over her head as if in great agony; her head turn[s] on her shoulders and, with one final writhe of her whole body, she sinks down, a blackened mass on the ruins of the town."[83]

However, the Bhaers' alternative family is able to contain these socially regressive impulses by teaching children to shed the brownness that indicates their "savage" origins and value the whiteness associated exclusively with national values instead.[84] Though repeated throughout the novel, the exclusive association of whiteness with social acceptability is epitomized by Goldilocks, who makes an appearance at Plumfield. "A mixture of child, angel, and fairy," Goldilocks takes her name from "the golden hair which she inherited from her blonde mamma," and which envelops "her like a shining veil."[85] Not in need of social regeneration like the children at Plumfield because she is the daughter of Jo's affluent sister and brother-in-law, Goldilocks appears in the text as a timely reminder to the boys and Nan of the appeal of affiliation with society and the incentives for conforming to its codes.[86] As the representative of these codes, Goldilocks immediately is able to "fill every heart with tenderest sympathy" and thereby achieve immense influence over all the children. Because of the "natural refinement that makes her dainty in all things," she demands that those around her develop more rigorous hygiene regimes. Fearing to hear "do away, dirty boy," the boys use "more soap during her visit than at any other time" and make sure that they do not approach her with "unclean hands." Even Nan is "subdued" by the "well-bred lady" who identifies her as a "wild animal" after witnessing her savage nursery play. Goldilocks's lasting influence over Nan becomes clear when, a number of months later, Nan writes a natural-science report on the sponge and admits that, although she does not like "to wash her face" with it, she uses the sponge regularly because she "wishes to be clean."[87] After the Thanksgiving Day "washing, brushing and prinking that would have done anyone's heart good to see," the children convene to watch Goldilocks act out a classic drama of racial evolution. Playing Cinderella, she tugs at the "brown gown" that covers her body and keeps her from enjoying the affluent life to which she aspires. The "rags" drop away and reveal "a gorgeous sight" underneath—a "pink and white" gown that suggests the "true" whiteness of her body and her right, because of it, to be "a tiny court lady."[88]

Even the most rebellious boys who enter Plumfield are coerced to value the whiteness that indicates their social evolution from "savage" to citizen. Immediately on entering Plumfield for the first time and being told by Jo that he has acquired both a "home" and "a father and a mother," Nat is sent upstairs to "have a bath." The bathroom contains an extensive array of cleaning devices — "two tubs, besides foot-baths, basins, douch-pipes and all manner of contrivances for cleanliness." They are immediately put into operation by Nursey Hummel, who removes the soil from Nat's "grimy little hands" and "dirty face" and cuts his "rough neglected hair" to reveal the "good forehead" it hides. Once "washed and done up in a blanket by the fire," Nat experiences for the first time "the new and delightful sensation [of] cleanliness." He is never the same again, for the washing begins the process of regenerating Nat's neglected body and soul. Under the beneficial influence of Plumfield life, Nat's "eyes begin to shine," his "once thin cheeks" become "plump and ruddy" instead of brown and thin, and, in a process that uncannily mimics human evolution itself, his "bent shoulders slowly straighten."[89] While Nat flourishes, the friend that he brings to Plumfield resists the regenerative lessons the Bhaers try to teach him. Dan's resistance is registered both by his antisocial behavior and by his persistent brownness. As the test case of the family's power over scientific models of the natural world, Dan initially prefers the company of animals to human beings and resists the efforts of Plumfield's impressive plumbing. Unlike Nat's "long and fair" face, Dan's face remains "square, brown and strong," with particularly "brown cheeks." The "big, brown hands" that resist washing and cause his expulsion from Plumfield, however, are also his ticket of reentry. Jo spots "a shirt sleeve with a brown hand sticking out of it" in the bushes one night and carries into the house a "ragged, dirty, thin, and worn-out" boy. The pain and illness that his itinerant life have produced finally break down Dan's resistance to both Plumfield's affective power and the whiteness it requires. As Dan's broken bone is set and his "lips become white" from the pain, he confesses to "Mother Bhaer" that he has "come home" at last.[90]

The Bhaers ensure that Dan will become an upstanding member of U.S. society by channeling his enduring interest in the natural world into the creation of a natural-history museum. Initially "conquered" by Jo's "soft words," Dan is able to endure his prolonged confinement to the house and the process of being "tamed by pain" only because she offers him a makeshift cabinet of curiosity in which to put his specimens. Claiming that she will see in "the pebbles, mosses, and gay butterflies good resolutions carried out, conquered faults, and a promise well kept," Jo asserts the important role that science can play in the individual's social progress.[91] In so doing, she represents the prevailing view held by late-nineteenth-century museum advocates like Frederic De Peyster, president of the New-York Historical Society, who contended that natural-history museums "add strength to all moral and religious ideas" because they "rouse the public mind to the noble impulses [of] scientific discovery."[92] Other prominent public men agree with De Peyster, and P. T. Barnum speaks for the vast majority of American citizens when he declares that natural history is the "most important" study for "the youth of a rising generation" because it teaches "man his superiority over brute creation."[93] Dan's successful internalization of this superiority is accomplished only after he transforms his personal cabinet into a "fine, little museum" for public uplift.

Dan's public institution successfully reinforces in even the most recalcitrant boys the important "idea of progress" by transforming the animals it exhibits from competitors to subjects of intellectual analysis.[94] Named after its benefactor, who, like the most prominent capitalists of the 1870s, endows an institution for the viewing of nature to "elevate" the poor, the "Laurence Museum" dramatically redefines the boys' understanding of their relation to the natural world. Initially, the boys tend to compete with animals, pitting their physical prowess at gathering nuts against that of the "busy squirrels," for example. The squirrels "work the best" and collect more nuts, but once the boys adopt the objective gaze of the scientist and learn how to analyze the natural world around them, they are able to discover where the squir-

rels hide the nuts and steal them back.[95] It is this very "new view" of the
environment that natural-history museums attempt to inculcate, according
to Eilean Hooper, to encourage national progress.[96] Equating "knowing"
with "seeing" rather than the other senses, the natural-history museums
becoming popular during the 1870s present objects from the natural world
exclusively to the view of their visitors and collectively organize museum
objects to represent, and thereby reinforce, the new scientific evolutionary models and, more particularly, humans' placement within them.[97] The
natural objects collected in the Laurence Museum do remind the "dirty-
handed" collectors of their relation to the various assembled animals and
savage idols and thus of the need to go "off to wash."[98] But when Dan, as
museum curator, is presented with a long-desired microscope, he finally
metamorphosizes into an illustrious man of science who contributes to,
rather than retards, civilization's progress.

As we have seen, the child protagonists that Alcott features in her sentimental novel are transformed through the educational reforms that evolutionary scientists argue will turn even the most unruly children into irre-
proachable citizens and thereby ensure the nation's optimal development.
Plumfield re-creates the developmental process in its educational model—
acknowledging each child's animal nature and encouraging his evolution
from "savage" to "civilized" citizen—to make successful citizens out of antisocial children. By using scientific theories that argue that the nation's superiority depends on its evolutionary progress, Alcott shows how the child's
consent to civic affiliation furthers a national narrative that precedes but is
perpetuated through popular sentimental discourse. Further, her child protagonists make explicit the racial premises underpinning national narratives
even as they come to accept these national ideals as "natural" and therefore
unavoidable. Although frequently ignored in favor of Alcott's *Little Women*,
Little Men is less a departure than an explicit reiteration of sentimental fiction's representation of the child. With this explicit account of the racial
components of the child's civic regeneration as a context, the next section
analyzes the two sentimental novels that were most popular with readers at
the beginning and end of the genre's era—Cummins's *The Lamplighter* and
Burnett's *Little Lord Fauntleroy*—to trace the sentimental child's enduring
role in maintaining the racial contours of civic life.

THE WHITE IMAGE

The most popular book of the 1850s after *Uncle Tom's Cabin*, Maria Cummins's *The Lamplighter* (1854) captured and sustained the interest of a wide range of readers in large part because it showed them, through the career of its racially indeterminate, socially ostracized child protagonist, how to improve their own circumstance by gaining social recognition and prominence.[99] That betterment, not surprisingly, involves the acquisition of the racial characteristics that will transform Gerty Flint, the child protagonist of *The Lamplighter*, from social outcast into conceptual mainstay of a cohesive collectivity. While Amy Kaplan and Amy Schrager Lang have recently identified Gerty's importance as an icon of U.S. imperial and class structures, respectively, their analysis of her as a young woman rather than as an eight-year-old child has left uncharted the important alliance she forges between race and nation precisely because of her representative status as a child.[100] When the reader is first introduced to Gerty, she is as ideologically and physiologically dark as the indigent among whom she lives, but she quickly learns to alter her self to conform to the social imperatives of the community to which she desires to belong. The novel opens by insisting that the "sallowness" of Gerty's "complexion" is not only skin deep but a direct reflection of the "darkened" state of her understanding. Both her external and internal darkness are produced by "the mud and filth which abound in those neighborhoods where the poor crowd together" and where even the whitest objects — "the beautiful snow," for instance — cannot maintain their "purity and whiteness" for long.[101] In Cummins's novel, the dirt that inevitably rubs off on the skin of these social outcasts leaves a subcutaneous trace in their characters, and they become clearly, and repeatedly, distinguishable as "furren boys."[102] Yet if Gerty is literally raised amid the dirt that surrounds and characterizes those existing outside of the community she desires to enter, she is not reducible to it, and it is the focus of Cummins's novel to show readers how such a child develops into an icon of national virtue for all who encounter her. Crucial to this process, however, is Gerty's capacity to absorb the explicitly racialized behavior and identity defining that culture. If "good taste is inborn," as the narrator declares, Gerty's capacity to internalize and then demonstrate it, in other words, is the direct result of the lessons that she receives at the hands of the fair-skinned child representatives of the community of which she desires to be a part.

Gerty is first introduced to a community organized on principles of civic virtue by the child who epitomizes these principles for all who gaze on her. Looking into the parlor windows of the affluent homes that she passes on the street, Gerty is transfixed by a child with "fair hair" that falls "in long ringlets over a neck as white as snow."[103] The parlor, as the nineteenth-century social commentator Russell Lynes writes, was not only "a room in the house, but a room in a world apart, a sort of island filled with treasure to which one could on very special occasions retreat."[104] The parlor into which Gerty peers offers just such a rich visual opportunity, but the child at its center reinforces not the child's separability from but centrality to the social structure on display. "Not belong[ing] to himself but public property," according to Benjamin Rush, the child, even when safely ensconced within the American parlor, must represent and uphold "those virtues and values [so] critical to the republic's survival."[105] Taught the "honesty and willingness to sacrifice for the good of the nation" that "guarantee that civic virtue would be sustained" in future generations, the child therefore looks after the "welfare of [the] country" by representing "the principles of virtue and of liberty" that are "the cornerstone of national survival."[106] Regardless of venue, "American youth," as the nineteenth-century child memoirist Lucy Larcom recalls, was therefore infused with the distinct idea that "this universal Yankee nation" was peopled with "good patriots."[107] Thus, the parlor that can be in danger of becoming, in Harriet Beecher Stowe's estimation, too sequestered from communal life — "a cold, correct, accomplished fact . . . an undeniable best parlor . . . too good for human nature's daily food" — functions as the principal private room in which public manners were most on display, in large part due to the child at its center.[108] Within the primary physical space offering "the public world of strangers" important lessons in civic virtue, the child ornamenting the parlor, therefore, teaches disorderly individuals like Gerty, who freely mingle on "the urban street," how to train their "minds and habits of thinking and reasoning" so that they can achieve the "*self*-government" on which, according to Catharine Maria Sedgwick, "effectual and lasting government" depends.[109] Thus, by identifying the "fair hair," "blue eyes," "cherub face," and "little round, plump figure" of the child ornamenting this ideologically weighted space as crucial to understanding this process of social affiliation, Gerty begins to internalize the racial ideals that the child represents as necessary prerequisites to social inclusion.[110] In so doing, she begins the process that will enable her to occupy such a place in her own right and represent its values to all who, like her, look longingly upon it.

It is, however, the "white plaster image" of a child that Gerty receives from her new benefactor, Trueman Flint the lamplighter, that enables her to internalize the whiteness that the child represents as integral to national life. The whiteness of the little Samuel that True gives to Gerty is much remarked on by characters and narrator alike. Although there were "some black ones too" sold by "those furren boys" from Gerty's old neighborhood, True chooses the white one for his new charge because of its unique capacity to associate the behaviors of the Samuel—prayer and spirituality—with not only a physiological but an ideological "lightness" of being.[111] "Her eyes fixed intently upon the white image" that she receives, Gerty asks what the Samuel is doing when, with hands folded in prayer, he looks to heaven.[112] In so doing, she begins her education in the Christian principles that prove powerful enough to "cure" Gerty of the passionate temper learned from her first, working-class home and identified repeatedly as "her dark infirmity."[113] After learning about prayer and God, Gerty conforms physically as well as behaviorally to the "white image" she hugs "close to her bosom" by looking to the "sky bright with stars" and wrapping her hands around the Samuel in prayer as she falls asleep.[114] While Gerty attempts, in a rude imitation of the white icon, to appropriate its ideological importance, it is only through extended association with Emily Graham that she adopts the principles that equip her to become a national icon in her own right. Remarkably "pale, with light complexion," Miss Graham successfully imparts "light to the child's dark soul" and teaches her how to "receive into her heart the first beams of that immortal light" by the example she sets as well as how she looks. Yet the process of "cast[ing] light upon the darkness" of Gerty's soul transforms the child's external as well as her internal state. Although, as her childhood friend Willie Sullivan tells her, she has not "got long curls, and a round face and, blue eyes" like the child they both admire in the parlor window, when she "shines" with "right" feeling, she becomes "the brightest looking girl" he has ever seen.[115] After Gerty suffers the loss of her Samuel at the hands of a malicious housekeeper but nonetheless manages to maintain the behavior characterizing the child she admires, she becomes lightened by the new ideals of forbearance that now govern her. Thus, the narrator concludes that the most "brilliant rainbow" is not "half so beautiful as the light that overspread the face of the young girl," and this metaphorical lightness subsequently translates into a physical "pale[ness]" that is repeatedly remarked on by admiring onlookers.[116]

In turn, the lightness that Gerty's character and person acquire not only inducts her into the community from which she was once ostracized but transforms her into a powerful exemplar of its values for all who look upon her. No longer considered "horrid-looking," Gerty is transformed into a child of "admirable looks" by those who watch her walk down the street, with True Flint and Emily Graham on each arm.[117] But if Gerty attracts much attention in public because of her behavior and looks, it is in the parlor that she most powerfully represents the civic values that she now embodies. Gerty's capacity to create a parlor out of her new living space in the lamplighter's humble house signals her newly acquired ability to demonstrate as much civic virtue as the very best American child. Thus, Trueman Flint's room comes to reflect in its newly achieved "outward neatness and purity" the "inward peace" that typifies both the nation and the child who represents and protects it.[118] Just as Gerty is able to create a harmonious parlor out of the lamplighter's disorderly room, so, too, is she essential to the Graham household, where she acts as a living embodiment of its most valued communal principles and, as a result, becomes its most highly valued object. Before she makes her appearance in the Graham's parlor, Gerty is unanimously identified as "the most perfect" person to inhabit it, graced with "beautiful manners" that should serve as a "pattern" for all other young people. Her entrance is anxiously anticipated, and "all eyes turn upon her" to observe "Gertrude's motions . . . attentively" as she "crosses the large saloon with characteristic grace, and as much ease and self-possession as if she were the only person present." While her "features are still the same" as they were when she lived outside of the community she has come to uphold, in every other regard she "has altered very much" and become "a fine-looking girl," with "something very attractive about her face."[119] As such, she is able to remind the parlor's occupants of the communal principles they are in danger of forgetting when they ridicule one of their visitors. Declaring that it is the responsibility of every person in the parlor to develop and maintain the right civic virtues, Gerty reminds her chastened listeners that the fundamental tenets of proper "civilizing" life must never be forgotten wherever such a life is expected to flourish, particularly in the parlors that display civic values for all to see.

While the narrative thrust of *The Lamplighter* is Gerty's gradual transformation of herself into a pure white child icon of civic values for those needing social guidance, the child protagonist in Frances Hodgson Burnett's *Little Lord Fauntleroy* is, from the novel's opening, such a powerful representative of U.S. civic identity that he can effortlessly uphold, protect, and, most important, extend the nation's precepts, despite the increasingly racial diversity of the nation's population.[120] Anxious that an uninterrupted decline "in the size of native-born white families," coupled with a dramatic influx of immigrants, was causing "the white middle-class" to be "overrun by a population they considered, in Darwinian and eugenic terms, less fit to rule society," as Estelle Freedman, Matthew Guterl, Gary Gerstle, and Arthur Mann have shown, late-nineteenth-century readers found in Burnett's child protagonist a dynamic and reassuring national representative able to uphold the whiteness underpinning national identity not only by frustrating the efforts of immigrants to strip him of his social significance, but also by exporting American values to an ideologically hostile parent country.[121] Collapsing distinctions between real and fictional children by making Cedric the most popular boy's name of the 1890s and by purchasing the Fauntleroy suit for an entire generation of boys (figure 8), readers of *Little Lord Fauntleroy* endeavored to transform their own children into national representatives of the enduring centrality of whiteness to the nation, regardless of the changing racial makeup of the nation's populace. Therefore, just as Burnett claimed that it was her son Vivian's ardent fascination with the American Revolution—a fascination that caused him to declare himself publicly to be "a strong Republican"—that was her inspiration for a novel in which "American principles" were pitted against both the racially diverse immigrants within the nation and "the still-hardened class system" of England, American readers, conversely, used Burnett's child protagonist as a model for transforming their children into internationally persuasive representatives of U.S. civic values.[122]

The child protagonist of Burnett's text, like Vivian, "attract[s] every one's attention [by telling] The . . . story of the Revolution."[123] Yet Cedric proves to be irresistibly appealing to his audience because he not only expresses but also embodies American national identity with his "handsome, strong,

Figure 8   Children wearing velvet suits inspired by *Little Lord Fauntleroy* style. Courtesy Library of Congress, Prints and Photographs Division (LC-USZ62–67632).

and rosy" complexion and "golden hair" — "soft, fine, gold-colored . . . hair which curl[s] up at the ends and [falls] into loose rings."[124] His fairness intensifies as he discusses "the Declaration of Independence" with Mr. Hobbs, the local grocery man. When Cedric is "told the story of the Revolution," he becomes "so excited that his eyes sh[ine], his cheeks become . . . red, and his curls [are] all rubbed and tumbled into a yellow mop."[125] Thus, if his "American blood tells," as his grandfather, the Earl of Dorincourt, fears, it only transforms Cedric into an even more compelling image of whiteness for those who watch and listen to him. Liking to talk "polytics," Cedric declares himself publicly to be "a 'publican" and insists on his Americanness when he tells his grandfather that his "papa was a very brave man — as brave as George Washington." Contesting his grandfather's "grim" assertion that Cedric is an "Englishman," Cedric declares, "I am an American. I was born in America. . . . You have to be an American if you are born in America. . . . If there were another war . . . I should have to — to be an American."[126]

The national identity that Cedric's whiteness represents to all who encounter him ensures that he operates as a persuasive representative of U.S. civic ideals wherever he goes. As a youngest son, Cedric's father, Captain Errol, has "gifts" his older brothers do not — namely, "a beautiful face and a fine, strong, graceful figure," a "bright smile, . . . and brave and generous" manners.[127] But because these gifts go unrecognized under the law of primogeniture governing the British aristocracy, Captain Errol emigrates to America and marries an American. After his uncles and his father die, Cedric becomes the next in line to inherit the Earl of Dorincourt's estate and title. Expecting to find the new American inheritor living in an unkempt rented room, Mr. Havisham, the earl's attorney, is impressed with the neat and tasteful appearance of the widowed Mrs. Errol's parlor. When Cedric enters the ideologically weighted parlor, he immediately reinforces the attorney's dawning conviction that national taste and refinement, rather than "American impudence" and "beastly, impudent bad manners," govern the child he has been instructed to relocate to England. Not only "one of the finest and handsomest little fellows he had ever seen," Cedric is also "the best-bred," because Mrs. Errol has taught him to "think [the] kind [of] thoughts always" that, as Webster, Paine, and Rush contend, represent and therefore uphold the nation's ideals. To be so trained, according to the narrator, transforms a child from even the most humble origin into one who can be a powerful national icon—into finally nothing less than "a king."[128] The national identity that Cedric epitomizes is heightened rather than reduced once he moves to Great Britain to live with his grandfather and inherit the earldom. Though the earl initially chooses "to think that Cedric's beauty and fearless spirit [are] the results of the Dorincourt blood," he comes to understand during the course of the novel that the fierce love of American independence that Cedric has acquired in his American home is the source of the appeal that makes him "every inch a lord."[129]

Yet it is the tyrannical earl's education in and gradual acceptance of the U.S. civic selfhood that Cedric represents, rather than Cedric's transformation into a lord, that forms the primary focus and imaginative energy of Burnett's text. Initially thinking that "those American children" are nothing more than "a lot of impudent little beggars," the earl is confounded by the "graceful, easy carriage" that suggests a refinement wholly unexpected in the "fearless little fellow" who stands before him. Yet, as the earl learns, Cedric's "beauty and . . . brave, childish grace" are a function not so much of his British as of his Anglo-American heritage. Looking at his "cross and hard-hearted" grandfather "with clear, unsuspecting eyes" that do not see "the ugly part of his nature," Cedric applies to his new British family a national lens that is powerful enough to persuade his uncle to conform to what the novel insists represents the U.S. civic identity that Cedric epitomizes. Dumbfounded "to see each of his ugly, selfish motives changed into a good and generous one," the earl finds that his grandson is able to clear "all the atmosphere from the big gloomy room and make it brighter." Integral to this brightening is Cedric's representation of his grandfather as not a "gory tyrant," like the British ruling class who oppressed the Colonies, but, rather, as a democratic overseer of his tenants' well-being. Because of the "frank, true, kindly nature, the affectionate trustfulness" that produces in Cedric the unshakable conviction that his grandfather "is not a tirent [sic] at all," the earl is persuaded to conform his behavior to realize Cedric's national vision. It is contemplating "that small boy with the mop of yellow love-locks" who entertains him with descriptions of "the Fourth of July and the Revolution . . . and the Republican Rally in all the glory of its banners and torches and rockets" that makes the Earl want to be a "benefactor of the entire human race, and the soul of nobility" rather than the "most vicious, savage, ill-tempered" master his servants and tenants have ever had. Thus, contemplating the combination of "childish courage" and blond curly locks that Cedric possesses causes the earl to conclude that his "long life in which there had been neither generous deeds nor kind thoughts" must be changed to conform to Cedric's vision of him.[130]

However, the full extent to which Cedric has transformed the earl and the governance he practices to conform to a U.S. liberal-democratic model become fully apparent only when Cedric's right to the earldom is challenged by the very kind of dark American interloper that many Anglo-Americans had come to fear by late century. "An American of the lower classes" who is "ignorant, vulgar . . . absolutely uneducated and openly mercenary [if] very handsome in a coarse way," the dark-faced and black-haired mother, as well as her dark child, cannot, according to the earl, share his "noble blood and lofty lineage," because they do not look or behave like the American child who has reconstituted British aristocratic selfhood and its rule in his image. Demonstrating its mother's "queer[ness]" as well as inheriting her "big black eyes and black hair," the second child is universally recognized to be, like its mother, "a person from the lower walks of life," who is "uneducated and untrained . . . and quite unused to meeting people" of "the right sort." Motivating the earl to unearth Minna's plot and to restore Cedric to what has come to be understood by all as his rightful place, this dark child represents a threat not only to U.S. national identity, but also to a British way of life newly reconstituted along Anglo-American lines. Once each child has been restored to his rightful social place, the novel ends by predicting that Cedric will reconstitute not only his grandfather's outlook, but all British social practice and the juridical laws that govern it, around the racially appealing civic self that made him such a favorite with his grandfather in the first place. Thus, when commoners and aristocrats alike convene to celebrate his birthday on the Fourth of July, all temporarily "forg[e]t to feel any restraint," but look democratically at the "beautiful, innocent little fellow . . . with his brave trustful face" and come collectively under the power of the American ideology that his "brave and just and true" countenance represents.[131] This final image of an American child reigning supreme over the British aristocracy, as well as over the racial others who threaten his ideological hegemony, illustrates the child's capacity to reach beyond the nation's borders to reconstitute the parent nation in the child nation's image.

RACIALIZED READING

While critical accounts of the nineteenth-century sentimental novel have documented its capacity to create identificatory bridges across racial difference in an effort to reclaim such texts as part of an American literary canon, it is equally important to recognize how popular novels like *Little Men, The Lamplighter,* and *Little Lord Fauntleroy* solicit consent to governance among their readers by representing race as an integral element of social affiliation and civic selfhood in the first place. It is important to recognize, in other words, how the child these novels feature not only builds bridges between white characters and racial others, but, as importantly, reinforces the sharp racial differences that make such bridges necessary. Laura Wexler has commented on the paucity of critical attention devoted to "the direct and indirect effect of the widespread reading of mid-nineteenth-century sentimental fiction upon those who were not white, middle-class, Christian, native-born readers."[132] As the preceding pages have suggested, this fiction, through its child protagonists, encouraged all readers not only to sympathize with the plight of racial others, but also, as importantly, to develop, regardless of their own racial identity, an investment in whiteness as a necessary prerequisite for social affiliation and thereby to contribute to the very racial hierarchies sentimental novels often seek to redress.

In so doing, the child that has historically both posed and helped to resolve the challenge of soliciting individual consent to national governance continues, through the racial narrative that it represents, to facilitate consent to major reallocations of social responsibility that begin to occur in the middle of the nineteenth century. The child, as Marilyn Ivy has observed, plays a crucial role in displacing "the possibilities of politics and community in late twentieth-century America into the domains of a privatized imaginary" that finally subsumes the possibility of collective social action.[133] But this impulse has its historical origins, as Ian Hacking points out, in the nineteenth century when the "emerging welfare state" placed increasing attention on the image of the child to "radically increas[e] state control over families." Less concerned with "the protection of children" than with the "increase of state power," federal and state governments used the image of the child to transform mounting social problems facing the nation into signs of personal and familial, rather than civic, failure. "Beginning in the Victorian era," the

image of the child therefore began to serve as a "rhetorical device for divert-
ing attention [away] from society" and onto the self to justify a steady decline in social responsibility.[134] By functioning, as Walt Whitman writes, as
the "text [that] the reader of the book," as well as its author, must complete,
the child encourages the all-absorbing identification that Ann Douglas and
Gillian Brown have shown distracted nineteenth-century readers of popular fiction from the pressing social problems coincident with the "realities
of the advancing capitalist economy."[135] Representing not so much an alternative to civic responsibility as a primary means through which individuals
consent to assume an increasing amount of it, the child functioned as a
primary device through which the state solidified control over its citizens.

The racial narrative that child protagonists in popular novels like *Little
Men*, *The Lamplighter*, and *Little Lord Fauntleroy* therefore represent facilitates, as well as coincides with, this larger shift toward the social regulation
of the self. The children who do not or cannot transform themselves into
white citizens as Gerty and Dan can remain on the margins of these texts —
often as objects of outreach for children who can — and in so doing represent the increasing social problem that such citizens pose for the state. As
the child advocate and reformatory-school leader Louise Rockford Wardner wrote to promote legislation such as the 1879 Industrial School for Girls
bill, "Each unprincipled, impure girl left to grow up" unreformed poisons
society as many times as she reproduces and therefore should be committed
early in life to one of the many experimental reformatory schools that child
savers were founding in the late nineteenth century.[136] Jane Addams devoted much of her adult life to creating benevolent institutions like Hull
House, aimed at promoting the childhood "innocence," "tender beauty,"
and "ephemeral gaiety" that characters like Gerty achieve.[137] Books like
Jacob Riis's *The Children of the Poor* (1892), Edward Townsend's *A Daughter of
the Tenements* (1895), and Franklin H. Briggs's *Boys as They Are Made and How
to Remake Them* (1894) feature the child to encourage major reconsiderations
of both the individual's social responsibility and society's responsibility to
its citizens. Yet the whole culture of social outreach in the United States, as
Illinois Governor John Altgeld, a prominent late-nineteenth-century child-
welfare reformer, observed, was designed not to eradicate but to "intimi-
date and control the poor."[138] In his 1897 address to the Illinois House of
Representatives, Altgeld reminded political leaders that it is not the poor

but the "greedy and powerful" who have the power to destroy the nation, and therefore that "our country" will only fully realize its "great vitality" by "listen[ing] to the voices of the struggling masses."[139]

To the extent that nineteenth-century fiction obscures these voices by promoting a model of social affiliation that is premised on the whiteness the child represents, such fiction generally helps to sustain the social order that Altgeld critiques, even as such fiction may encourage some readers to challenge racist social institutions like slavery. We need to recognize that, among other things, we are consenting to this set of social practices when we identify with the child protagonist, when we chart the social progress of our selves through Dan or Gerty or Cedric. We need to understand that nineteenth-century fiction constructs not only the child but, through this child, the fiction of unilateral consent to the social circumstances that might enable some readers to discover how to move from dingy street to ornate parlor, but that guarantees that there will always be a dirty, dark, and poverty-stricken child outside on the street looking longingly in.

four

⤭

TRANSNATIONAL TWAIN

As we have seen, the child was the cornerstone on which the conviction that the United States was a white nation rested from the nation's genesis through the slavery crisis, even when the wide range of literary, political, and social discourses featuring the child were not explicitly addressing questions of race relations or racial equality. This enduring conviction of the nation's whiteness facilitated its expansionist era, as scholars from Reginald Horsman to Theodore Allen have amply documented, but white supremacy continued to function as an imperfect crusading ideology, shot through, as Eric Love has recently pointed out, with more contradiction than is often recognized.[1] Thus even as political commentators such as Reverend Theodore Parker continued to argue that the "peculiar characteristics of the Anglo-Saxon . . . his restless disposition to invade and conquer other lands" explained U.S. expansionism, white racial formation was a continuous process, catalyzed and altered by a wide range of social forces throughout the second half of the nineteenth century.[2] Given the child's longstanding conceptual significance to nation formation, it is not surprising that the child was pivotal both to sustaining the nation's racial identity during this increasingly expansionist period and to critiquing the racial premises underpinning U.S. imperial nationalism. Nowhere is the child's dual role more apparent than in the writing of Mark Twain. As Albert Stone noted almost half a century ago, the child serves as an important "instrument for social criticism" throughout Twain's career, and conversely, Twain's child, as Steven Mintz has recently observed, "has served as a lightning rod for popular fantasies and anxieties" about American culture.[3] Amy Kaplan makes a passing reference to the child's importance to Twain's attitude toward U.S. imperialism when she argues that the little Kanakas child Twain describes in *Following the Equator* represents, for Twain, an "implicitly racialized discourse of national identity" that depends on distinctions between "savage and civilized, American and European, masculine and feminine" to justify the nation's commitment to slavery, as well as its absorption of territories like Hawaii.[4] Yet in her attention to U.S. imperialism as a "dyadic contest" for gender dominance between a "masculine America and a feminized Europe," Kaplan overlooks the full conceptual significance of the child through whom the nation came into being as a distinct geopolitical entity and through whom Twain formulated his critique of U.S. race relations, as Shelley Fisher Fishkin has persuasively observed.[5]

As the following pages illustrate, the child represents how U.S. national identity depends as much on collaboration with as on distinction from the very European nations against which the United States has historically tended to define itself. Thus, the child in whom Twain is interested serves as an important instrument for representing the complex transnational influences that continued to underpin U.S. racialized nationalism in the second half of the nineteenth century. Even as the child proved central to the Colonies' separation from Great Britain and to the formation of an autonomous, infant nation, as we have seen, such repeated representations of the child not only constitute the new nation in opposition to European nations "grown old," as Noah Webster writes, through "folly, corruption and tyranny."[6] Rather, as Twain's commentary on the child makes clear, such accounts of the child also register the extent to which U.S. national identity is shot through with a racial subtext that aligns the new nation with a longstanding multinational commitment to upholding and extending white supremacy. The child, featured in a wide range of political, literary, and social texts circulating in the United States and abroad, therefore, not only represented a coherent narrative of the United States' political independence from other nations; it also registered, through its representation of race, the transnational collaborations constituting and ongoing within the nation it exemplified. In so doing, the child functioned as a particularly rich discursive site, both authorizing a distinct national identity and, in its depiction of the integral place of race in shaping that nation's international relations, revealing the conceptual instabilities embedded within, and threatening to undermine, the nation.

The child's capacity to represent the transnational racial logic underpinning U.S. national identity is of urgent concern at the current critical moment when Americanist social, literary, and political scholarship has undertaken to chart the transnational forces operating within and beyond U.S. national culture. Even as important recent analyses have documented the child's conceptual centrality to the formation and stabilization of U.S. national identity, the tendency of these landmark studies to overlook the racial meanings inhering in the child has circumscribed consideration of the full range of ideological work in which the child is engaged not only in sustaining national cultures, as we saw in the preceding chapters, but also in establishing transnational cultures.[7] The myth of racial purity not only constitutes individual nations, as scholars have long observed.[8] It also creates transnational communities. Therefore, the idea of race serves as one of the primary vehicles through which nations can be "transformed by contact and interaction with each other," as John Carlos Rowe, among others, points out.[9] Because we cannot chart a history of the modern world without acknowledging the history of nation-states bumping up against each other, as Cornel West reminds us, it is important to understand how the child not only represents race as an organizing principle of individual nations but, as importantly, illustrates such nations' shared commitment to reinforcing whiteness as a conceptual mainstay of a global community.[10]

We can begin to excavate these unrecognized dimensions of Twain's child protagonist by placing it within the context of the child through whom Harriet Beecher Stowe rethought the racial politics of *Uncle Tom's Cabin*.[11] While Leslie Fiedler has argued that Twain was preoccupied by Stowe's success in the marketplace, Alice Crozier and Judie Newman have more particularly noted the striking similarities between Stowe's *Dred* and Twain's *Pudd'nhead Wilson*.[12] Both featuring a central pair of children, one of whom is free and the other enslaved, these two texts read together suggest that Stowe exerted a more extended and complex influence on Twain's career than is usually recognized in comparisons of Stowe's Uncle Tom and Twain's Huck. Repeatedly identified as a "*child*—a gay, beautiful unformed child," Stowe's girl protagonist Nina insists on her own enduring status as a child rather than "a woman grown" to protect her own "perfect liberty and free[dom]."[13] Yet if there is for Nina "a feeling of dread . . . a most dreadful feeling" associated with the civic representation "without liberty" that marriage signifies, Stowe insists that Nina must develop a civic self that retains the best aspects of her child identity to challenge her brother's attempts to govern her slave community along racist lines.[14] Many have commented on Nina's failure to recognize racial identity—that is, her failure to recognize her slave Harry as her half-brother—and yet this refusal is not so much a conceptual limitation of Stowe's racial critique as one of its central features. Because the imaginative task Stowe sets herself is not to reinforce the racial knowledge that organizes civic life but, rather, to emphasize how racial prejudice shapes social interaction, she places narrative emphasis on the effects of racial thinking rather than on the recognition of characters' racial lineage. It is this approach to civic governance—an approach that Nina approximates with her unique brand of child citizenship—that enables her to become an effective "mistress of the fortress—commander-in-chief" once her brother challenges her rightful authority.[15] Nina's approach to civic representation dovetails with the language of consensual governance that pervades the text and works to authenticate her as Clayton's ideal partner in his lifelong project of realizing racial equality within social communities. While Clayton's dream remains unrealized, the net social benefits of the kind of citizenship Nina epitomizes can be seen in the novel's final scene, where "*forty* destitute children" peacefully coexist—"black and white" with "no distinctions of color"—and are nurtured by a black woman who declares that she "loves" "white chil'en, when they 'haves themselves . . . jest as good as black."[16]

Stowe's exploration in *Dred* of the full range of the child's racial representations was a career-long interest of Twain, as Fishkin has indicated in her important analysis of the actual child who served as Twain's inspiration for Huck. Yet the full range and texture of Twain's literary engagement with the child as an icon of racialized nationalism become apparent only once we place such texts as his *Pudd'nhead Wilson* not only in conversation with U.S. racial commentaries offered by such texts as *Dred*, but also within the transnational context in which Twain was working in the early 1890s. Recognizing the child's capacity not only to distinguish the United States from other countries, but to associate the United States with countries like Germany through the racial narrative it represents, Twain uses child protagonists to offer an important and thus far unrecognized critique of the racial contours of this transnational alliance between the United States and Germany. By approaching the child protagonists at the center of Twain's 1894 *Pudd'nhead Wilson* and *Those Extraordinary Twins* from the vantage point of Twain's less-well-known German writings—of his 1891 translation of Heinrich Hoffman's German children's stories *Der Struwwelpeter* or his 1891 essay "The German Chicago," for example—we can begin to see the transnational, as well as the national, racial commentary embedded in Twain's work. Contemporary U.S. and German popular political commentary represents a thus far untapped mine of critical information on the two nations' joint commitment to upholding the idea of racial purity—a mine of information that is crucial to understanding the scope and significance of Twain's transnational commentary. In what follows, I chart the child's fundamental importance to the process of forming these transnational alliances between the United States and Germany, as well as to Twain's critique of such alliances. This excavation of the child's utility in mapping the transnational connections between the two countries reveals how whiteness can emerge and operate as a powerful conceptual linchpin of increasingly postnationalist, global communities. Attending to the child's importance in forging transnational alliances, in other words, reveals that the child's recently recognized capacity to destabilize the nation's current geopolitical borders under global capitalism and its related technologies is part of a longer history in which the child forges the very transnational structures it subsequently helps to undermine.[17]

"THE REPUBLIC OF THE WORLD"

The child consistently featured in U.S. and German political rhetoric not only helps to organize each "nation's essence" around an Anglo-Saxon founders' love of liberty, but in so doing makes Germany and the United States into a collective, interlocking transnational expression of the supremacy of the Anglo-Saxon race.[18] The child at the center of U.S. and German political narratives during the late eighteenth century and nineteenth century did not simply embody the idea of national regeneration by upholding the myth of racial purity on which modern nations like Germany and the United States are founded but created an innovative, enduring transnational collective based on white supremacy. In the case of the United States, as we have seen, not only is the "infant empire" that early political commentators like Thomas Paine depicted as a pure-blooded Anglo-Saxon child forced to separate from a corrupt parent country in order to uphold its race-based love of liberty, but the young nation's ongoing success depends on the child, who must continue to represent and protect the love of liberty that characterizes the nation.[19] Declaring that, because "ninety nine in a hundred [Colonists] are white, . . . we . . . should be free" rather than Britain's "Negroes," John Adams relied on the idea of white supremacy to argue for separate nationhood by construing British rule as racial debasement, and the child reinforced this alliance between race and nation, upholding with the racial narrative it represents the idea that "Liberty," as the *Newport Mercury* asserts in 1767, "undoubtedly belongs to Americans."[20] Just as young citizens "*make* their country as they go along" and "carr[y] their country and government in their minds" by upholding the racial principles defining U.S. national identity, so, too, is the child integral to the racial logic governing German national identity.[21] Because the true German child, according to the nineteenth-century German political commentator Houston Stewart Chamberlain, has "a marked instinct for race" that reflects the Anglo-Saxon heritage from which the nation springs, the child is crucial to Germany's efforts to "reawaken the Germanic spirit of independence" in its citizens by reminding them of their shared racial heritage.[22] Able to eradicate the "Un-Germanic qualities [that] nestle in the heart of the best Teutons" due to the "chaos of racial mixing," the child not only represents the racial principles defining the German nation, but also functions as an important political tool in Germany's late-century effort to extend the reach of the "new empire" through a racial logic that privileges "the purest Germanic descent."[23] As such, the child served as an important point of origin from which many German, as well as U.S., citizens derived a sense of the racial superiority of their nations, even as this child reinforced the essential differences between the various races inhabiting each nation.

Yet the child upholds white supremacy as a cornerstone not only of individual German and U.S. national identity, but also of an enduring, if often overlooked, transnational alliance between the two nations. The "expanding knowledge of America and growing interest in its characters and fortunes [that] began to show themselves in Germany at the time of the American Revolution," according to Edgar Hemminghaus, illustrate Germany's early, enduring understanding of the two nations' joint racial and political heritage.[24] This heritage precedes even as it precipitates U.S. nation formation. Indeed, the "government of the United States," according to John Fiske's 1885 *American Political Ideals*, "is not the result of special creation but of evolution" that proves that New Englanders are "lineally descended from . . . the early Aryans."[25] As an extension and direct expression of the "rustic democracy" that their "Aryan forefathers" preserved in the "purest form" in the "impregnable mountain fastnesses of upper Germany," our "American history" therefore "does not begin with the Declaration of Independence" but, rather, "descends in unbroken continuity from the days when stout Arminius in the forests of northern Germany successfully defied the might of imperial Rome."[26] Bringing their "laws, manners, and institutions . . . with them from the woods of Germany" and transferring "them to the woods of America," according to Robert Knox, these Saxons create "in the free States of America" a perfect expression of their racial character.[27] Americans, Fiske argues, must consequently understand "Washington and Lincoln" to be bringing to fruition political efforts that extend "very far back in the history of the Aryan world," and "Hamilton and Madison" to be giving form and expression to the political principles which were latent in and protected by their Teutonic forebears.[28] James Nourse concurs in his 1847 *Remarks on the Past and Its Legacies to American Society* that "our American liberty had its origin in the German forests," where Anglo-Saxons created early "Germanic nations distinguished by their aptitude for free institutions" and committed to "reconciling order and liberty, and teaching mankind the science of government."[29]

With its "national life" integrally aligned with the United States through the conjoined racial heritage that a "universal-history" approach reveals, according to political commentators like Fiske, Germany during the late nineteenth century in turn depended on the child to uphold the racial principles that had historically organized U.S. political culture but that were being jeopardized by emancipation. Commentators like Fiske asserted that the United States might "come out stronger than ever" after the Civil War, but the transformation of former slaves into citizens posed a threat to the racial premises underpinning national order—a threat that Germany was committed to avoiding in its newly unified nation.[30] As a result, the child not only aligned the two nations but helped to initiate an important new phase of German nationalism resulting from the deaths of Wilhelm I and Friedrich III in 1888 and the dismissal of Bismarck in 1890.[31] If "the years around 1890," as Rüdiger vom Bruch and Peter Burg, among others, have pointed out, represent a historical fault line in German nation formation, the aggressive building of the German nation-state during this period depended on the idea that "a unique racial quality" distinguished Germany from "other nations."[32] As Chamberlain summarized, Germany could succeed in founding a "firm national union" only if it instilled in all its residents "the consciousness of the possession of a distinct, pure race," and, as we have seen, the child was crucial to Chamberlain's notion of how to succeed in this important national task.[33] Because the "instinct for individual freedom . . . and public freedom" that defines these racially pure "Germanic races" can be nurtured only if the nation's leaders are "genuinely Germanic," or of the "purest Germanic descent," each citizen must uphold the racial purity the child represents to keep Germany from deteriorating into a "union of mongrels" who are "not [of] a common origin and common heart-beat."[34] This vision of an explicitly white German nation, propounded in political rhetoric of the 1880s and 1890s and defined in the 1885 *Brockhaus*, was implemented by popular nationalist groups like the Pan-German League, which formed with the sole purpose, according to its 1894 handbook, of "invigorat[ing] German national feeling, especially the cultivation of the consciousness of racial belonging."[35] Seeking to "fight with all its might, whatever hinders our national development" and to pursue "an energetic policy for Germany through the world, especially a continuation of German colonialism," the Pan-German League and other groups, in turn, featured the child in their political rhetoric to cultivate among citizens an explicitly Aryan German national identity that was superior to, and could therefore immediately subdue, any threat that other racial groups might pose to its nationalist logic.[36] Therefore, even as the United States "raise[d] the edifice of human freedom" from the moment the Puritans first nurtured "the Germanic principle," the "inhabitant[s] of Germany" increasingly took up "the question" of the racial "character" of a "world republic in its practical light" that "the American[s] forget," according to *The New Rome* (1853), as they confront the challenge of absorbing newly emancipated citizens into the national corpus.[37]

We can begin to see how the child helps Germany to uphold this ideal of a "world republic" by turning to the popular "missing-link shows" that featured the child both to illustrate the evolutionary distance of nations like the United States and Germany from their nonwhite neighbors and to link such nations together as transnational expressions of racial superiority. While freaks might enable spectators to recollect "a younger, child self," as Leslie Fiedler contends, such a self, as child freaks like "missing links" make clear, does not precede so much as uphold the national cultures in which they and the individuals viewing them circulate.[38] Children like the eight-year-old "missing link" Krao (figure 9) therefore came to epitomize, for the unprecedented number of Germans and Americans who visited her in the early 1890s, an unequivocally racial explanation for the constitutional and political structure of each nation and the "world republic" they collectively constitute. Indeed, the "idea of the missing link made remarkably clear sense" to late-nineteenth-century Germans and Americans and was intensely promoted in both countries, as Nigel Rothfels, James Cook, and Andrea Stulman Dennett have illustrated, because it facilitated an account of national superiority in which different races "represent[ing] earlier stages in human development" were construed as "evolutionary ancestors of modern Europeans."[39] Responding to the "desire of Germans . . . to learn as much as possible about other peoples of the world . . . during the period in Germany . . . in which the state fundamentally changed from a predominantly inward looking confederation of largely independent political entities to a remarkably powerful and politically unified colonial empire," German scientists transported the "ape-child — a girl of seven to eight years old" from "the forest of Laos" to Germany to provide a racial explanation for Germany's national past and future progress.[40] With her "whole body . . . covered with black hair" and "her extraordinary prehensile powers of feet and lips," Krao, according to George Gould and Walter Pyle, came to represent, for the large audiences she drew, the concept of irreconcilable racial difference that had historically underpinned both countries and that increasingly enabled Germany, as the protector of the world republic, to embrace "military and naval expansion, imperialism, and war."[41] Intensely promoted by posters depicting a hairy child drawn against a jungle background, Krao,

Figure 9 "Krao, the Ape Girl."
Courtesy Harvard Theatre Collection, Houghton Library, Harvard University.

like the fair children put on display at such events as New York's 1877 Great National Baby Show therefore became a focal point around which citizens bolstered a sense of collective purpose through the racial narrative the child represented.

"WHITE AND FAIR TO SEE"

The child at the center of nineteenth-century scientific, social, and political commentary locates whiteness at the center not only of German and U.S. national identity but of the "world republic" they collectively create. If Germany, as Holger Kersten has pointed out, holds a particularly "prominent position among the many depictions of foreign nations and people" in Mark Twain's work, I suggest that Germany attracts Twain's particular attention in 1891 not only because of the very favorable public response to his second visit but, more particularly, because of the structural similarities that he notes, during that trip, between the racial logic that Germany and the United States share.[42] In his writing of the early 1890s, Twain features the child that affiliates Germany and the United States to comment on the two nations' joint engagement in the transnational project of upholding white supremacy. We can begin to see how Twain uses the child to comment on the transnational racial logic aligning Germany with the United States by turning to his 1891 translation of Heinrich Hoffman's *Der Struwwelpeter*. Completed while he was in Germany and considered by some to be the "most important" literary outcome of his 1891 summer in Berlin, Twain's reworking of the popular German children's stories provides an important, and thus far overlooked, critical commentary on the transnational racial logic binding Germany to the United States.[43] Twain insists on the significance of adopting a transnational perspective when analyzing his work when he asserts that he finds the "answer" to the structural dilemma that his 1894 *Pudd'nhead Wilson and Those Extraordinary Twins* pose only when he and his "manuscript" move "back and forth across the Atlantic two or three times." By "read[ing] it and stud[ying] over it on shipboard" as he traverses the geographic and conceptual distance separating the United States from Europe, Twain is able to "see where the difficulty lay" in the relations between his two stories and to "pull one of the stories out by the roots" in "a kind of literary Caesarean operation."[44] By taking seriously what Twain insists on in this oft-cited passage—that it is only by recognizing the transnational dimensions of U.S. race relations that he can resolve the narrative dilemma his two texts pose—we can see how Twain in turn features the child in the twin texts he "births" to comment on the transnational racial bonds that the child helps to sustain between nations like Germany and the United States. We can see, in short, how Twain's insistence on the twins' prior childhood experience as an attraction in "a cheap museum in Berlin" carries important and thus far unrecognized conceptual significance for the racial narrative the child protagonists of his 1894 texts represent.[45]

We can begin to see how Twain's child protagonists represent and finally critique the transnational racial contract in which the United States and Germany are engaged by turning to Twain's 1891 translation of *Der Struwwelpeter*. By adding the term "Missing Link" to the original text and then exploring the missing link's interactions with three white German children, Twain interrogates the child's ideological importance as an exemplar of the racial purity that "explains" national identity. By illustrating how the child creates rather than codifies the racial purity that structures national unity, Twain points out that the child does not so much "explain" as produce the idea of racial purity on which the German nation-state is premised and on which it draws unprecedented imaginative energy after 1890. The three white child protagonists of Twain's translation of "The Tale of the Young Black Chap" (figure 10), one of the stories in the Hoffman collection, for example, initially view the fourth child—a "Moor"—in ways that reproduce the education in racialized nationalism that Germans visiting the missing-link shows at Berlin's Castan's Panoptikon and Frankfurt's Zoological Gardens were receiving as Twain wrote his "Slovenly Peter" stories. However, Twain explores how the public spectacle of the child "missing link," as the German illustration accompanying Twain's text helps to show, does not so much reinforce as call into question the racial hierarchies on which nations like Germany and the United States rely.[46] It is because Ludwig, Kaspar, and William refuse to heed the advice of the wise teacher Nicholas not to "laugh, scoff and wink, and mock at that poor Missing Link / Because his skin is black as ink" that the boys are punished by being forced to acquire the racial identity they ridicule—that they are racially transformed by a punitive dip in the "mighty Nicholas'[s] . . . ink-stand" into children who are "all black as sin—Much blacker than that Niggerkin." When he describes how the

Du siehst sie hier, wie schwarz sie sind,
Viel schwärzer als das Mohrenkind!
Der Mohr voraus im Sonnenschein,
Die Tintenbuben hinterdrein;
Und hätten sie nicht so gelacht,
Hätt' Niklas sie nicht schwarz gemacht.

Figure 10   "The Tale of the Young Black Chap." From Mark Twain, *Slovenly Peter*.

three initially white German children would still be "white and fair to see" had they "but hid their glee" at ridiculing "a coal-pitch-raven-black young Moor," Twain insists that it is the children's ridicule of the missing link because he cannot "bleach out at will, be white like you" that is responsible for turning them into "Ink-Blots following dark as night . . . the Moor," who is now "marching in the light."[47] Once transformed by the ink into the literal stuff of racialized text, Twain's child protagonists reveal the constructedness of the racial purity on which national narratives featuring the child rely to explain national supremacy. By showing race to be "something that makes and unmakes itself," as Renan observes, Twain's translation uses the child that has historically helped to uphold racial hierarchy as a constitutive element of nation formation to challenge the general assumption that racial purity explains the accelerating imperial expansion that he sees going on in Germany and that is generally accepted by Germans as a natural expression of Germany's racial superiority.[48]

Yet if Twain uses the child not so much to reinforce whiteness as an organizing principle of German national identity as to indicate the final inadequacy of the idea of race to justify Germany's imperial nationalism, he also begins in his translation to consider the impact of such a critique on U.S. national identity and the reunification efforts under way in the United States after Reconstruction. By associating the term "missing link" with another that he adds to the same story—"Niggerkin"—Twain suggests the relevance of his reworking of the German child protagonists' commentary on race and nation for those "native-born white Americans" who—just like their German counterparts—became increasingly concerned about the impact that an "emerging multiracial society" of freed slaves, "Chinese, Japanese, and Mexican immigrants" would have on U.S. national identity "in the half century following the Civil War."[49] J. D. Stahl has contended that Twain "substitutes something quintessentially American in the process" of translating *Der Struwwelpeter*, but his reworking of Hoffman's child protagonists, I suggest, instead begins to interrogate the relevance of Germany's model of racialized nationalism for a United States in the process of reunifying after Reconstruction.[50] Twain, in other words, begins to reconsider in his reworking of the German text how the sleight of hand through which the child upholds the alliance between race and nation in Germany might in turn structure efforts at U.S. national reunification—efforts that, as Charles Chesnutt notes, worked to reiterate the nation's founding association with the "all-pervading, all-conquering Anglo-Saxon race."[51]

"THE GERMAN CHICAGO"

Major U.S. reunification efforts with which Twain was familiar, such as the 1893 Chicago Columbian Exposition, feature the United States' and Germany's shared racial history and the child that represents it to help "the North and the South, with the extinction of slavery," as Chicago Expo President Thomas W. Palmer asserts, "come to know each other better and to love and respect each other more."[52] David Blight has recently shown that "white supremacy" operated as a "silent, invisible," but powerful organizing principle in the "politics of reconciliation" in the post-Reconstruction period.[53] And the fair that Richard Harding Davis described as "the greatest event in the history of the country since the Civil War" drew heavily on the nation's longstanding alliance with Germany to reinforce the racial principles that had long structured the nation. Newspapers like the *Chicago Tribune* and the *New York Times* agreed that Germany's was by far the "most complete exhibit of all foreign nations" represented at the expo, and the prominence of Germany's exhibit dramatically overshadowed African American representation, as Du Bois, among others, noted.[54] As Ferdinand Barnett summarized in the final essay of *The Reason Why the Colored American Is Not in the World's Columbian Exposition*, "The Exposition practically is, literally and figuratively, a 'White City,' in the building of which the Colored American was allowed no helping hand, and in its glorious success he has no share."[55] With such displays as the Krupps Gun Works Pavilion, which contained the 124 ton Krupp gun and emphasized its unprecedented scale by placing a young German boy against the forty-six-foot rifle, Germany offered visitors to the expo the most spectacular evidence of the national progress that fair nations could enjoy.[56] If the expo was created, according to its president, to display how "our country has profit[ed]" from "the successes . . . of other nations of the earth," Germany, as "the greatest exhibitor at the Fair," provided numerous "magnificent displays of the resources of that great Empire" that, like the Krupps exhibit, clearly attested to the importance that the racial heritage Germany shared with the U.S. played in ensuring the nation's future success.[57] Thus, the "German village" and German building that prominently displayed the innovations so "indicative of national disposition" compelled every visitor, according to *The Story of Columbus and the World's Columbian Exposition*, inevitably to ask, "What does not this country owe to the German?" Giving both "name and character to some of our leading States," Germany, *The Story of Columbus and the World's Columbian Exposition*, concluded, so infuses "our vast domain" as to make "American skill and genius" unique among "all the world."[58] Acknowledging Germany's profound influence on late-nineteenth-century U.S. culture, Twain's 1891 essay "The German Chicago" predicts what the Chicago Columbian Exposition demonstrates: — that because Berlin is slightly "blonder of complexion" than Chicago, Germany offers "plenty of things . . . worth importing to America."[59]

By featuring the child with its innovative Children's Building, the Chicago Columbian Exposition represents white supremacy as a conceptual mainstay of a newly reunified and strengthened nation. According to the expo's president Palmer, the Children's Building was intended to offer visitors a "school where the impulse to aspiration and knowledge may be stimulated and . . . where memories may be revived and traditions garnered. . . . Intended to be . . . an educational exhibit" that showed "the most improved methods adopted in the light of the nineteenth century for the rearing and education of children," the Children's Building featured the child to show how national success was a direct result of the nation's racial origins.[60] "Commencing with the infant in its earliest and most helpless stage" and including "an exhibition of infants' clothing of all nations and times," the Children's Building not only used the child to foreground the nation's racially pure past, but insisted on the unequalled development of the nation's children, encouraging "young people all over the country" to prove their superiority by taking "the children's building as their work in the great Expo" and assisting "in raising a portion of the money for their building." The Children's Building therefore proved essential, according to Palmer, to the expo's goal of teaching "the American people"—whether they be the "colored boy picking bananas in Key West, or [the] Swedish emigrant at the headwaters of the Mississippi"—to recover a nationally unifying story of white supremacy that binds racially and regionally diverse American citizens to the idea of a unified, racially pure nation.[61] The child, as a result, worked to convince visitors, according to James Shepp and Daniel Shepp, that vast, insurmountable differences existed between "American sunshine and soil, American skill and genius" and the achievements of all other nations, and, in so doing, helped to reconstitute "the states and territories of our own country," according to Palmer, into one great "people of North America," who are proud of their superior "institutions," "commerce," and "quick civilization."[62]

It is such a child—a child that realigns community through its capacity to represent a transnational racial narrative—that Twain draws on in *Pudd'nhead Wilson and Those Extraordinary Twins*. We can begin to excavate the transnational dimensions of the racial narrative the child protagonists represent by considering Twain's insistence that his texts are indebted to the freakish spectacle of twinning that the conjoined twins Giovanni Baptista and Giocomo Tocci offered their audiences. The 1894 edition of *Pudd'nhead Wilson and Those Extraordinary Twins*, as Susan Gillman has pointed out, features on its cover a picture of Twain looking at a sign for the "Wonderful Twins."[63] Yet if these conjoined twins become a rich vehicle for Twain as a spectator, in turn, to comment on U.S. racial logic, as Gillman and others have importantly illustrated, their extensive exhibition in Germany at the Berlin Panoptikon in 1891, before their arrival in the United States, is crucial to the commentary that Twain produces.[64] While Eric Sundquist, Cathy Boeckmann, and Brook Thomas, among others, have pointed out that *Pudd'nhead Wilson* and *Those Extraordinary Twins* offer a "parody of versions of the southern racism that helped reunite North and South after Reconstruction,"[65] these and other important accounts of Twain's racial commentary have tended to overlook the significance that Twain's repeated references to the conjoined twins' two-year history traveling "all about Germany . . . with a freak-show" have in his commentary on the role that race plays in U.S. reunification efforts of the 1890s.[66] By the twentieth century, conjoined twins function as a rich metaphor for East Germany and West Germany,[67] but their importance in nineteenth-century Germany, according to Jan Bondeson and Nancy Fredricks, resided in their ability to "embody problems of identity and difference" for a nation increasingly committed to upholding the racial logic of the "world republic."[68] Not simply representing the nation's racial purity, conjoined twins like those described by *Anomalies and Curiosities of Medicine* (1896) — twins of "different colors," with "two-colored faces," or "with one side of the face white and the other black" — reveal a racial hybridity often occluded but nonetheless present within the individual.[69] More than these other "double monsters," the Tocci brothers on whom Twain fashions his extraordinary twins were understood to be "the most remarkable twins that ever approached maturity."[70] Demonstrating a unique "intimacy of attachment" that, as Robert Harris tells 1892 readers of the *American Journal of Obstetrics*, illustrates their extensive regions of common sensibility, the Tocci boys in body are "so intimately blended that their interior anatomy is an interesting study" for those wishing to determine a precise relationship between self and other.[71] Exhibited at the Panoptikon in Berlin in 1891 after being written up by Rudolph Virchow, the Tocci twins showed their audiences how the "distinctly individual and independent" — even opposing — "sensations and emotions" that, *Anomalies and Curiosities of Medicine* (1896) insists, define each brother nonetheless constitute a shared, essentially hybrid body that represents for the interested observer how different identities might combine to constitute a collective subject.[72] The hybridity that these conjoined twins epitomized sparked general interest in "double monsters," making conjoined twins of all races, such as Millie Crissie (figure 11), sites of powerful cultural meaning.

The twins' circulation as a spectacle in Germany therefore highlights the

2 Headed Girl, MILLIE CRISSIE.
(Copyright secured.)

Figure 11 "2 Headed Girl: Millie Crissie."
Courtesy New-York Historical Society (77730d).

hybridity at the center of the child subject, a hybridity that challenges the logic of racial purity on which Southern communities like Dawson's Landing are premised. As a result, Angelo and Luigi, Twain's fictional representation of the Tocci brothers, do not so much offer citizens a welcome distraction from the social order governing their lives as reveal to them the logical fallacy undermining the racial premise on which that order has been based. Angelo and Luigi are able to "turn the town on its head" not so much because the fact that "they've been in Europe" offers citizens a diversion from Dawson's Landing as because their experience there as "side-show riff raff, dime-museum freaks" enables them to reveal to the residents of Dawson's Landing the final insufficiency of the logic of racial hierarchy to govern their community.[73] "One . . . a little fairer than the other, but otherwise . . . exact duplicates, . . . the two most distinguished-looking pair of young fellows that the West had ever seen" not only reproduce the problem that Tom and Chambers pose to Dawson's Landing—the problem of firmly fixing racial identity in the child—but heighten that problem by placing difference within one body.[74] If town opinion on Luigi and Angelo can be "clean[ly] and exact[ly]" divided, with "half of the town" siding with Luigi and "the other half" with Angelo, their body, in other words, poses a greater problem for the judicial system under which both twins have consented to be governed in the act of becoming U.S. citizens. Unwilling to consider what the fact that each twin's "identity is so merged in his brother's" might mean for civic governance, the court insists on upholding a notion of individual citizenship that punishes innocent and guilty brother alike rather than reconstitute its approach to representation and due process around the new model of conjoined, hybrid citizenship the twins present.[75]

Temporarily frustrating due process in Dawson's Landing, the conjoined citizenship that Angelo and Luigi exemplify in turn offers an important model for understanding Chambers's and Tom's subsequent challenge to their community's understanding of the social significance of race. Once we understand the conjoined identity that Luigi and Angelo model for the citizens of Dawson's Landing as an outgrowth of the cultural meanings that their collective body acquires as a result of its circulation in Germany, we can see how such transnational meanings structure the racial significance that Twain's child protagonists acquire. In Dawson's Landing, the purity of bloodlines determines social position, and "when a person could prove descent from the First Families of that great commonwealth" of Virginia, he is "exalted to supremacy."[76] However, this racially pure origin, while imaginatively powerful, remains unattainable by even the most prominent of the community's citizens. While Pembroke Howard and the Driscolls are "very popular with the people" because of their "proved descent from the First Families" from the time when "that State still ranked as the chief and most imposing member of the Union," they cannot successfully reproduce the racial purity they seem to represent, and "so the cradles [remain] empty" until a slave woman both bears a child and raises the child Mrs. Percy Driscoll bears before dying.[77] The cradle switch that transforms Tom Driscoll into the slave child Chambers and Chambers into his white master, in character as well as name, loosely replays the plot of Twain's earlier "The Tale of the Young Black Chap" in that both the 1891 tale and the 1894 texts explore the final transferability of racial identity. Yet it is not so much that Tom frustrates the justice system because it initially fails to recognize him as black as that the black blood in his veins, as well as the Driscoll blood that he and others assumed made him white, are in fact the same—that the Essex blood of his black mother, like the Driscoll blood, connects Tom to "de highest blood dat Old Virginny ever turned out," as Roxy reminds him, and to ancestors who, by including "Cap'n John Smith" as well as "Pocahontas" and "a nigger king outen Africa," illustrate how pure blood, be it "black" or "white," is essentially racially mixed.[78] The answer of the United States to the question "Who is black?" as F. James Davis notes, has long been, "Any person with *any* known African black ancestry."[79] If this strict racial cataloguing is most acute in the United States, as we have seen, it is not unique to it but, rather, the result of a long transnational history in which German as well as U.S. national identity is organized through the idea of white supremacy. As a result, the definition of black that develops in the South and becomes naturalized as the nation's social and legal definition by 1896 with *Plessy v. Ferguson*, as Twain illustrates with his 1894 conjoined texts, is not only the end product of a protracted transnational alliance that upholds the constitutive importance of racial purity to national supremacy, but also a conceptual impossibility because, finally, it must include *all* citizens. The answer to the question, "Who is black?" therefore is not "Tom" or "Chambers" but "both," because Tom, like the conjoined twins, encodes within himself the essentially mixed racial identity that, Twain suggests, resides within each citizen—even those most committed to the project of racial purity that posits white supremacy as a cornerstone of national identity. Therefore, even as Dawson's Landing resolves the radical social challenge that the child's essentially mixed racial identity represents by subsequently expelling Tom from the community, its residents cannot negate the fact of racial hybridity that Tom and Chambers as child subjects represent. In the decade after he modeled Huck on a black child named Jimmy, Twain continued to use child protagonists like the black chap to point out the mistaken assumptions that enabled the idea of racial difference to continue to prevail within the United States.

"THESE CHILDREN OF OUR AMERICA"

Written the same year that Twain translated *Der Struwwelpeter*, José Martí's "Our America" contends that it is "these children of our America" who serve to remind citizens that because "there are no races," that "there can be no racial hate [in] the blond nation of the continent."[80] Yet even as the child functions in Twain's writing as a powerful representative of the fact that, as Renan contends, "there is no pure race" and thus the "greatest nations are essentially mixed blood," the child, as we have seen, represents not only the irrelevance but the persistence of the idea of racial purity to transnational, as well as national, identity.[81] The increasingly transnational America that emerges in the early twentieth century—an America that, according to Randolph Bourne, is "coming to be, not a nationality but a transnationality, a weaving back and forth, with other lands, of many threads of all . . . colors"[82]—continues to depend on the child that, as we have seen, has historically maintained transnational alliances through its capacity to represent race. Preserving the very logic of "superior and inferior races" that Bourne calls for increasingly racially diverse Americans to reject, the child helps to ensure that the problem that W. E. B. Du Bois famously predicted would be the problem of the twentieth century is indeed that of the color line. "Germany," Du Bois asserts in *Darkwater* (1920), has a "greedy appetit[e]" to conquer "the dark world," and so Germany's "struggle for the largest share in exploiting darker races" will precipitate world war by the first decades of the twentieth century.[83] Yet even as Germany and other "white" nations like the United States continue to figure the individual of "dark . . . descent" as a "holy-child" in order to further their imperial ambitions,[84] the child, as we have seen, also holds out for Twain, at least, the rich possibility of rethinking the racial basis of national and transnational formations—a possibility that Du Bois and Martí will explore further, as I will show in the concluding chapter.

five

HENRY JAMES, PAULINE HOPKINS,

AND PSYCHOLOGIES OF RACE

A s we saw in the preceding chapter, the child consolidates even as it offers
the possibility for refuting the racial contours of national affiliation
and transnational alliance. The psychological models of self emerging at the
same time that Randolph Bourne was calling for a rethinking of race's place
in national formulations absorb and reflect this U.S. commitment to white
supremacy more than has been generally acknowledged. Thus, the child
that psychologists posit as the point of origin for the self becomes a rich
source for exploring the racial contours of the modern self. In his 1919 "A
Child Is Being Beaten," Sigmund Freud, for example, makes marked if passing reference to the constitutive role that American slavery plays in the formation of individual psychosexual consciousness when he notes that it is "almost always the same books" — books such as *Uncle Tom's Cabin* — "whose
contents give a new stimulus to the beating-phantasies" of his patients.[1]
Though beating in *Uncle Tom's Cabin* is a direct expression of the racial logic
that structures U.S. slaveholding, Freud does not address the role that race
plays in the psychological formations that the child develops in response
to reading Stowe's novel. He implies that, although initially awakened to
beating fantasies by the reading of *Uncle Tom's Cabin*, the child inevitably
edits racial content out of its newly awakened fantasy life by "compet[ing]
with these works of fiction" and "by producing his own phantasies [of the]
wealth of situations and institutions in which children were beaten."[2] Thus,

in the act of making the racially inflected beatings depicted in *Uncle Tom's Cabin* part of its own psychology, the child scripts out the specificity of the U.S. racial conflict that inspired Stowe's writing. Like Freud, Henry James identifies the founding importance of Stowe's novel for young readers' development when he concludes in *A Small Boy and Others* that, for its child audience in particular, *Uncle Tom's Cabin* was "much less a book than a state of vision," requiring that readers "wal[k] and tal[k] and laug[h] and cr[y]," but never merely read, the novel.[3] However, if Freud edits racial content out of the psychic reality that he uses the child to represent, James, I suggest, explores the founding significance of race in constituting the self that the child comes to represent in psychological discourse once slavery is abolished and the political work of Stowe's "picture" is seemingly done.

This chapter explores late-nineteenth-century American psychological and literary narratives' equation of the child with the self, arguing that the child these narratives collectively depict conceptually depends on race to both constitute and contest the self with which it is increasingly equated in late-nineteenth-century and early-twentieth-century psychological and scientific discourse. The following pages begin the process of charting the centrality of race to the self the child denotes by locating the writing of prominent early American psychologists like James Mark Baldwin, G. Stanley Hall, and William James within a tradition of U.S. post-Reconstruction racial commentary rather than within the European psychological tradition with which they associate their work and to which they claim their work is exclusively indebted. In so doing, this chapter illustrates, first, that American psychology depends on U.S. racial logic for the model of identity it uses the child to represent; and second, that two radically different contemporary U.S. writers—Henry James and Pauline Hopkins—engage with these psychological models to explore, and often to critique, the legacy that American psychology's conceptual dependence on race has on the American self with which the child is equated. By identifying the centrality of racial identity to an emerging American psychology, James and Hopkins collectively illustrate how a fledgling American psychology harnesses a burgeoning contemporary commitment to narratives of racial difference to aid in its conceptualization and popular acceptance. Then they illustrate how the stories of psychological identity and development that this new psychology uses the child to script have at their core a racial content. Andrew

Heinze has recently shown that U.S. psychology's emergence at the end of the nineteenth century "was profoundly implicated with the dynamics of immigration, acculturation, and race."[4] However, the role that these racial dynamics played in the emergence of U.S. psychological discourse and in shaping the child at its center has remained relatively unexplored, even as scholars like Sander Gilman have more generally documented the prominent place of racial thinking in the development of European and, more particularly, Freudian psychology.[5] As the following pages suggest, by imbuing the child that functions as the point of origin for U.S. psychological definitions of the self with contemporary racial logic, American psychologists harnessed the explanatory power of postwar racial logic to generate for late-nineteenth-century Americans a cohesive and compelling account of their psychological make-up. Commenting on this equation of child with tacitly racialized self, James and Hopkins interrogate the potentialities and the pitfalls of such an alliance for the radically different versions of self with which their fiction is concerned.

My interest in the chapter's first section is less to document the presence of racial otherness in Henry James's work, as a number of critics have ably done,[6] than to suggest that James represents contemporary psychological understandings of race as forming a latent, inevitable element of the child identity with which much of his 1890s short fiction is interested. Many have noted that James's frequent depictions of child protagonists during the last decade of the century reflect a renewed interest in his own childhood and in the self that the child comes to represent by late century.[7] Less well understood has been how these child protagonists also include James's commentary on the role that contemporary psychological accounts of race play in the constitution of the self that the child denotes. Understanding how such children as Miles, Flora, and Maisie reflect the role that race inevitably plays in constituting a self requires that we attend to the ways in which U.S. postwar accounts of racial identity increasingly posit race as existing not on the skin but in the self—as a subcutaneous element of identity that can be determined not so much by the color of one's skin as by one's developmental progress, aptitudes, and behavior. Charting the extent to which these psychological accounts of racial identity organize the interior lives of James's child subjects not only offers a new analytical framework for reading his texts, but also opens the conceptual field in which we consider race in James's writing. Showing how contemporary accounts of racial otherness constitute the "rosy sprite" Flora as well as the "swarming" Jewish children of the East Side reveals that racial concerns, as Kenneth Warren has suggested, shape "James's aesthetic even when his texts [are] not specifically 'about' race in any substantive way."[8] More particularly, doing so contributes to our understanding of the range of subject matter that is "specifically 'about' race" in the first place. In short, by looking, as did nineteenth-century psychological scientists, beneath the child's surface layer of skin, we find in James's child protagonists a representational world of racialized subjectivity that places race at the center of the child consciousness that nineteenth-century Anglo-Americans increasingly locate as the conceptual point of origin for the self.

RACIAL RECAPITULATION

Despite American psychologists' insistence on the exclusive importance of European scientists like Pierre Janet and M. Binet to their models of individual development, they nonetheless depended on late-nineteenth-century U.S. sociological accounts of race to constitute models of the individual self that the child represented and with which it was increasingly equated. Because the child, as the prominent Princeton psychologist James Mark Baldwin asserts in *The Mental Development in the Child and the Race* (1894), has "not learned its pedigree" or social standing yet, it is a perfect subject of study for those who wish to chart the genesis and development of the "true self."[9] Yet the self that the child represents — or, more particularly, the self described by American psychology — draws from sociological narratives that are used in the post-Reconstruction period to reinforce the essential nature of racial differences. Social commentators like Atticus Haygood insist that there is "no more slavery in our country" after the Civil War and Reconstruction and even go so far as to request that African Americans "stop digging up slavery as an everlasting theme,"[10] but they can do so only because narratives of racial difference, as critics have recently pointed out, have replaced, and re-anchored, eroded social distinctions between slaves and citizens.[11] Therefore, Haygood can insist that the "most unique chapter in our national history" is over and that "slavery is entitled to its grave," because he has exchanged the logic of slavery for a logic of racial identity in which the

"emancipated negro . . . can never perform aright the duties of free citizenship" due to his essential inferiority. Though the "poor Africans" have made
substantial progress as a race since their relocation to the United States and,
as Haygood insists, are better "fitted for freedom in 1865" than they were
"when the slave-ships first landed them in America," their racial identity
makes them essentially less able to shoulder the responsibilities of citizenship than those of Anglo-Saxon origin. Therefore, though slavery is dead,
the "race problem" has replaced it with a greater and seemingly unending
vitality, as Haygood makes clear when he writes that it "is likely to be our
problem as a Nation always."[12]

Late-nineteenth-century American psychologists employ such contemporary narratives of essential racial difference in the developing models of
individual consciousness that they use the child to illustrate. "The analogy
between race and individual development" is not only "very clear," according to Baldwin, but absolutely necessary for American psychologists, for
"no consistent view of mental development in the individual could pos-
sibly be reached without a doctrine of the race development of consciousness."[13] In such an analogous model, a developmental series typifying racial
progress is repeated, or recapitulated, in "the infant's growth." Propounded
by G. Stanley Hall, among many other nineteenth-century scientists, recapitulation theory contended that each child repeated in microcosm its
race's entire developmental history and that the child's every "instinct and
feeling" were therefore an index to its "remote ancestral past."[14] Recapitulation theory proved a generative model for emerging American psychological theories of child development like Hall's 1883 *The Contents of Children's
Minds*, one of the earliest serious attempts to examine the psychology of
the child. As chair of a new psychology department at Johns Hopkins University, Hall promoted a model psychological laboratory grounded in his
training in Europe but influenced by U.S. post-Reconstruction racial models
like recapitulation theory. In such a model, each child must pass through
all the previous, "less evolved" racial stages of development as part of the
maturation process, and so even the highly evolved white child temporarily
acts and thinks like less-evolved races in the process of finally proving the
specific evolutionary sophistication of the race to which it belongs.

American psychological studies documented the fact that different
races supposedly achieved different developmental levels of consciousness.

Therefore, distinctions between races are directly reflected in the seeming differences among individual progress that variously raced children represent.[15] Because its ancestors never advanced to a higher intelligence level, for example, the "negro child," as Anna Tolman Smith summarizes, remains "psychologically different from the white child," unable to evolve beyond the "imperious sexual impulse" and susceptibility to superstition that reflects its race's inferior developmental state.[16] As a result, black children, according to Howard Odum, "innocently . . . reflect all that is not innocent; guiltless, they show the superlative of filth and indecency." Odum concludes that "the amount of knowledge of evil and evil practices possessed by small children is unthinkable. . . . [T]he unconscious depth of depravity to which the children have already come is appalling."[17] These traits impede the black child's "judgment, observation, reasoning, motor control, logical memory, [and] use of words," according to Josiah Morse.[18] Thus, if initially "remarkably precocious when taught in school by the side of white children," black children, according to the turn-of-the-century psychologist M. J. Mayo, cannot finally keep the characteristics that define them as a race from intruding into their "interest in study" and "interrupt[ing] their progress," which thereafter falls "behind their white competitors" and requires that they leave school for their own and their classmates' good.[19] As part of the racially specific evolutionary progress it represents, the white child, conversely, must pass through these less evolved stages of development but inevitably moves successfully beyond them, thereby ensuring that "skin color" becomes an accurate "index of intelligence and mental ability."[20] Thus, even though all organisms develop "serially in regular stages," the growth stages of higher-functioning beings are accelerated, according to Baldwin, and directly represent later stages of development without those individuals seeming to have to learn all the earlier stages. Benefiting from its race's mastery of "a great mass of phylogenetic details," the more evolved individual seems essentially different "from the crude imitative consciousness in which it had its beginning," and from those individuals who demonstrate such a consciousness. In such a model, all individuals follow the same developmental trajectory, but the "growth of the individual" functions as a direct index to the "very marked modifications of the race record" indicating that one race is more evolved than another.[21]

While it is easy to see how this account of psychological development might produce racist commentary in American psychological tracts, I am interested not so much in documenting the prevalence of overtly racist language in nineteenth-century psychology as in identifying the historically specific racial logic embedded in the core of its theory of the individual. Drawing on the racial logic propounded by social commentators like Haygood, prominent psychologists like Hall often argue that, "after slavery," the "Negro" loses "his mental equilibrium . . . from stress and strain which would not affect a race mentally stronger" and thereby deteriorates under the social pressures of freedom and citizenship.[22] In this social model, the Negro's degeneration enables "the white race's" regeneration, and the social challenges produced by the "race problem" enable the white race "to gather itself up for an extraordinary new unity and further step in advancement."[23] Such a degenerative account of "the Negro" not only reflects a burgeoning postwar racism that reinforces white superiority, but, as important, it reveals the extent to which racial logic is embedded within psychological discourse, structuring how that emerging discourse imagines the individual that the child represents. Despite their declared indebtedness to European psychological models, it becomes difficult for American psychologists to imagine or describe individual development outside the terms of evolving nineteenth-century U.S. racial-identity formations, as Hall makes clear when, in his seminal 1890s psychological treatise *Adolescence*, he argues that at a certain point a child's development inevitably resembles "that of the sudden emancipation of the Negroes in the South."[24] As Hall's analogy illustrates, it is not only that the white individual can come dangerously close to resembling "the Negro," but that what comes to count as "the Negro" by the late nineteenth century is embedded, and remains latent, within each individual. Whether it be "the Negro [in slavery] who did not worry . . . but led a humble if somewhat animal life in his little cabin" or the Negro after slavery who promptly degenerated under the pressures of freedom, the individual as American psychologists script him carries within himself and at his core this less evolved, newly racialized essence.[25]

It is to this world beneath the skin that late-nineteenth-century scientists like Hall, Mayo, and Odum consistently turn to find a firm outline and anchor for the racial differences that are always present, if not always easily visible, in the individual.[26] Summarizing the prevailing scientific view, as well as his own findings regarding sure indicators of racial identity, James

Bardin concludes in *Popular Science Monthly* that even the most convincing visual markers of whiteness cannot erase a given race's "mental character- istics," which are "as distinctly and as organically a part of the race as its physical characteristics" and therefore continue to "distinguish" the races even when "physical characteristics" give the lie to racial identity.[27] It is for this reason, Bardin contends, that "we can never make the Negro like the white man mentally," even if he bears the most convincing physical resem- blance. A person with these indelible and "characteristic mental peculiari- ties" is therefore destined to "remain a Negro psychically," regardless of the race to which he appears to belong. And because his "psychical reactions to the influences of our civilization are entirely different from our own," all reality "will take on a different meaning in the Negro's consciousness" than in "the white man's."[28]

Sure indicators of the mental traits that differentiate the African Ameri- can from the Anglo-American when color cannot, according to Hall and Thomas Garth, among others, are the extremely strong sensations that cre- ate a susceptibility to believing in the supernatural and a tendency toward sexual excess early in life. Because "the Negro race is indeed more highly rated than any other race in sensory development," Garth finds that the sheer "strength of their sensations" produces a distinguishing set of be- haviors.[29] William James's one-time colleague and friend, Hall, documents these behaviors in detail in "The Negro in Africa and America." Contend- ing that "no two races in history" have "psychic" traits as vastly different as "the Caucasian and the African," Hall proceeds to itemize the psychological differences that make any visible distinction in "the color of the skin" only a superficial "sign of many far deeper differences" between the races.[30] Most notable is "a strong belief in invisible powers" that makes the "Negro's" life too easily "dominated by spirits" rather than reality. Inheriting with his race an extremely active imagination that makes "the next world," rather than the present, real, the Negro in America has an "intense emotionality [that] predisposes him to believe in supernatural agencies." Daily life is therefore controlled not by reason but by "superstition" and the "sorcery, voodoo- ism, [and] witchcraft which can be traced back to Africa." The extremely vivid "tropical imagination" and "very keen sensitiveness" to stimuli that distinguishes the African American from other races create not only the tendency to believe that "spirits do all that is unusual," but also what Robert

Bean summarizes as a marked "lack of self-control in connection with the sexual relation" that leads to precocious sexual activities and interests.[31]

Within the context of these contemporary psychological accounts of the differences between races and of racial identity's inevitable centrality to the self, then, the question that concerns the governess in both *The Turn of the Screw* and *What Maisie Knew*—does the child have a moral sense, in the case of Maisie, and what does the child know, in the case of Flora and Miles?— are questions not simply about the children's sexual knowledge but also about the racial influences that shape their identity. That the question of the children's sexual precocity might easily translate for late-nineteenth-century audiences into a question of their racial make-up is not meant to suggest that Miles, Flora, or Maisie have "black" blood in their veins per se but, rather, that James uses contemporary psychological accounts to consider how the self that the child represents might be constructed through racialized discourses. By representing the importance of racial difference to his fictional child's unfolding, developing self, James uses psychological models that rely on and use the child to reinforce racial difference to insist on the place of that difference within every self. James was repeatedly encouraged by his brother William to write about child psychology in the late 1880s and early 1890s, and in fiction like *The Turn of the Screw* he admitted his interest in depicting "the fact of infant depravity."[32] While contemporary critics of the text agreed in general that "the question of good and evil in childhood is well described," even if some found "the extent of the corruption cruel and untrue," those contemporary models of race that take the child as their interrogatory subject to a large extent lend shape and texture to these representations of childhood evil.[33] All three children have a fairness that is much commented on, yet the texts are concerned with what eludes visual representation but is shown in the child's behavior. The question that compels both texts and adult protagonists—what invisible matter makes up these child subjects?—is exactly the question asked by psychologists who search the child for signs of those particular characteristics that distinguish one race from another.

The answer in both texts becomes explicable within the context of contemporary psychological accounts of the child, which emphasize the racial influences at work in the child's developmental progress even as they use the child to enunciate the contours of racial identity in the postbellum period.

These influences, as William James notes in the series of immensely popular lectures that he gave in 1895 and subsequently published as *Talks to Teachers* (1899), can directly affect the child's ability to benefit from traditional education.[34] Hall concurs with James and argues that once such children's "minds develop irregularities," their educability ceases and they need to be "sifted out of school for both its good and their own."[35] It is this question of educability that is of primary concern in both Henry James texts. While the cause of Miles's dismissal from school and the question of whether "he is really *bad*" focus the governess's attention in *The Turn of the Screw*, *What Maisie Knew* tracks the repeated conflation of erotic with educational plots that finally keeps Maisie from the formal education offered at such institutions as "the splendid school at Brighton."[36] As Hall and William James suggest is the case when children experience particularly volatile developmental phases, both child protagonists, for different but not unrelated reasons, show the lack of educability that debars them from formal education and evokes the specter of racial difference at work within their developing selves.

The "precocious experience" and "easily . . . almost infinitely quickened" perceptions acquired outside of school are developed rather than contained through the children's associations with adults who they recognize as racial others.[37] The racial identity of characters like the Countess, the Captain, and Quint seems generative of the knowledge the children internalize through association with them. In *What Maisie Knew*, for example, a number of adults who encourage in Maisie the "capacity to understand much more than any [child] had perhaps ever understood before" appear before her as a panoply of "brown" individuals.[38] Mr. Perriam resembles "quite her idea of a heathen Turk," of "a person who comes from the East," or, alternatively, as Mrs. Wix contends, "a heathen Jew," whereas her first glimpse of one of her father's companions likewise reveals an "almost black" Countess.[39] This "brown lady" is indistinguishable from the bevy of "bright brown ladies" who advertise the sideshow Flowers of the Forest and who are "brown all over—in a medium suggestive of tropical luxuriance."[40] The signature red hair that Stanley Renner argues indicates a particular physiognomic propensity for sexual appetite in Peter Quint likewise indicates an Irishness that for James, as well as for many nineteenth-century Americans, unequivocally signaled a "foreign note" and distinct racial identity, as Noel Ignatiev has

shown.[41] The "evil time" that Quint initiates in the children's lives is therefore a direct reflection of the "matters in Quint's life"—the "secret disorders
[and] vices"—that become a sign of his racial identity.[42] The prescience that
the children show because of their association with these individuals transforms their surroundings into projections of their racialized identity—into
"phantasmagoric" and ghost-filled spaces into which they both stare "half-
scared," looking for clues to help them understand "the evil" being "poured"
into their "little gravely-gazing souls."[43] Precisely such an image of Miles
blindly searching for the ghost he cannot see concludes *The Turn of the Screw*.

By encountering racial difference as an unavoidable, constitutive element
of the developing self, James's child protagonists in turn require their adult
watchers to consider the ongoing place of racial alterity within themselves.
By leaving their watchers wondering about their own potential to carry
within themselves the "fresh system of misbehavior" that they detect in the
child, James's children require that adults ask themselves, as does Miles's
governess—"if he *were* innocent what then on earth was I?"[44] The self that
James's children represent for their interested watchers therefore remains
not so much divorced from, as existing in, shifting, synthetic relation to
late-nineteenth-century psychological ways of conceptualizing of selves as
racialized subjects. By exploring the potential for racial difference to exist
in all selves, regardless of the race to which they visibly appear to belong,
these stories challenge firmly fixed notions of racial purity. Just as Twain's
1890s texts use the child to challenge the place of race in the nation, so do
James's fictional children point out the mistaken racial premises of modern
selfhood. James's child protagonists, in other words, pose the question that
James would in *The American Scene*: "Which is the American which is not
the alien . . . where does one put a finger on the dividing line?"[45] If one of
"the child's values" for James is that it represents the individual's "vessel of
consciousness" not as disconnected from, but as integrally bound to, contemporary social constructs of race, the child, as we have seen, inevitably
complicates the neat distinctions such constructs tend to create between
races.[46] Insisting on the place of racial difference within each self, James's
child lends a "precious element of dignity" to the people "involved" with
it not because it offers them an alternative to culture—not because it reminds adults distracted and absorbed by nineteenth-century society of their
own lost, presocial "spirit of infancy," as Emerson contends—but because

the child encourages them to understand the self as constituted through a racial logic that places difference at the center of even the whitest individual.[47] In so doing, James's child protagonists challenge readers to rethink their understanding of self and of the social framework that conceptualizes that self along an axis of racial difference.

HIDDEN SELVES

If Henry James depicts the inevitable place of racial alterity within the child and the psychological self it represents, Pauline Hopkins critiques the impact of U.S. psychology's conceptual dependence on racial logic for those individuals who are socially identified as racial others. Like James, Hopkins explores how American psychology's dependence on post-Reconstruction racial logic structures the self, but Hopkins takes African American consciousness as her exclusive focus, considering in detail how this dependence affects African American identity. As the title of her 1902 serial novel *Of One Blood; or, the Hidden Self* suggests, Hopkins uses William James's popular 1890 essay "The Hidden Self" as an organizing principle for her fictional account of the different identity formations that distinct bloodlines produce.[48] In making a case for the value of Hopkins's sensation novel, scholars have recently used the second half of her title as a way to understand the first. In short, they have argued that Hopkins not only was familiar with William James's contention that there is a "hidden self" within the individual but appropriated James's term to express the social condition of the African American after Reconstruction.[49] Just as James's student W. E. B. Du Bois declares in an 1897 essay for the *Atlantic Monthly* that the African American experiences an inevitable "double-consciousness" proceeding from "two souls, two thoughts, two unreconciled strivings; two warring ideals in one dark body,"[50] so, too, does Pauline Hopkins in these accounts use James's description of a "consciousness split into parts which coexist" as a way to express the psychosocial condition of the late-nineteenth-century African American.[51] Using contemporary notions of a hidden or doubled self as a road map for reading the cultural meaning of blood in Hopkins's novel has certainly produced important accounts of how Hopkins figures blood and its social meanings in her text. However, I suggest in the rest of this chapter that reading Hopkins's title from front to back — that is, assessing the impact that blood and, more particularly, historically specific ideas about its social meaning have on contemporary psychological notions of the self that the child represents — reveals an equally important social commentary on American psychology's impact on African American selfhood that thus far has remained hidden in Hopkins's text. Reorienting how we think about Hopkins's fictional text in relation to the historical one with which, as her title indicates, she is in dialogue therefore reveals how late-nineteenth-century American psychology's conceptual dependence on racial difference intersects with African American identity and how Hopkins's text in turn offers an important, so far unrecognized critique and, finally, revision of such scientific models of identity.

As much as the multiple self theorized by European psychologists like Janet and Binet, it is the less-evolved, degenerative, and racialized self described by U.S. psychologists, I suggest, to which William James refers when he describes to readers of *Scribner's Magazine* the problem that "two different selves or persons in one man" pose to scientific discourse. Though he declares his exclusive indebtedness to "Janet's observations and hypotheses" and "the observations of M. Binet," the hidden self that James delineates for his popular U.S. audience takes much of its shape and imaginative energy from contemporary U.S. sociological theories of racial difference.[52] Indeed, James not only uses the contemporary psychological notion that interested his brother Henry of an essentially degenerative, racially distinct other at the core of the more evolved individual as an organizing principle of his theory of the multilayered psyche, but he also relies on the popular metaphor of a second or hidden U.S. history of racial inequality to describe his scientific model to a popular audience. It is "the dust-cloud of exceptional observations [and] of occurrences minute and irregular" that "float . . . about the accredited and orderly facts of every science" in which William James declares he is interested in his essay.[53] Although such accounts are regularly dismissed by science as irrelevant, unsubstantiated, and therefore insubstantial, James contends that such events are "real" but merely indiscernible to traditional scientific practice. To find evidence of and begin to understand this "mystical consciousness," James asserts that we must "look behind the pages of official history" to another, undisclosed history.[54] It is precisely to such a second, supplemental history that William Wells Brown points readers when he asks them in *Clotel* to look beyond Plymouth Rock and to see, on the same day that the *Mayflower* arrives, a second ship "low and rakish . . . hastening from the tropics to the New World, freighted with . . . the first cargo of slaves on their way to Jamestown."[55] The two ships—one seeding the nation with "prosperous, labor-honoring, law-sustaining institutions" and the other with "slavery, idleness, lynch-law and ignorance"—represent, as James Clarke declares in *Anti-Slavery Days* (1884), the essentially double history of the nation and those who people it.[56] Just as the United States contains within it two stories—one dominant and one, as Clarke puts it, "untold"—so does the individual in which James is interested in "The Hidden Self" contain within himself "a secondary self, or selves [that] coexist with the primary one" in uneasy, ongoing tension.[57] This second self, according to James, has the capacity to disrupt a person's "normal flow of life" at any time, due to the "perverse" nature of these "buried fragment[s] of consciousness."[58] Represented by popular cartes de visites and photographs of the child as a representative of an essentially doubled, multiple identity, the self that William James describes, as James Mark Baldwin reiterates, cannot be an "isolated-and-in-his-body-alone-situated abstraction."[59] Composed of "a network of relationships among you, me, and the others," this essentially multilayered self can "throw the emphasis on one pole sometimes, calling it me; and on the other pole sometimes, calling it you or him," and in so doing remains, in Baldwin's account, in a vital, essentially dialogic relation with that which it is intimately related.[60]

Like his account of its place in canonical scientific discourse, William James's characterization of this hidden self draws from contemporary descriptions of racial identity and, more particularly, from the scientific terminology that U.S. doctors used to prove the inferiority of the African American. The extent to which this particular racial logic organizes James's account of the psyche becomes clear once we place his description of the symptomatic patient's hidden self within the context of accounts in prominent American medical journals of the degenerative African American. Medical findings published in the 1880s and 1890s in important journals such as *Journal of the American Medical Association*, *New York Medical Journal*, *Medical News*, and *North Carolina Medical Journal* agree not only that the African American is degenerating under the pressures of emancipation, but that reduced or aberrant visual capacity—a crucial symptom of one's hidden self in James's account—is the most common symptom of this degeneration.

Just as the Negro who, according to Thomas McKie, has keen vision "far surpassing that of the Caucasian . . . while enslaved" finds himself, with emancipation, suddenly subject to a plethora of eye diseases that lead to partial blindness, "hallucinations and delusions," so, too, does the individual under the sway of active multiple selves, according to James, find her eyes and vision to be severely compromised.[61] While the Negro, once "thrown upon his own resources" and "subject to the same demand as the white race," according to one writer for the *New York Medical Journal*, is exposed "to diseases that lead to eye complications" because he does not have the "same vital power of resistance" as whites,[62] individuals most troubled by their subconscious or hidden self are those of "the 'visual' type," according to James, and their symptoms are almost exclusively visual aberrations. "Visual derangements," such as "nystagmus or trembling of the eyeball" are often proof, according to Max Nordeau, of African Americans' degeneration.[63] Perceiving the world through a "trembling, restless . . . field of vision, devoid of firm outline," the degenerate has "all sorts of gaps in his field of vision producing strange effects." Unlike "the consciousness of a healthy, strong-minded man" who has an "eye [that] sees all objects distinctly . . . in the full light of day," the degenerate feels himself to be "surrounded by sinister forms" and is plagued by "defective observation" that produces a "distorted and blurred view of the external world."[64] Like this degenerate, the individual who experiences cognitive dissonance between what James terms "the upper self" and "the under self" is troubled by "hallucinations," "fixed blindness" and "hysterical blindness."[65] Often an individual so troubled will "ignore . . . one eye" that she experiences as "blind," according to James, until "the other, or seeing eye, is shut," at which point the blind eye "will do its share of vision perfectly well." Even when both eyes seem functional, the individual under the influence of multiple selves "often has to invent an hallucination by which to mask and hide from [the primary's self's] view the deeds which the other self is enacting." As a result, patients are often found "unconsciously writing down words which their eyes [are] vainly endeavoring to 'see.'" Subject to a partial blindness and distorted vision that are symptomatic of a consciousness that is "split into parts which coexist but mutually ignore each other," such an individual reproduces as the substance of its second and hidden self the degenerative African American identity that prominent late-nineteenth-century American psychologists argue remains embedded, but most often latent, within each individual.[66] Thus, the second self that James presents to his readers is nothing less than the inevitable specter of racial difference that each individual, no matter how evolved, carries within himself and to which he remains in dialogic relation.

Familiar with James's theory, Pauline Hopkins insists in her fictional response to it on contemporary psychologists' conceptual reliance on popular ideas of racial difference.[67] Yet while Hopkins, like Henry James, explores the centrality of these ideas to the psychological models contemporary scientists produce, she more particularly focuses on the impact that such models have on African American identity. When we read *Of One Blood; or, the Hidden Self* along with Hopkins's less-well-known historical compilation on which her novel draws, *A Primer of Facts: Pertaining to the Early Greatness of the African Race and the Possibility of Restoration by Its Descendants* (1905), it becomes clear that Hopkins is producing a powerful critique of late-nineteenth-century scientific formulations of racial difference and the psychological models that rely on them by positing an alternative scientific account of racial identity in which "the Negro" is not essentially degenerative but socially regenerative. A compilation of "the works of the best known ethnologists and historians," *A Primer of Facts* provides an alternative account of the social meaning of blood and thereby challenges both dominant scientific narratives of racial difference and the psychological theories of individual consciousness that, as I have illustrated, derive from them in the late nineteenth century.[68]

Written almost contemporaneously with *Of One Blood*, Hopkins's historical text provides an important, and overlooked, roadmap for assessing the full extent of her novel's critique of contemporary U.S. psychology's reliance on racial logic. Analysis of *A Primer of Facts* makes clear that her fictional text is part of an ongoing commentary not only on the social condition of African Americans, but also on the scientific models that normalize that condition. Insisting that "Yellow, Black, and White" are all "born of the same father and mother" and are thus all "of one race and color," *A Primer of Facts* begins its response to contemporary scientific accounts of race by describing the human body as containing all racial variations within its multilayered epidermis. All "human skin," according to Hopkins, "consists of three structures: the cuticle or external surface, the middle structure and [the] true skin." In this epidermal palimpsest, the cuticle is "transparent

[and] colorless," as is the third or "true skin," but the second skin, initially "jelly-like and colorless," contains cells that change to the color of whatever enters them. "These cells are empty or partially filled with a colorless substance" in the white race, only changing temporarily when "red matter enters the cells of the middle skin" during a blush, for example. However, in the African race, these cells are constantly filled with this red matter, causing permanent darkening of the skin. As Hopkins writes, "The coloring matter which enters the cells of the middle skin of the African race is the same red matter, concentrated, which flushes the cheek of the white man under strong emotion."[69] Because both cells and fluid are the same in all individuals, and it is only the degree of the latter that causes a different color to appear on the external or cuticle skin surface, black and white skins signify incremental rather than essential differences. Asserting that "in human races, running through all shades of complexion, there is but one color, modified and intensified from the purest white to the purest black," Hopkins insists that skin variations reflect the individual's degree of separation from a common point of historical origin.[70]

To exemplify this concept, Hopkins likens human skin to the skin of fruit. Just as black fruit goes through various color changes: from "green, then white, next slight red which deepens daily to a final intense red or blackness in color," so, too, is the blackness of skin no more than the visible endpoint of various developmental color changes. Indeed, the blackness of the fruit is nothing more than an intensification of the fruit's "red color matter," according to Hopkins. Like the skin of fruit, then, the skin color of even the "blackest African is simply concentrated red"—the shared biological "color" of all humankind. Thus, crucial for Hopkins's project is the claim that skin color is no different from any other individual characteristic—that just as the same mother and father might produce children "with different color eyes and hair," so, too, is the hue of one's skin color an arbitrary byproduct of an individual's second, hidden skin layer.[71] Her challenge to popular scientific accounts of essential racial difference depends on the contention that all individuals are composed of a multilayered biological self in which the extent to which one's hidden, second skin cells are full or empty is less important than the fact that variation is possible.

While on the one hand, this physiological account of the role that blood plays in coloring a multilayered biological self resembles contemporary scientists' models of the progressive individual development that the child represents, on the other hand, it enables Hopkins to re-describe the African American as socially superior to and subsequently regenerative for the white race.[72] And in so doing, Hopkins challenges popular scientific claims that the African American is essentially inferior and degenerative. If "all races have sprung from the same parent stock," and so all humankind is "of one race," Africans' choice to take "purple and nothing else" as their "real color" reflects their superiority as a people, according to Hopkins. Purple is the color produced by the African's second skin layer; as Hopkins argues, it is a "regular established law of physiology [that] an adequate quantity of red blood, blending, forms the purple of the blackest African complexion." However, it is also a symbolic color, reflecting the Africans' advancement as a people. It is "a royal shade" and is "adopted" by Africans as a signifier of a collective identity not only because it is "emblematic of the complexion of their kings and queens," but because it represents the quality of their own blood. Ethiopians show a "delicate perception" in choosing purple as a representative color that proves that they contain in their skin and, therefore "are," what the color symbolizes. "A mixture of red and blue," purple "implies the existence of blue in the [African's] blood." Moving between literal and figurative meanings, Hopkins argues that "blue veins" hold the "blue," aristocratic blood that in the "white race" produces "its blue eyes" as well as accounts of its social advancement. Both physiologically and ideologically, then, the "purple color of the African" proves that blue reflects an ideological as well as physiological element of his blood.[73]

The proof that *A Primer of Facts* provides that unparalleled social advancement is literally encoded in the blood of the African American via his distinct Ethiopian ancestry is crucial in countermanding scientific accounts of his inevitable biological and social degeneration and, by extension, the psychological theories that feature the child to illustrate them. That such a rejoinder is urgently needed becomes clear from Hopkins's account of the state of contemporary public speech about the social and intellectual potential of African Americans. By the 1890s, Hopkins estimates that "every leading intellect" on the question of African American advancement "has been intimidated" into silence, and "a horde of Southern writers, speakers and politicians" subsequently "fill the air with their doleful clamor against a proscribed race," uncontested by even the slightest "protest." Given "the front of the stage in presenting" the history of racial difference and reasons for it, such public spokespeople are literally rewriting history as they speak and presenting as a natural, incontestable, and accomplished "fact" their racial superiority. "Solemnly impressed with the magnitude of our wicked-ness and hopeless depravity by partisan white and colored speakers, . . . cultured men and women of color" sit in "silence" in conventions and as-semblies where these public discussions occur and are unable to contribute to the "burning question" of racial equality because they lack basic informa-tion. At such a crucial juncture, Hopkins tells all readers who are "descen-dants of Africans in America" that it is their "obligation" to intervene with educated and corrective speech of their own. The best way to do so is to be-come "thoroughly familiar with the meagre details of Ethiopian history" to "foster race pride" while providing another, alternative history of the regen-erative potential of African American identity.[74] Hopkins's *A Primer of Facts* is one such speech act. It compiles scientific, historical, and ethnographic details not only to offer scientific "proof" of African American equality, but also to delineate the "great advancement in science and the mechanical arts" that Africans have made and thereby to show "the living reality of Ethiopian knowledge" in modern society. Such an account is important because "the present crisis of our racial history" and "of the Republic," according to Hop-kins, can be averted only by redressing what she considers a "lamentable ignorance of the commonest scientific and historical facts."[75]

While such imaginative rewritings and recoveries of "lost" history en-able marginalized groups and individuals to build cohesive political iden-tities, as Joan Scott has pointed out, the full scope of Hopkins's revisionist project becomes apparent only once we use the alternative history that her *A Primer of Facts* provides as a means of interpreting her novel.[76] Once we do so, it becomes clear that Hopkins attempts to reconstitute African Ameri-can identity for her silenced readers not simply by using Anglo-American psychological theories to describe its complexity or by compiling an alter-native history of African identity but, rather, by imagining the full social impact that such an alternative history would have on an African Ameri-can self and on a dominant "science" that, as one of the characters in *Of One Blood* states, "has done its best to separate the [preeminent] race from Northern Africa."[77]

While William James's theory plays a pivotal role in such a project, and

Of One Blood makes repeated reference to "the hidden self" that lies "quiescent in every human soul," the relationship of the novel's protagonist, Reuel Briggs, to both self and science is inevitably mediated through a heritage of mixed blood that complicates the very premises of dominant science. The novel opens with the young Harvard scientist pondering the "haunting significance" that he finds in the "new discoveries in psychology" and in a newly published book titled, *The Unclassified Residuum.*[78] Because of his mixed blood, Briggs is not only a student of, but also subject to, the "exceptional observation" that James identifies at the beginning of his essay as representing this "unclassified residuum." "Effects of the imagination," including "divinations" and "apparitions," form the substance of Briggs's self, as well as of his scientific inquiry, and indicate, as he will discover, the presence of royal African blood in his veins. It is the convergence of this hidden, racialized self, and the knowledge it gives him, that combines with his scientific practice to give him the potential to "astonish the world." Though students disagree about whether he is Italian or Japanese, they concur that he is a "genius in his scientific studies . . . whatever land claimed him as a son," but what they do not recognize is the constitutive role that his undisclosed racial identity plays in that scientific genius.[79]

To synthesize his racial identity successfully with his scientific expertise, Briggs must confront the personal and sociological implications of "the Negro problem" to which psychological discourse contributes by featuring the child as a representative of the self.[80] Like most "cultured men and women," according to Hopkins, Briggs has no language with which to comment on the "race problem."[81] When asked explicitly what he thinks about "the only burning question . . . about which [he] is silent," he declares that he has "a horror of discussing the woes of unfortunates, tramps, stray dogs and cats and Negroes." Yet Hopkins places him within "a new era in the life of the nation" that begins with the "passing of slavery from the land." This new era influences "the undiscovered country within" Briggs and, by extension, his psychological theories of the individual. Briggs begins to understand the relevance of his African American identity to his psychological make-up and scientific inquiry when "the passing shadow" of a woman in one of his visions becomes real at a concert of "Negro music." Like the rest of the "self-possessed, highly-cultured New England assemblage" in attendance, he sees "all the horror, the degredation [*sic*], the awfulness of the hell" of slavery as he listens to the woman sing. Yet he is "spell-bound" in a way essentially different from the other listeners because he "sees" in the woman, Dianthe, not only the momentary revivification of slavery but proof of a strong "mental sight" that indicates the exceptional perception accruing exclusively to his race, according to psychologists. Dianthe becomes the occasion for the public exercise of this power in the scientific community when Briggs reanimates her seemingly lifeless form for his medical colleagues and teachers. Although he is told by the head physician and all the surgeons who surround Dianthe's body that the theories of mesmerism and animal magnetism with which he declares he will resuscitate her "smack of the supernatural, charlatanism, and dreams of lunacy," Briggs uses his race-based knowledge to invest Dianthe and, by extension, himself with mysterious life. If, as Briggs defines it, "life is that evidence of supernatural endowment which originally entered nature" to form the human self, then both he and his patient gain it as he demonstrates his scientific theory. While Briggs's "whole person took on the majesty of conscious power, and pride in the knowledge he possessed" as he disseminates that knowledge to a skeptical scientific community, once he proves his theory by revitalizing his patient, a "potent presence radiates" from him, producing "respect mingled with awe."[82]

Once Briggs brings the full power of his racial self to bear on science, he not only adds to scientific knowledge with a "celebrated case" that is featured in "all the scientific journals" of the day,[83] but he also reconstitutes scientific practice around the racial identity that psychology used the child to subordinate. In short, by discovering his own African heritage and the alternative developmental history encoded within it, Briggs reorients science around an alternative figuration of a socially advanced African individual identity. Unable to support himself and Dianthe within the U.S. scientific community because, unknown to Briggs, employers have discovered his racial identity, he enlists as medical staff on an expedition to Africa to discover the buried treasure left in an ancient Ethiopian city, Meroe. Motivated by dreams of "fame and fortune he would carry home to lay at a little woman's feet," Briggs has an investment in the expedition that is initially identical to those of the other men. While it will do the "Negro race good" if the discovery is made, the men, as one of his colleagues says, have two motivations: "to get a few more dollars and fresh information." Like the others,

Briggs initially sees Africa through the lens of a "healthy American" perspective in which the "march of progress" is discernible by "the sound of hammers on unfinished buildings that tell of a busy future and modern homeliness." With "no railroads, no churches, no saloons, no schoolhouses," Africa appears to Briggs to carry "no promise of life" and "no future" for himself or his scientific society, only "the monotony of past centuries dead," literally as well as figuratively buried. Structured by accounts of social development in which Africans degenerate before the greater integrity and vitality of the white race, these expectations that an exploration of Africa will reveal only dead "old things" that will enable the finders to "impart our knowledge to the people of our land, who are eager to know the beginning of all things" fails to take into account the full history and ongoing reality of African identity. One professor contends correctly that the group will find evidence that will "establish the primal existence of the Negro as the most ancient source of all that [is] valued in modern life." Proving that "Ethiopia antedated Egypt," and thus that "the race of Negroes" that garners "extreme contempt" in U.S. psychological and sociological discourses is in fact responsible for all "our arts, sciences and even the use of speech," is to reveal the partisan interests that undergird widely accepted scientific models of individual identity. By redefining these scientific accounts as self-interested rather than as objective truth, such an alternative history challenges established ways of thinking and knowing the past. As one explorer exclaims when he hears the professor's hypothesis: " 'Great Scott!' You don't mean to tell me that all this was done by *niggers*?' " By documenting how "the Anglo-Saxon has climbed to the position of the first people of the earth today" and how "the African people have fallen to reach the abjectness of the American Negro," such an alternative history refutes once and for all theories that align the child with the self to naturalize the idea of transhistorical, essential racial difference.[84] Thus, the exploration of Africa by which Briggs intended to establish himself at the forefront of Western scientific progress ends up reconstituting Anglo-American scientific ways of knowing and the accounts of social progress that reinforce it around an African identity that precedes and preempts such models of knowledge.

This revisionist history not only repositions Africa as the originator of cultural advancement and progress. It also reaffirms, through Briggs, Africa's ongoing centrality to contemporary U.S. society and the scientific models it produces. Self and scientific knowledge merge when Briggs is carried against his will to the hidden city of Telassar by living descendants of Ethiopian society and is told that he is their lost king—the long-awaited individual who will "restore to the Ethiopian race its ancient glory." While he tries to "convince himself that he is laboring under a wild hallucination"— that his second sight is only temporarily intruding upon a fixed, prevailing world of well-established scientific fact—his "senses all give evidence of the reality of his situation," and he comes to accept this second consciousness and the new self it reveals to him. By subordinating Anglo to African identity, this new self not only fulfills all "the dreams of wealth and ambition that had haunted" him when he was an obscure and impoverished student at Harvard. It also alters the world as he and others initially knew it. Not only finding in the lost city of Meroe "evidence of the correctness of the historical records" that prove the Africans' historical preeminence, Briggs— now known by his royal name, Ergamenes—also receives the "record of the wisdom and science of [his Ethiopian] ancestors." This scientific text initiates him into the ancient Ethiopian scientific methods on which his Harvard textbooks were tacitly based and thereby teaches him "all that he longs to know." As he ponders this "proof of supernatural powers," he wonders "what the professors of Harvard" would say to this "knowledge of science that all the wealth and learning of modern times could not emulate." Ashamed that he had "played the coward's part in hiding his origin" from his American colleagues, Briggs claims this hidden African heritage and the "second self" that is coterminous with it as part of his true identity. Once he does so, he is able to do what Hopkins encourages her readers to do. He is able to "restore the race of his fathers" to their rightful, preeminent place within contemporary scientific and psychological discourse that, as we have seen, locates the child as the center point of the self to reinforce the inferiority of African American identity.[85]

"YOU, ME, AND THE OTHERS"

As the preceding discussion illustrates, placing Hopkins's and James's writing in conversation with Anglo-American psychological accounts of the self that take the child as their point of origin reveals that the truly hidden, and delimiting, element in scientific models of self is their dependence on and indebtedness to the contemporary accounts of racial difference from which they want to distance their work. Just as Henry James features the child to depict racial alterity as an inevitable, finally constitutive element of the self, so does Hopkins engage with psychological models of the self to challenge readers to rethink how they conceptualize knowledge and selfhood. Thus, Hopkins's and James's writing taken together offers, among other things, an intervention in and revision of definitions of racial difference that scientists have both relied on and perpetuated in the postwar period. Responding to contemporary psychological accounts of race in the making of the self, James and Hopkins ask readers to conceive of individual identities not as essential and predetermined (as nineteenth-century scientists would have them do) but, instead, as contextual by-products of strategic ways of thinking about the past.

Such a request continues to have relevance for American literary practice. The current critical impulse to redress absences in the canon with recovery projects and influence arguments too often transplants current understandings of the politics of individual and national identity into historically remote periods rather than conceptualizing of the terms as historically discrete and contingent. To "recover" nineteenth-century texts requires, among other things, determining whether, how, and why they posit individual and national identity as salient terms. In the case of *Of One Blood*, Hopkins scripts selfhood into narrative being in direct response to its increasing lack of availability to African Americans as a result of late-nineteenth-century scientific discourse and inevitably shapes its meaning for African Americans out of the conceptual tools that this contemporary scientific discourse makes available to her. The African American as well as the Anglo-American self that she and James imagine is therefore composed, as their contemporary Baldwin notes, of an intricate "network of relationships among you, me, and the others."[86] It is this essentially contiguous self—a self that, regardless of its skin color, comes into a sense of its own identity through recognition of the contingency rather than discontinuity of racial identity—in which Hopkins and James are interested. Indeed, it is the project of determining the final potential of this particular notion of self for all Americans, regardless of race, in which Du Bois becomes interested, as we will see in the concluding chapter.

six

RACELESS STATES:
W. E. B. DU BOIS
AND CUBA

"In the treatment of the child the world foreshadows its own future and faith. All words and all thinking lead to the child—to that vast immortality and wide sweep of infinite possibility which the child represents."[1] So contends W. E. B. Du Bois in his 1928 commentary on the task of realizing liberal democracy in the twentieth century. Because "all our problems center in the child," Du Bois continues, if "democracy is a failure" we can "make it succeed" by turning our attention to the "immortal child."[2] The social possibilities that inhere in this "immortal child" seem at odds with the child Du Bois had described twenty-five years earlier, in "Of the Passing of the First-Born."[3] Unlike this mortal child whose early death Du Bois depicts as an "escape" from the "living death" that the impossibility of raceless citizenship in U.S. society has on black citizens, his immortal child seems to suggest that antiracism remains a possibility—albeit unrealized—in a U.S. liberal-democratic tradition. With these two child representatives as a backdrop, this final chapter explores the shifting place of race in Du Bois's developing political vision of the possibilities of individual citizenship within the nation-state. "In a Jim Crow world the effort to abandon the idea of race as a political instrument" is necessarily doomed, as Ross Posnock reminds us, but this fact must not cause us to ignore how early-twentieth-century black intellectuals like Du Bois developed the earlier thinking of writers like Twain, James, and Hopkins to explore the full range of possibilities for individual representation within the racial state.[4] Using the child that had long represented a racially inscribed polity "as a weapon *against* the status quo of white supremacy," Du Bois not only described the ways in which civic selfhood continued to be denied to blacks after Reconstruction; he also explored the ongoing possibility of creating "a collective national identity" founded on a "society purged of all racial distinctions."[5] Approaching the child as a representative not simply of the autonomy and liberty characterizing liberal-democratic citizenship but also of dependence enabled Du Bois to explore the possibilities and the limitations of civic representation and to tease out the question of social justice in a racial state. Liberal societies and the ideal of freedom have become so intertwined and complementary, as John Tomasi has pointed out, that it becomes difficult, if not impossible, for liberalists to theorize the place of dependence in democratic society. As a result, the idea of autonomy, as Eamonn Callan observes, keeps "sneaking in through the backdoor of political liberalism."[6] By insisting that the racial hierarchy that "explained" the nation's ideals of liberty and freedom actually delimited liberal democracy, and by exploring how racial difference could revivify the nation's commitment to democratic principles, Du Bois challenged the United States to reconstitute the terms through which the nation had long defined itself. Du Bois, in short, recognized that the child's racial representations not only worked to sustain independence as the default position of individuals in U.S. civic society, but also curtailed the achievement of true civic equality by maintaining racial inequity as the conceptual backbone of U.S. political culture.

Crucial to understanding how the child comes to encapsulate Du Bois's understanding of socially just relations between all individuals within the liberal-democratic state are contemporary developments that occur in each at the time that Du Bois was refining his political thinking: on the one hand, the American psychological and philosophical models of self propounded by John Dewey, Josiah Royce, and William James, and on the other hand, Cuba's struggle to establish a raceless independent nation. That Du Bois was heavily influenced by the innovative psychological and philosophical traditions developed by Harvard faculty while he was a student is a widely recognized fact. Less familiar is his interest in Cuba's struggle for independence from Spain, a struggle that depended on both a multiracial army that was integrated at all ranks and a powerful rhetoric of antiracism that became more dominant in the years between the legal end of slavery in 1886 and the outbreak of the third and final war beginning in 1895.[7] Most scholars have tended to overlook the significance of Cuba for Du Bois's thinking, focusing instead on his attention to Haiti and its influence on his commitment to Pan-African nationalism. Yet Du Bois remained interested in Cuba throughout his career, making many trips to Cuba, engaging in extensive correspondence with Cuban political leaders such as Fernando Ortiz, and writing as well as speaking not only about U.S. policies in Cuba but also about the raceless nationalism to which Cuban insurgents had been committed. Struggling to achieve independent nationhood at a time when U.S. notions of self and state tended to be mutually constituted through an increasingly rigid account of racial difference, Cuba offered a timely alternative formulation of how race could facilitate, rather than impede, the realization of a socially just state. Responding as much to Cuba's unique struggle to create a nation—where, as José Martí asserts, there is no fear of a race war because both nation and citizens are more than white, mulatto, or negro[8]—as to the philosophies and psychologies that located the self firmly within its social context, Du Bois featured the child to explore the possibility of renegotiating the increasingly fixed place of race in constituting both self and state. He turned to the child, in short, to consider through the dual lenses that pragmatism and Cuban independence offered the ideal social location of the African American self.

"NO NORTH, NO SOUTH, NO BLACK, NO WHITE"

To white Americans, the decade of the 1890s was a gilded age, but to African Americans, it was the darkest age since the Civil War and a period of retrogression in black–white relations. As the historian Rayford Logan has commented, "The last decade of the nineteenth century and the opening of the twentieth century marked the nadir of the Negro's status in American society."[9] Racial discrimination and oppression reached new levels of intensity and social acceptance, leading Charles Chesnutt to comment in 1903 that "the rights of the Negroes are at a lower ebb than at any time during the thirty-five years of their freedom, and the race prejudice is more intense and uncompromising."[10] Just finishing school at such a critical moment,

Du Bois consequently contemplated the situation of the African American with a unique sense of urgency, and the question he pondered, according to Zhang Juguo, was "how to lead black people out of the seemingly boundless darkness of African American history."[11] Otto von Bismarck offered Du Bois one compelling model of social leadership, because, as Du Bois recalled in his *Autobiography*, Bismarck "united the internecine peoples into a powerful country" and "foreshadowed in my mind the kind of thing that American Negroes must do, marching forth with strength and determination under trained leadership."[12]

Despite Du Bois's recognition of a powerful political leader's importance in any effort to correct racial inequality on the national level, he contended that the solution to the "Negro problem" depended on the common efforts of all of the nation's citizens, regardless of their race. Asserting that race prejudice was caused by misunderstanding, misinformation, and ignorance of African Americans, and that "the two races should strive side by side to realize the ideals of the republic and make this truly a land of equal opportunity for all men,"[13] Du Bois devoted himself early in his career at Atlanta University to educating both blacks and whites about the real conditions of African Americans' lives to repudiate the racial logic that had long governed the nation. With studies like *The Philadelphia Negro* and *The Negro American Family*, he hoped to prove to white readers that there was no adequate historical evidence for claiming that the black race was inherently inferior to other races, and his commitment to publishing Atlanta Conference studies such as *Some Efforts of Negroes for Social Betterment* (1898) was based on the idea that scientific study of the "Negro problem" would act as an effective weapon against racism.[14] Aimed at repudiating racial thinking for the good of the nation, these 1890s publications, along with speeches like "Jefferson Davis as a Representative of Civilization," were part of Du Bois's effort to persuade all citizens that any nation "whose principle is the rise of one race on the ruins of another is a farce and a lie."[15] Thus, individuals should collectively work to achieve "greater respect for personal liberty and worth, regardless of race" throughout the nation so that "the ideal of human brotherhood [could] become a practical possibility."[16] Both celebrating black identity and hoping to help create "a truer world" where "men will judge men by their souls and not by their skins," Du Bois contended that black and white citizens "both act as reciprocal cause and effect [of prejudice] and a change in neither alone will bring the desired effect. Both must change or neither can improve to any great extent."[17] Driven by the desire "that some day on American soil two world-races may give each to each those characteristics both so sadly lack," Du Bois was therefore actuated, as Adolph Reed has recently shown, by "the ideal of fostering and developing the traits and talents of the Negro, not in opposition or contempt for other races" but, instead, to bridge the breach separating the races.[18]

Du Bois's ideas during the 1890s about how to transform the United States into an antiracist nation that was able simultaneously to acknowledge and transcend racial thinking coincided ideologically as well as chronologically with Cuba's struggle to achieve an independent, raceless nationhood. Even as Du Bois registered increasing frustration that the U.S. government would "rather go half way around the world to conquer a weak people at the cost of hundreds of millions than provide Atlanta University for the paltry sum of money [needed for] the African Americans studies program,"[19] he recognized the importance of blacks both inside and outside the United States to Cuba's efforts to create an independent nation founded on racial equality. As he declared in *The Horizon*, despite the fact that "Black men . . . freed Cuba," Anglo-Americans "snatched the victory" away from them and "kicked the 'niggers' back to their places" while "conspiring to perpetuate 'white' rule." Therefore, "the rape of Cuba" is one of the "blackest things in recent American history—fit to be written down beside the Seminole 'wars' and the looting of Mexico."[20] Du Bois's attention to Cuba's frustrated struggle to found a racially equitable independent nation is usually ignored or overshadowed by his simultaneous and often overlapping attention to Haiti's struggle to become a black republic. Yet the model of antiracist nationalism that Cuba tried, unsuccessfully, to achieve—in stark opposition to Haiti's racial republic—is crucial to understanding the complex dimensions of Du Bois's career as an advocate for racial equality. Between 1776 and 1825, as most of the colonies of North and South America acquired their independence, Cuba remained loyal to Spain. However, by 1868 Spanish rule had become sufficiently constricting that a handful of prosperous white men struck for independence by freeing their slaves, placing free men of color in local positions of authority, making former slaves soldiers, and calling all black men citizens. The three rebellions leading up to circumscribed

Cuban independence — the Ten Years War (1868–78), the Guerra Chiquita (Little War; 1879–80), and the final War of Independence (1895–98) — were all waged by an army (the Liberation Army) unique in the history of the Atlantic world because of its racial equality.

In essays, speeches, newspapers, and memoirs, white as well as nonwhite Cubans consistently claimed that the struggle against Spain had produced a new kind of individual and a new kind of collectivity. They argued that war had forever united black and white; and they imagined a new kind of nation in which equality was so ingrained that there existed no need to identify or speak of races — a nation in which, as the mulatto General Antonio Maceo wrote, there are "no whites nor blacks, but only Cubans."[21] José Martí, founder of the Cuban Revolutionary Party in 1892; Juan Gualberto Gómez, a mulatto journalist educated in Paris and Havana; and Rafael Serra y Montalvo, a journalist who began his career as a cigar worker all wrote of the union of blacks and whites in anticolonial war and located the symbolic and material birth of a nation in the alliance between black and white men. By declaring that there were no races and asserting that racism was an infraction against the nation as a whole, they helped defeat Spanish claims about the impossibility of Cuban nationhood. As General Maceo wrote on May 16, 1876, to Tomás Estrada Palma, president of the rebel republic, "This democratic Republic, which has established as its principle foundation liberty, equality, and fraternity, does not recognize racial hierarchies."[22] Stating that "all inhabitants of the Republic [were] entirely free [and] all citizens of the republic [would be] considered soldiers of the Liberation Army," Article 25 of the 1868 decree on abolition caused slaves to join the Cuban forces by the thousands. As one observer noted, they "marched in companies giving cries of long live Liberty and the whites of Cuba, who only yesterday had governed them with the harshness of the whip . . . today treat them as brothers and grant them the title of free men."[23] Rebel propaganda likewise declared that "all men are our brothers, whatever color their skin, whatever their race. . . . Liberty for all men, of all races, of all peoples, in all climates!"[24] A December 1869 rebel periodical similarly proclaimed that "every Cuban (white or black for we are all equal) . . . [e]veryone without distinctions of color . . . can serve . . . their Patria and Liberty.' " One rebel handbill directed at black manual laborers succinctly summed up the role that race played in founding the Cuban nation as follows: "The blacks are

the same as the whites. . . . The Cubans want the blacks to be free. The Spaniards want the blacks to continue being slaves. The Cubans are fighting the
Spaniards. The blacks who have any honor should go fight together with the
Cubans. . . . Long live liberty!"[25] These claims were substantiated by daily
interactions between blacks and whites, as Murat Halstead observed when
he described "Negro soldiers on guard" and "black workingmen . . . quickly
admitted" into the highest echelons of Cuban rebel leadership. Thus General Weyler's declaration that his policy toward blacks was "just the same
as to others" and his decision to constitute his cavalry escort of black men
reflected the extent to which he "esteemed them as soldiers."[26]

In the writings of Martí and black insurgents like Ricardo Batrell Oviedo
we can most clearly see the foundational importance of the idea of racial equality to Cuban independent nationhood. Professing that race was
merely a tool used locally to divide the anticolonial effort and globally by
men who invented "textbook races" to justify expansion and empire," Martí
concluded that, "to dwell on the divisions of race, the differences of race . . .
[was] to hamper the public good."[27] For Martí, the Ten Years War exemplified a Cuban history in which "the Cubans rose up in war, . . . broke the
shackles of their slaves; [and] converted, at the cost of their lives, [a] Spanish
indignity into a nation of free men." As a result, "Blacks and whites became
brothers . . . facing death, barefoot all and naked all, blacks and whites became equal: they embraced and have not separated since . . . the souls of
whites and blacks [rise] together through the skies."[28] "There will never be
a race war in Cuba," according to Martí, because the Cuban revolution "re-
turned the black race to humanity, and made the dreadful fact [of slavery]
disappear—"by giving life to the black man of Cuba, she was the one that
lifted the black man from his ignominy and embraced him—she, the Cuban
revolution."[29] This utopian vision of Cuban nationalism had a profound influence on independence efforts because, as Salah Hassan has pointed out,
Martí's political rhetoric captured the political and cultural forces in which
an increasingly modern Cuban populace lived in the 1880s.[30] Oviedo's mem-
oir reflects the power of Martí's political vision even as it seems to bear out
Martí's predictions that an antiracist Cuban republic was being born. The
black insurgent recalls seeing two soldiers alternately carrying each other
across a battlefield as each needed aid. This spectacle of black and white
brotherhood, for Oviedo, epitomized "democracy, with all its beautiful at-

tributes . . . there existed 'human reciprocity'—a reciprocity that all civilized peoples, nations, and men struggle to attain." Representing the spirit of "the true 'Cuban people'" where there were "no races," such an image helped not only Oviedo but all Cuban revolutionaries realize the nation for which they fought.[31]

This vision of a raceless Cuban nation depended, in large part, on reclaiming as a central trope of Cuban national identity the image of the child through which U.S. and Spanish political commentators dismissed the insurgent effort. Richard Henry Dana's *To Cuba and Back* (1859), for example, likened Cuba to a "child at play" with the idea of self-government but unable to achieve it because its citizens lacked the qualities inhering in "the Anglo-Saxon race"—qualities essential to realizing self-government.[32] Declaring that "you cannot reason from Massachusetts to Cuba," Dana dismissed Cuba's early struggle for "self-government" by describing Cuban citizens in the terms he used to characterize their children: "sallow, frail . . . and disposed to tyranny" because of "the effect of slavery and of despotic institutions."[33] Forty years later, as Cuba struggled once again for independence, the poet Robert Manners reiterated Cuba's status as "the loveliest child that Nature gave" to the care of the superior, "freedom-loving" United States to dramatize how the racial identity of "Cuba's valiant children" brought them under Spanish rule and necessitated the continued oversight of a racially superior nation.[34] Transforming the child who represented U.S. founding principles of liberty and freedom into incontestable proof of Cuba's racial inferiority, and therefore its inability to govern itself, writers such as Dana and Manners effectively undermined Cuba's independence efforts in the minds of the majority of American citizens. Such deployments of the child worked to distinguish "our own American nation," which, according to Italo Canini, was composed of "the positive, practical and daring spirit of the Anglo-Saxon" from Cuba, which combined Spanish blood with "large infusions of the blood of an ignorant and inferior race of the negro."[35] Influenced by such political commentary, Theodore Roosevelt read *The Superiority of the Anglo-Saxons* on his way to Cuba and described how Edmond Demolins's description of "the reasons why the English-speaking peoples are superior" helped him ensure that the Rough Riders would easily control Spanish and Cubans alike.[36] The racial difference between the United States and Cuba that the child codified therefore proved that Cuba could never "attain true liberty and establish sound and lasting republican institutions," because "license and anarchy, not true liberty, is the state of things [in] the countries of Central and South America, which can hardly be called Republics but rather caricatures of a Republic."[37]

Cuban nationalist heroes like Maceo, Martí, and Raimondo Cabrera, however, featured the child that discredited Cuba's independence efforts in the writings of non-Cuban political commentators to argue that Cuba could be nothing less than an independent, and antiracist, republic. As John Blanco has shown, Martí's political language transformed the terms of patrimony to advocate for a new nation remarkable not for its antecedents but for its infinite youth and futurity.[38] Declaring that it is precisely because "Cubans are the children of their progenitors whose vices and virtues they reflect" that they must "beg for Autonomy as the saving anchor for the Colony and for the Nation," Cabrera, like Martí, deployed the image of the child that was used to dismiss Cuban independence efforts to argue that the child colony, just like the Thirteen Colonies that the child represented to American citizens, must claim independence "because the motherland refuses to listen to its clamors."[39] By appropriating U.S. political language that featured the child to justify its own independence effort and to undermine Cuba's, Gonzalo de Quesada, Cuban minister to the United States, like Cabrera, proceeded to show readers that "the cause of the present revolution in Cuba" replicated the causes of the American Revolution—namely, "taxation without representation."[40] After declaring that "the Cuban people have the same reason for their Great Revolution that America had when she threw off the yoke of oppression," Quesada addressed "the American people" directly, asserting that, just "as your forefathers fought for independence, so the brave army of my compatriots is struggling to make Cuba free." Thus, "the terrible struggle of long-suffering Cuba" must appeal "to all freedom-loving people and every person in America should know how just and holy is the cause for which so many Cubans are shedding their blood."[41] Declaring that it is only "natural that an intelligent and spirited people like the Cubans should demand the right to govern themselves," Quesada concluded that the "best blood of Cuba's native-born population" drove the insurgent effort, producing "a war between two peoples who are distinct in all characteristics which mark the differences between nations."[42] Thus, Tomas Estrada Palma contended when confronted with a Spanish compromise, that Cuba would listen to no compromise but would only deal with Spain on the basis of absolute independence for Cuba because it is time for the Cuban people to satisfy their just desire for a place among the free nations of the world.

Martí used the child to which U.S. social commentators likened Cubans not only to assert Cuban national ideals but to critique U.S. policy in Cuba, as well. In "The Truth about the United States" (1894), Martí declared that "the truth about the United States must be made known to our America" so that "an excessive faith in the virtue of others does not weaken us in our period of foundation. . . . Publicly loving all that is fair-skinned as if that were natural and proper," U.S. citizens "try to cover their own origin, which they see as mestizo and humble"; as a result, they delimit the promise of liberty that the child had originally represented for U.S. colonists.[43] Asserting that "children are the hope of the world" in the preface to his children's periodical *Le Edad de Oro* (1889), however, Martí posited the child as the future of a Cuban nationalism that could escape the pitfalls into which the United States had fallen. "These children of Our America," he asserted, in "Our America," will be able to "save" Cuba from repeating the "grave blunders" of which the United States is guilty, because they will uphold the lesson Cuba has learned from the United States' example. Originally having "a childlike confidence in the certain help of the United States," Cuba has learned the lesson that proves its final readiness for self-government: that "there is no solid ground" from which to create an independent, raceless nation "but the ground on which one was born"—where the child represents a citizen unencumbered by race and therefore works to create a new antiracist republic. Turning to their own abiding belief that "there are no races," Cuban statesmen who "arise from the nation" therefore, of necessity, uphold the ideals the child represents more authentically and advocate for the insurgent nation's political commitment to racelessness more successfully than any alien nation that uses the child to enforce a racial logic that infantilizes it.[44]

Representing these true principles of freedom and liberty for all men regardless of their race, the child featured in Cuban insurgent rhetoric therefore worked to create an antiracist Cuban nation—in direct opposition to the child featured in U.S. political rhetoric that upheld racial difference within and outside the United States. As Martí insisted in *Le Edad de Oro*,

"We are working for children because they are the ones who know how to love, because they are the hope of the world—the happiest country is the one which has best educated its sons, both in the instruction of thought and the direction of their feelings." Believing that "there will be no true growth for the nation . . . until the child is taught" to uphold its ideals, Martí turned from the child who represented the concept of a raceless Cuban nation to the real children who must be trained to protect and maintain its political reality.[45] In so doing, he echoed even as he revised the thinking of early American political commentators like Benjamin Rush and Thomas Paine by pointing out that the Cuban child must in no way resemble the inchoate child citizens that the United States was raising. Indeed, much of the United States' mistaken understanding of Cuba's struggle could be traced to the nation's failure to raise its young citizens to uphold the principles of "North American liberties" and freedoms that Cuba's much-beloved Lincoln represented. In "A False Conception of Public Education" which he wrote for the Cuban newspaper *La Nación* in 1886, for example, Martí critiqued "public education in the United States" because it produced "dull and indifferent children . . . without the grace of childhood, or enthusiasm of youth." Plagued with "a niggardly sense of life" that represents nothing less than "a national cancer," Martí contended, the United States systematically had failed to nurture "the originality which each child carries within himself" and instead had chosen to "suffocate people from childhood on," leading, among other social ills, to the accelerating racial prejudices riddling U.S. society.[46] With the exception of individuals like Bronson Alcott, who Martí lauded in *La Nación*, U.S. social and political philosophers undermined rather than facilitated the nation's founding ideals of liberty, and they did so through their treatment of the child on which U.S. national integrity depended. "To be a citizen of a republic," Martí reminded his audience, "is a difficult thing, and one must rehearse for it from childhood" if one is committed to the project of "quicken[ing] and enlarg[ing] . . . a national soul."[47] With his articles on educational theory and pedagogy, his writings for children in his immensely and enduringly popular *Le Edad de Oro*, and his representation of the child's conceptual centrality to creating a raceless Cuban nation, Martí hoped to found a nation that would avoid the racism, inequality, and hypocrisy that in his estimation characterized the United States.

Martí's concern that U.S. racial logic would undermine the unique form of race-free nationalism that the child represented in Cuban political rhetoric was well founded, for even as Cuba's rebel leaders denied the existence of race, and a powerful multiracial army waged anticolonial war, their efforts to achieve independence coincided with an international rise in racism characterized by the rise of scientific racism and accelerating imperialism. Therefore, if Du Bois's prophesy that the problem of the twentieth century would be the problem of the color line finally proved more accurate than Martí's prediction that "this is not the century of struggle of races but rather the century of the affirmation of rights,"[48] it was in no small part due to the United States' successful disarmament of the fragile antiracist and anticolonial promise of Cuba's nineteenth-century revolution. Cuban rebels fought to create a raceless nation in the fifty-year period that began with Southern affirmation of racial inequality, but because they encountered European and North American thinking that linked biology to progress and divided the world into superior and inferior races, American involvement in Cuba worked to uphold and extend U.S. racial principles rather than the idea of racelessness that the child represented as a central component of the Cuban revolution. Once the explicitly anticolonial, antislavery, and antiracist movement came under the influence of a nation inventing Jim Crow segregation and acquiring a far-flung empire, U.S. soldiers, officers, journalists, and cartoonists propagated images of Cuba as a land of dark, childlike savages and of Cuban insurgents as black men unwilling to fight. General William Shafter's assistant wrote that Cubans are "a lot of degenerates . . . no more capable of self-rule than the savages of Africa." Shafter agreed, declaring, "Self-government! Why these people are no more fit for self-government than gunpowder is for hell," while General Ludlow concurred that "the Cuban character . . . is devoid of executive and practical power . . . thus they lack the prime elements of effective national action."[49] Therefore, just as Spanish leaders like Provincial Governor Camilo Polavieja had tried to make the rebellion imitate their interpretation of it, declaring, "We must remove all white characteristics from the rebellion and reduce it to the colored element, that way it will count on less support and sympathy," so, too, did U.S. forces shape Cuban independence efforts to conform with the racial contours of U.S. imperial logic, despite the fact that, as Halstead observed, "the black rebels were among the bravest of the fighters for freedom."[50] Insurgent leaders like General Calixto García unsuccessfully attempted to refute these rewritings of Cuban insurgency by reminding U.S. leaders that "my ragged, hungry soldiers have endured with the resolute sincerity of the American of Saratoga or York-town" the hardships of war and therefore deserve to be treated not as "a conquered people" but as partners in the struggle for independence.[51] How-ever, despite the protestations made by leaders of U.S. occupying forces like Leonard Wood that the United States was "giving the Cubans every chance to show what is in them, in order that they either demonstrate their fitness or their unfitness for self-government," once the United States conquered Spain, American officers "prohibited Cuban soldiers from entering the city that many of them had been born in and at the capitulation the Cubans were not represented, despite the aid they had gratuitously given" to the capture of Santiago.[52] Despite the fact that this exclusion made soldiers "feel as the patriots under Washington would have felt had the allied armies cap-tured New York, and the French prohibited the entry of the Americans and their flag," according to one Cuban, U.S. commitment to racial inequality shaped rebuilding efforts which drew on the "Native White Population," as Horace Fisher observed, to establish an "orderly government."[53] There-fore, by relying on the "Spanish race," which demonstrated "an individual initiative equal to our own," U.S. administrators planned to form a govern-ment in Cuba that would subordinate "the mixed and colored races" to the "great races."[54]

Despite its commitment to featuring the child to install U.S. racial prin-ciples in Cuba, some U.S. political commentary depicted Cuba as a power-ful cure for the racial difference the child had long upheld in U.S. political culture — as the place where black and white U.S. soldiers could experience the antiracism that Cuba stood for and therefore might import a race-free environment into the United States. The writers of *Under Fire with the 10th U.S. Cavalry, A Purely Military History of the Negro* (1899) found in Cuba a powerful refutation of late-nineteenth-century U.S. racism. Black soldiers being transported to Cuba were the recipients of the benevolent "patriotism displayed by the liberty loving people of this county" until they reached "the South, where cool receptions told the tale of race prejudice even though these brave men were rushing to . . . defend the flag."[55] How-ever, the authors predicted that "the same strong spirit and quickened conscience which took up the cause of Cuba will surely secure justice to the American Negro."[56] In their account of U.S. involvement in Cuba, "White regiments, black regiments, regulars and Rough Riders, representing the young manhood of the North and the South, fought shoulder to shoulder, unmindful of race or color, unmindful of whether commanded by an ex-Confederate or not, and mindful only of their common duty as Americans." Declaring that "there was no North, no South, no black, no white. We were at once a compact national force," many soldiers agreed that "both white and colored soldiers had a brotherly affection for each other while on the way to Cuba, in Cuba and on our way back to the U.S.," but some black soldiers continued to wonder "why can't it be so at home?"[57] Through their military action in Cuba, according to President McKinley, African Americans were going far toward justifying Lincoln's liberation of the black race for those who remained unconvinced of the black man's patriotism: "If any vindication of that act was needed, it was found when these brave black men ascended the hill of San Juan Cuba, . . . vindicated their own title to liberty on that field and . . . gave the priceless fight of liberty to another suffering race."[58] The authors agreed that "it was in the memorable siege of Santiago and the never to be forgotten charge up San Juan Hill that [the black soldier] challenged the admiration of the American people and solicited the tumultuous applause of every liberty loving nation throughout the civilized world."[59] A few newspaper men and black activists even argued that "the timeliness and importance of this Afro-American military colonization of Cuba" had the potential to reshape U.S. race relations in the South. "If Cuba becomes a state of the American union," the *Springfield Republican* said, "then no better place could be found in which to assert and establish the principles of free government."[60] "Freedom . . . once being firmly established in Cuba, will then be asserted in South Carolina, Mississippi and Louisiana where liberty now 'lies bleeding' under the heel of a ferocious white minority rule race despotism."[61] Asking readers to "get together and show the imperialists . . . that the liberty ideals of 1776 are still a potential force in the world's affairs," the author of "Immortal Doctrines of Liberty Ably Set Out by a Colored Man" predicted that "Cuba is destined to become the one all embracing liberty issue around which Americans everywhere will have to fight finally for their own freedom rights."[62]

Yet most of the U.S. black press insisted that U.S. policy in Cuba extended and reinforced rather than solved U.S. racism and was quick to identify the hypocrisy involved in fighting a war allegedly to free Cuba when freedom was systematically denied to blacks at home. With the quick victory of American arms in Cuba, black newspapers warned that the process of reconstruction on the island would copy that in the American South after the Civil War, with prejudice and Jim Crow substituting for freedom and independence. As the Richmond *Planet's* 1898 article "The Insurgents and the Government" predicted, "The treatment accorded the colored people soon after the war, the relegating of them to the tender mercies of those against whom they fought in the South is to be repeated in an intensified form upon the soil of the 'Pearl of the Antilles.' "[63] Declaring that "all of the horrors of South Carolina, Mississippi, Louisiana, and Texas will be repeated" in Cuba, the *Planet* asked its readers to "hope that this dark-skinned race may be able to meet the issue more successfully than we have done in a country whose flag is a misnomer, and whose laws are openly defied." Charles Baylor agreed that, because "nearly all the leaders and fighters in the Cuban army of liberation are men, who if in South Carolina, Mississippi or Louisiana, would be made to ride in the 'Jim Crow Cars,' " the Cuban leaders who were fighting to achieve "those sublime liberty ideals proclaimed by the British-American colonists of 1776" were destined to be frustrated.[64] Recognizing that "the welfare of the negro race is vitally involved in the impending policy of imperialism" because "the whole trend of imperial aggression is antagonistic to the feebler races," the author of "McKinley's Inconsistencies" declared that the National Afro-American Party recognizes "in the spirit of Imperialism, inaugurated and fostered by the administration of President McKinley, the same violation of HUMAN RIGHTS which is being practiced by the Democratic Party in the recently re-constructed States, to wit: the wholesale disfranchisement of the Negro."[65] The "violation" in McKinley's policy was epitomized by the president's behavior on his 1899 tour of the Southern states. The Washington *Bee* addressed the president in an "Open Letter," pointing out that he "catered to Southern race prejudice [by] . . . receiv[ing] white men at the Capitol in Montgomery, Alabama, and black men afterward in a Negro church, . . . [by] preach[ing] patience, industry, moderation to your long-suffering black fellow-citizens, and patriotism, jingoism and imperialism to your white ones"—in short, "[by] win[ning] the support of the South" for his "criminal aggression" in Cuba through "shut[ting] his eyes, ears, and lips to the 'criminal aggression' of that section against the Constitution."[66]

"BROWN AND BLACK PEOPLES"

Cuba's ill-fated struggle to achieve an independent, raceless nation—and more particularly, Cuba's redeployment of the child that the United States used to dismiss the idea of an antiracist republic—exerted an important influence on Du Bois's thinking about race, nation, and citizenship.[67] Yet this influence has tended to be overlooked in favor of analysis of those black republics, like Haiti, that inspired Du Bois's career as a "talented tenth" race activist. The U.S.-Cuba encounter, however, sheds important light on Du Bois'a self-admitted frustration with the plight of the race man, who was always in danger of becoming "provincial" and a "prisoner" of the group he represented.[68] Admitting that "the McKinley campaign of '96" was pivotal to the evolution of his political thinking, Du Bois described in detail how McKinley's presidency transformed him from a Harvard student whose "main thought was on my studies" into an active agent in "the midst of political controversy." "By the time McKinley got to work," he recalled, "I began to awaken" and "to realize" that I had been "wrong in most of my judgments."[69] Du Bois's resulting judgments about U.S. past and present racial policy consistently acknowledged the nation's failure to pursue "a policy of honesty in Cuba."[70] In the lecture he delivered at the 1891 annual meeting of the American Historical Association, for example, Du Bois highlighted Havana's historical importance to mapping the U.S. slave trade,[71] while in "The Future of the Negro Race in America" (1904) he described "nineteenth-century efforts to civilize the heathen" in places such as Cuba.[72] Contemplating Cuba's renewed importance to advocating for racial equality "through the new imperial policy" of the United States, Du Bois declared that "our protectorate of Cuba" and other geographic locales represented "for the nation the greatest event since the Civil War and demands attention and action on our part."[73] Asking his readers to remember that "the twentieth century will find nearly twenty millions of brown and black people under the protection of the American flag, a third of the nation," Du Bois contended that once "Negro and . . . Cuban . . . stand united,"

America will "kno[w] no color line in the freedom of its opportunities."[74]
Yet once U.S. policy in Cuba was in effect, Du Bois descried "the spectacle
of . . . Cuba . . . trying desperately and doggedly to be 'white' in spite of the
fact that the majority of the white group is of Negro or Indian descent."[75]
Langston Hughes would subsequently agree that while "Cuban law recognizes no differences because of race or color" and "citizens of all colors meet
and mingle, . . . colored people in Cuba" have suffered since "white Americans [gained] control" and those "colored visitors," like himself, "looking
anxiously for a country where they can say there is no color line" are destined to be increasingly disappointed.[76] Like Booker T. Washington's commentary on Cuba, these accounts suggest that Du Bois continued to value
the "absence of that higher degree of race feeling" in Cuba that, in causing
"the color line" in Cuba to be drawn only "in a few instances," creates the
opportunity for different kinds of relationships between the citizen and the
state to develop.[77]

Once we place Cuba's frustrated commitment to antiracist nationalism
alongside Haiti's creation of a black republic, we can see how the two collectively inform Du Bois's thinking about the racial formations that structured
the United States. Du Bois not only "actively oppose[d] U.S. intervention-
ist and colonialist activities in Haiti and Cuba," as Herbert Aptheker has
pointed out,[78] but in public speeches "about Haiti and Cuba" he placed these
two different examples of race and nation side by side in order to consider
their relevance for the United States — to consider, in other words, if it is
"possible for a man to be both a Negro and an American without being
cursed."[79] Even as Du Bois, out of deep disturbance "over the situation in
Hayti and the action of the U.S.," wrote to the president of the United States
that Haiti is "the sole modern representative of a great race of men among
the nations" and that the United States therefore should facilitate independent nationhood in acknowledgment of "the great wrongs inflicted by this
land on the Negro race," such a policy, he continued, must be paired with "a
frank, high-minded" policy in Cuba if the United States wants to establish its
"moral hegemony" in the "Western hemisphere."[80] Recognizing that "the
day that Black men love Black men simply because they are Black, is the day
they will hate White men simply because they are White,"[81] Du Bois found
in Cuba an antiracism that challenged the logic that, as he wrote, made "the
race pride of Negroes not an antidote to the race pride of White people

[but] simply the other side of a hateful thing."[82] Even as Haiti's successful struggle for independent nationhood was premised on a logic of racial difference and Cuba's unsuccessful struggle attempted to eradicate race's national significance, both efforts at alternative nation building sought to create greater social justice for racially stigmatized individuals by rethinking the founding alliance between race and nation.[83] And Cuba's unrealized raceless nation, as much as Haiti's black republic, had an important influence on Du Bois's consideration of how race, nation, and citizenship might combine to form a racially equitable United States.

In his career-long depictions of the child that was central to the creation and destruction of Cuba's alternative republican ideal, we can chart Du Bois's exploration of the possibilities and pitfalls of realizing a true liberal democracy in the United States. Drawing on Cuba's refiguration of the child as a cornerstone of a raceless nation, Du Bois, in other words, featured such a child in his writings to imagine a different relation between self and state that was not based on race. Acknowledging in his early writings a slave history in which "children are taken from their parents as soon as they are weaned" to keep "the time of the mother from being taken up [with] her own children," Du Bois offered an important social history of African American life that emphasized the black child's unique, acute dependence. Emphasizing the fact that "parents [were] almost never consulted as to the disposition of their children,"[84] Du Bois depicted the black child under slavery as a partial subject intensely dependent on the social, yet beneath the social radar screen of liberal-democratic institutions that aim to transform child subjects into upstanding citizens. Yet not so much despite, but precisely because of, this unique social legacy in which racial prejudice works to produce among black communities "more poorly trained children" and inferior "family life," Du Bois concludes that whites "have something to learn" from such a child.[85] Indeed, the special African American social history that Du Bois documents provides its child with a unique capacity to reshape its social world. While one might assume that the "impaired chance for life which a debauched and immoral parentage bequeaths to childhood" might lead "infants in their graves to rise up in judgment" of the society that ill treats them, such a child, instead, suggests the possibility of "victories over self" that might in turn lead to "high standards of living" for all of the nation's inhabitants, regardless of their final ability to achieve social autonomy.[86] Suggesting that it is possible to wage "a heroic and successful fight" against "centuries of debasing slavery," such a child becomes a focal point around which Du Bois explores what such an altered liberal democratic world might look like.[87]

Within the context of the revisionist possibilities that such a social history of the African American child provides, then, the child at the center of such texts as *The Souls of Black Folk*, *Dark Princess*, and *Darkwater* represents Du Bois's attempt to imagine a just social world that values not only the independence of the classical liberal-democratic subject, but also the enforced, prolonged, and enduring dependence that a history of racial prejudice and a national commitment to white supremacy bequeaths to racial others. In addition to eradicating inequality by transforming dependent and therefore marginalized individuals into autonomous citizens, Du Bois's depictions of the child suggest that realizing social justice requires acknowledging those who, precisely because of the tangible historical costs of creating liberal-democratic institutions, are forced to remain partial, dependent, incomplete. Du Bois's depictions of the child, in other words, insist that there is in liberal democracy a politics of identity that privileges personal, as well as national, autonomy, freedom, and liberty and that, in so doing, delimits the very notions of social justice that identity politics subsequently seeks to secure for all individuals, regardless of their racial identity. If we want to take seriously the possibility of democratic selfhood that the child has represented in U.S. liberal-democratic discourse since the nation's inception, Du Bois suggests, we must reshape its founding assumption of equality to include not simply those of different racial identities or skin colors but, more fundamentally, the concepts of dependence, need, and insufficiency with which white-supremacist logic has long equated racial difference. When Du Bois asserts in *Darkwater* that introducing "the child to race consciousness . . . with intelligent guidance" rather than "prematurely" and "spontaneously" will correct a "world problem," he is therefore suggesting not simply that all races are equal and are consequently equally entitled to the liberal concepts of freedom and independence.[88] He is, as important, suggesting that the concept of social dependence that continues to be associated primarily with nonwhites (be they welfare mothers, criminals, drug addicts, or those below the poverty line) is not shameful. Thus, the drama with which *The Souls of Black Folk* opens — the drama of Du Bois's child self suddenly seeing himself "through the revelations of the other world" due to another child's refusal of his visiting card—suggests that basic human rights will be achieved not only once the prejudice that frustrates Du Bois's need for human recognition is eradicated but, more fundamentally, once the concept of individual need, as well as of independence and liberty, is recognized as equally important to and constitutive of liberal-democratic societies.

It is this unrealized possibility of creating a social world in which liberal citizenship can only be fully realized by acknowledging how racial difference operates as an empowering rather than compromising force with which Du Bois's 1928 novel *Dark Princess* concludes. Declaring that the royal male heir born to the protagonist and the Princess Kautilya will be "the Messenger and Messiah to all the Darker Worlds,"[89] the three Brahmin who, like wise men, emerge from the woods, promise to train the child so that he will be able to create a social order that blends different races, nations, and ideas of self and, in so doing, encompasses all the various relationships between selves and states that combine to create a just social order. Ross Posnock has suggested that the birth of the child at the end of *Darkwater* "memorializes earlier experiences in Du Bois's life . . . namely the death of his son in 1899,"[90] and that his obsessive love for the princess allows the male protagonist to indulge in the fantasy of abandoning social responsibility to the race. While I would argue with neither claim, I would rather suggest that the child product of this fantasy/remembrance represents not so much an escape from a commitment to social justice as Du Bois's final vision of its most successful advocate: a child who promises to create a social order that is truly just because it acknowledges the fundamental importance of racial diversity to liberal-democratic representation. Du Bois pursued the social possibility that this child represents the year after he finished *Darkwater*, when he helped John Dewey to form the socialist League of Independent Political Action and served as vice-chair during the league's four-year life. The league's goal was to think toward "a new kind of politics, a new kind of moral conception in politics [that requires] . . . some fundamental rethinking of our social and political relations," but to do so in a manner that was "partial and tentative, experimental and not rigid."[91] It is such a politics—a politics that emerges from recognizing the complex social work in which the child has been engaged since the emergence of the nation-state — of which we are still in need and to which these pages, I hope, have contributed.

I will close with one example of how such a politics might operate. Like Du Bois, William Faulkner recognized that the child offers a unique opportunity to explore how racial difference might enrich rather than compromise liberal representation. In *Intruder in the Dust* (1948), Faulkner explores the child's capacity to reshape a democratic social structure in which "the nigger act[s] like a nigger and the white folks act like white folks and no real hard feelings on either side," even when members of each group kill members of the other."[92] Accused of murdering a white man, Lucas Beauchamp "knew it would take a child" to successfully reform such a social system. Because "young folks" aren't "cluttered," Mrs. Downs insists, "if you ever needs to get anything done outside the common run, don't waste yo time on the men folks," but get the "children to working at it" instead.[93] The child that Lucas uses to save himself from lynching is not free of the racial prejudice that typifies his community, but his status as a child gives him a unique opportunity to rethink its premises. Like Richard Wright's *Uncle Tom's Children* (1938), *Intruder in the Dust* uses the child to insist on the enduring social injustice of a racially configured state — to bring "into the light and glare of day something shocking and shameful out of the whole white foundation of the county."[94] What is shameful is the fact that social integration is predicated on racial hierarchy, on whites thinking, "*We got to make him be a nigger first. He's got to admit he's a nigger. Then maybe we will accept him as he seems to intend to be accepted.*"[95] If Lucas's social transgression therefore precedes the actual crime of which he is accused, the primary focus and imaginative energy of the text is clearing Lucas not of the crime of murder but of the crime of refusing to accept the racial premises of civic affiliation. This task of averting a community's commitment to "make a nigger out of him once in his life anyway" falls of necessity to "a child . . . a swaddled unwitting infant in the long tradition of his native land" — "a witless foetus." Yet in the act of reshaping democratic justice to accommodate racial difference, the child is finally "weaned," transformed from a child into something else entirely.[96] If "the dismantling of white supremacy requires at the profoundest internal level, the rethinking and transformation of oneself," as Charles Mills has provocatively suggested,[97] then this rethinking must necessarily redraw the boundaries separating child from adult. It must involve what Martha

Nussbaum identifies as "some combination of adulthood and childhood" through which a more chancy and fearful but authentic liberalism becomes possible.[98] In short, we must begin to recognize that inhering in the child has been, and continues to be, a politics of identity that precedes and precipitates identity politics—a politics of identity that must be reckoned with if we are to create a truly better world for the next generation.

NOTES

INTRODUCTION

1 Shapiro, *Democratic Justice*, 68.
2 Phillips, *The Beast in the Nursery*, 155.
3 Perkins, "Opening Statement by the Chairman," 4–5.
4 Fenton, *Mental Hygiene in School Practice*, 17.
5 Grob, *Mental Hygiene in Twentieth Century America*, 73; National Committee for Mental Hygiene, Inc., *Report of the Maryland Mental Hygiene Survey with Recommendations*. For additional commentary on the mental-hygiene movement, see Richardson, *The Century of the Child*.
6 Kerber, *Women of the Republic*, 285, 283.
7 Dillon, *The Gender of Freedom*, 145.
8 Mills, *From Class to Race*; Reed, *Class Notes*; Robinson, *Black Marxism*.
9 Anderson, *Imagined Communities*. Felipe Smith (*American Body Politics*, 5) speaks to Anderson's inattention to race as follows: "The problem with Anderson's opposition of 'kinship' to 'ideology' is that it does not address the crucial third term — let's call it the 'ideology of kinship' — that functions in societies in which 'racism' or other 'isms' emerge as a culmination of long-standing practices and habits of thought." For recent critical accounts of the significance of race to Anderson's model of nationalism, see Castro-Klarén and Chasteen, *Beyond Imagined Communities*; Sidaway, *Imagined Regional Communities*, and Appelbaum et al., *Race and Nation in Modern Latin America*.
10 For commentary on the racial encounters constituting the United States, see Rogin, *Fathers and Children*; Slotkin, *Regeneration through Violence*; West, "The Dilemma of the Black Intellectual."

11 Brown, *Clotel*, 218.

12 Augusta J. Evans to General Beauregard, letter, March 30, 1867, Rare Book, Manuscript, and Special Collections Library, Duke University, Durham, N.C., reprinted in Sexton, *A Southern Woman of Letters*, 138.

13 Adams, "We Won't Be Their Negroes"; Paine, "The Crisis."

14 Du Bois, *Darkwater*, 30.

15 Emerson, "Self-Reliance"; Margolis, *The Fabric of Self*, 137.

16 Emerson, "Nature." For commentary on the association of the child with the self, see, most recently, Ferguson, "The Afterlife of the Romantic Child"; Kincaid, *Child-Loving*; Sánchez-Eppler, *Dependent States*; Steedman, *Strange Dislocations*.

17 Renan's 1882 "What Is a Nation?" is commonly identified as the first commentary on the racial components of modern nations. The modern nation-state "is nothing less than a racial state," as David Theo Goldberg has recently reminded us. "It is not just that the state is implicated in reproducing more or less local conditions of racist exclusion, but that the modern state has always conceived of itself as racially configured": Goldberg, *The Racial State*, 2. Renan's and other significant nineteenth-century considerations of race and nation include Du Bois, "The Conservation of Races," and Martí, "Our America." These and other landmark analyses can be found in Pecora, *Nations and Identities*, 162–76, 177–84, 190–99. For recent critical considerations of the racial state, see, for example, Cooper and Stoler, *Tensions of Empire*; Goldberg, *The Racial State*; Marx, *Making Race, Making Nations*; McClintock, "No Longer in a Future Heaven"; Nicholson, *Who Do We Think We Are?*; Omi and Winant, *Racial Formation in the United States*; Stoler, *Carnal Knowledge and Imperial Power*.

18 Jennifer Mason, *Civilized Creatures*; Susan Honeyman, *Elusive Childhood*; Angela Sorby, *Schoolroom Poets*; Ariès, *Centuries of Childhood*. For subsequent commentaries on the child's cultural significance, see, for example, Brodhead, "Sparing the Rod"; Graff, *Conflicting Paths*; Hawes and Hiner, *American Childhood*; Hiner and Hawes, *Growing Up in America*; Lerner, *Angels and Absences*; Mennel, *Thorns and Thistles*; Mintz, *Huck's Raft* and *A Prison of Expectations*; Preston and Haines, *Fatal Years*; Ryan, *The Cradle of the Middle Class*; Toynton, *Growing Up in America*; Yelland, *Gender in Early Childhood*; Zelizer, *Pricing the Priceless Child*; and Katharyne Mitchell, Sallie A. Marston, and Cindi Katz, eds., *Life's Work*.

19 de Tocqueville, *Democracy in America*, 39. For commentary on the child as a metaphor of the new nation, see Wishy, *The Child and the Republic*. See also Samuels, *Romances of the Republic*, for an incisive reading of early national images of the family.

20 Rancière, "Who Is the Subject of the Rights of Man?" See also Ferguson, "The Afterlife of the Romantic Child."

21 Sharon Stephens makes this important argument: see Stephens, *Children and the Politics of Culture*, 3–51.

22 For incisive accounts of the early United States' reliance on the idea of racial purity, see Dain, *A Hideous Monster of the Mind*. For accounts of the child's representative status for minority groups, see Coleman, *American Indian Children at School, 1850–1930*; Spencer et al., *Beginnings*; Takaki, *Iron Cages*.

23 Habermas, *The Postnational Constellation*, 71.

24 Notable exceptions to this tendency include Adams, *The Multicultural Imagination*; Bergner, *Taboo Subjects*; Brickman, *Aboriginal Populations in the Mind*; Lane, *The Psychoanalysis of Race*; Shepherdson, *Vital Signs*; Tate, *Psychoanalysis and Black Novels*; Žižek, *The Plague of Fantasies*, 45–86.

25 Jerome Levin points out that "the I" is the "personal pronoun in Old Gothic," which is "the ancestor of Anglo-Saxon." Saint Augustine's *Confessions* generally recognized the power of childhood experience in the shaping of personality and identity. Levin describes Augustine's turn to the child in psychoanalytic terms, arguing that Augustine "projected the preverbal urge for symbiotic union with the mother onto the cosmos": see Levin, *Theories of the Self*, 2–5.

26 Blake, "The Little Black Boy"; Taylor, *Sources of the Self*.

27 Lane, *The Narrative of Lunsford Lane*, frontispiece. See also Du Bois, *The Souls of Black Folk* (1983).

28 Hawthorne, "A Wonder Book" and "Tanglewood Tales," vii, viii. Diane Margolis relatedly argues that theorists of nationalism who take a developmental, familial approach to the topic tend to associate the nation with a parent and the citizen with a child: see Margolis, *The Fabric of Self*, 150–51. For additional commentary on psychological approaches to nationalism, see Searle-White, *The Psychology of Nationalism*.

29 Hawthorne, *American Notebooks*, 7:4, cited in Goodenough, "Demons of Wickedness, Angels of Delight," 226.

30 Whitman, "There Was a Child Went Forth," 2117–18.

31 Ibid., 2118.

32 Ibid.

33 Berlant, *The Queen of America Goes to Washington City*; Edelman, *No Future*; Kincaid, *Child-Loving*; Moon, *A Small Boy and Others*; Nealon, *Foundlings*; Warner, "Zones of Privacy."

34 See, for example, Blumin, *The Emergence of the Middle Class*; Degler, *At Odds*; Ryan, *The Cradle of the Middle Class*.

35 Arac, "Toward a Critical Genealogy of the U.S. Discourse of Identity."

36 Amy Gutmann begins this line of inquiry with her excellent essay "Children, Paternalism, and Education."

37 See Appiah, "Liberalism, Individuality, and Identity," 325. See also Appiah, *The Ethics of Identity*; Ross, "Commentary."

38 Liberalism, as Nancy Cohen observes, "has understood human beings as ratio-

nal, autonomous, and equal and has tended to assume an inherent conflict between society and the individual": Cohen, *The Reconstruction of American Liberalism, 1865–1914*, 7. Lionel Trilling initiates a liberalist tradition of turning to the child to locate an autonomous self when he asserts that the romantic child with which William Wordsworth is concerned in "The Immortality Ode" is an emblem of all selves: Trilling, *The Liberal Imagination*, 129–53.

39 Appiah "Liberalism, Individuality, and Identity," 330.

40 Mill, "On Liberty," 280.

41 Tomasi, *Liberalism beyond Justice*, 57.

42 Backus, "A Discourse Showing the Nature and Necessity of an Internal Call to Preach the Everlasting Gospel," 130–32.

43 Dewey, *Liberalism and Social Action*, 17.

44 Willard, *Liberalism and the Problem of Knowledge*, 4.

45 It is precisely this failure to understand Mill's writing that John Dewey identifies as causing the crisis in liberalism: see Dewey, *Liberalism and Social Action*, 39.

46 Chafe, "Race in America," 179.

47 Gikandi, "Race and Cosmopolitanism," 595, 599.

48 Mills, *The Racial Contract*, 14.

49 Nussbaum, *Hiding from Humanity*, 319.

50 See, for example, Ashby, *Endangered Children*; Avery, *Behold the Child*; Berrol, *Growing Up American*; Calvert, *Children in the House*; Clement, *Growing Pains*; Cross, *Kids' Stuff*; Fass and Mason, *Childhood and America*; Heininger, "Children, Childhood, and Change in America, 1820–1920"; King, *Stolen Childhood*; Lesnik-Obersteined, *Children in Culture*; Macleod, *The Age of the Child*; Murray, *American Children's Literature and the Construction of Childhood*; Reinier, *From Virtue to Character*; Seiter, *Sold Separately*; Scheper-Hughes and Sargent, *Small Wars*; West and Petrik, *Small Worlds*.

51 For commentary on children's literature and the child in literature, see, for example, Goodenough et al., *Infant Tongues*; Kuhn, *Corruption in Paradise*; McGavran, *Literature and the Child*; Westfahl and Slusser, *Nursery Realms*.

52 For accounts of the child and nineteenth-century sexuality, see, for example, Goshgarian, *To Kiss the Chastening Rod*; Kincaid, *Child-Loving*, and *Erotic Innocence*; Moon, "The Gentle Boy from the Dangerous Classes." For commentary on the child as a signifier of middle-class identity, see, for example, Blumin, *The Emergence of the Middle Class*; Degler, *At Odds*; Demos, *Past, Present, and Personal*. For commentary on the child as a representative of racial minorities, see, for example, Rogin, *Fathers and Children*; Takaki, *Iron Cages*.

53 The genealogy I am tracing from *Roberts* to *Brown* consistently has been overlooked in analyses of the 1954 decision, which overwhelmingly see legal precedent as beginning with *Plessy*. See, for example, Kelley, "*Plessy* and Early Chal-

lenges to the Doctrine of 'Separate, but Equal.' " As Kelley asserts, "*Plessy v. Ferguson* (1896) . . . established the precedent of 'separate, but equal' which shaped African American legal battles against segregation throughout the first half of the twentieth century": ibid., 19.

54 *Argument of Charles Sumner, Esq., against the Constitutionality of Separate Colored Schools in the Case of Sarah C. Roberts vs. the City of Boston*, 3.

55 Ibid., 32.

56 *Tourgée Brief—Records and Briefs of the Supreme Court*, 163 U.S. 537, cited in Ficker, "From Roberts to Plessy," 310.

57 In my reading of the white child's subversive social potential in *Plessy*, I depart from Susan Gubar's account of "the pampered white child" who is "waited on by a devoted black domestic": Gubar, *Racechanges*, 204.

58 Thurgood Marshall saw distilled in Kenneth Clark's doll experiments the "cumulative grief of three hundred years," and the use of Clark's research gave Warren's findings academic respectability. For additional commentary on *Roberts*'s importance to *Brown*, see Levy and Phillips, "The Roberts Case."

59 Ibid., 29.

60 Earl Warren, *Brown v. Board of Education*, 347 U.S. 483, reprinted in Whitman, *Removing a Badge of Slavery*, 305.

61 Rawls, *Political Liberalism*, 84.

62 Lane, *The Psychoanalysis of Race*, 4.

63 Ibid., 13. For a provocative account of psychoanalysis in the making of nationalism, see Žižek, "Enjoy Your Nation as Yourself!"

64 Steve Reicher and Nick Hopkins make an important distinction between nationalist uses of psychology and psychological understandings of nationhood: see Reicher and Hopkins, *Self and Nation*.

65 For some of the many critiques of psychoanalysis's and social-contract theory's inattention to global cultures, see, for example, Clinton, *Tocqueville, Lieber, and Bagehot*; Hayden, *John Rawls*; Semmel, *The Liberal Ideal and the Demons of Empire*; Žižek, *Tarrying with the Negative*.

66 For excellent recent examples of this kind of innovative approach, see Kerkering, *The Poetics of National and Racial Identity in Nineteenth-Century American Literature*; Levine, "Road to Africa," and "Circulating the Nation." My approach to the national draws from modernist approaches that consider nations as historical rather than natural phenomena and that emphasize that nations are modern in the sense that they are historically recent. Yet my attention to race's significance in the formation of nations derives in part from the work of scholars like Anthony Smith, who points out that, although modern, nations have premodern origins in ethnic communities and so are in part forged out of premodern forms of ethnicity and their deeply abiding ties. Finally, I implicitly acknowledge both Benedict Anderson's idea of a na-

tion as an imagined community that was first conceived in the American colonies and Eric Hobsbawm's important argument that modern nations' claims to continuity with the past are largely fictitious and thus that we must attend to the discontinuities riddling modern nationalisms. See Anderson, *Imagined Communities*; Gellner, *Nations and Nationalism*; Hobsbawm, *Nations and Nationalism since 1780*; Marx, *Faith in Nation*; Smith, *The Ethnic Origins of Nations*.

67 Semmel, *The Liberal Ideal and the Demons of Empire*. Influenced by the economic tradition that Smith initiated, the American political philosopher Francis Lieber was an influential and committed free-market internationalist. Arguing that "the great civilized family of men" required that each nation "regard other nations only as different members of the same household," Lieber extended the logic through which the United States naturalized its formation and affiliated individuals into itself to include other nations and peoples: Lieber, *Essays on Property and Labour, as Connected with Natural Law and the Continuation of Society*, 212.

68 Douglass, "What to the Slave Is the Fourth of July?" 127.

69 Meares, *Intimacy and Alienation*.

70 Margolis, *Selves and Other Texts*, 156. I am grateful to Jack Kerkering for alerting me to this text.

71 Hobbes, *Leviathan*.

1   NATION MAKING IN THE SLAVERY ERA

1 Woolman, *Considerations on the Keeping of Negroes*, 58–59.

2 Basler, *The Collected Works of Abraham Lincoln*, 7:23.

3 Castronovo, *Fathering the Nation*; Fliegelman, *Prodigals and Pilgrims*; Takaki, *Iron Cages*, 5–11.

4 Russ Castronovo has importantly shown how nineteenth-century racial practices "acted as an ideological buffer insulating the founding ideals from censure." He shows that because "the present absorbed all of the abolitionists' contempt; the present became a scapegoat in order to preserve the unsullied reputation of 1776." See Castronovo, "Radical Configurations of History," 180. My interest is to show not so much that black authors transform the child into a signifier of the contradictory ideologies undermining a cohesive national narrative but, rather, that the child functions as a powerful indicator of these contradictions in a wide range of political texts from the early national period through the Civil War.

5 Balibar, "Racism and Nationalism," 37.

6 Gould, "The Geometer of Race," 1.

7 Mills, *The Racial Contract*, 13, 3.

8 See, for example, Berlant, *The Queen of America Goes to Washington City*; Brown,

"Child's Play," and *Consent of the Governed*; Edelman, "The Future Is Kid Stuff";
Kincaid, *Erotic Innocence*; Moon, *A Small Boy and Others*; Nealon, *Foundlings*;
Samuels, *Romances of the Republic*; Warner, "Zones of Privacy."

9   Berlant, *The Queen of America Goes to Washington City*, 21.

10   I am grateful to Jack Kerkering for this observation. Examples of the asso-
ciation of blacks with children occur in numerous nineteenth-century texts.
For example, Mary Langdon writes of blacks, "They are mere children," while
Harriet Beecher Stowe repeatedly describes Tom as having a "childlike sim-
plicity" and "the soft, impressible nature of his kindly race, ever yearning
toward the simple and childlike": see Langdon, *Ida May*, 116; Stowe, *Uncle Tom's
Cabin*, 231, 275. For critical analysis of this trend, see, for example, Takaki,
Iron Cages, 108–44. Takaki concludes that "the black 'child/savage' represented
what whites thought they were not, and more important — what they must
not become. . . . The black 'child/savage' defined deviancy and served in effect
to discipline whites . . . into republican conduct": ibid., 126.

11   *Dred Scott v. Sanford*, 1857. U.S. Supreme Court, decision of Chief Justice Roger
Taney, in Rothenberg, *Race, Class and Gender in the United States*, 278.

12   *Report of the Decision of the Supreme Court of the United States and the Opinions
of the Judges Thereof in the Case of Dred Scott v. John Sanford*, 9.

13   Emerson, *English Traits*, 13, 28, 38, 75; Knox, *Races of Men*, 50.

14   Nourse, *Remarks on the Past and Its Legacies to American Society*, 206–207; letter,
June 10, 1827, cited in Perry, *The Life and Letters of Francis Lieber*, 70.

15   Bancroft, *Literary and Historical Miscellanies*, 3,5.

16   Ibid., 182; Nourse, *Remarks on the Past and Its Legacies to American Society*, 73.

17   Otis, *The Rights of the British Colonies Asserted and Proved*, 28.

18   General Congress at Philadelphia to the People of Great Britain, letter, September 5, 1774, Gilder Lehrman Collection, Morgan Library, New York (here-
after, GLC) 4774.

19   "Petition from the General Congress in America to the King, Published by
Order of the Congress at Philadelphia," October 26, 1774, GLC 219.01, 69, 143.

20   *Journal of the Proceedings of the Congress Held at Philadelphia*, May 10, 1775, GLC
05704, 182.

21   General Congress at Philadelphia to the People of Great Britain, letter, September 5, 1774, GLC 4774, 5; "To the Inhabitants of Great Britain," April 26, 1775,
in *Journal of the Proceedings of the Congress Held at Philadelphia*, GLC 05704, 139;
Continental Congress, October 20, 1774, GLC 2668; "A Declaration by the Representatives Setting Forth the Causes and Necessity of their Taking up Arms,"
July 7, 1775, in *Journal of the Proceedings of the Congress Held at Philadelphia*, GLC
05704, 120, 127.

22   *Journal of the Proceedings of the Congress Held at Philadelphia*, May 10, 1775, GLC
05704, 128.

23   *Journals of Congress*, October 1774, GLC 2668, 145.

24 "Petition from the General Congress in America to the King, Published by Order of the Congress at Philadelphia," October 26, 1774, GLC 219.01.

25 "A Speech to the Six Confederate Nations [of Indians], Mohawks, Oneidas, Tuscaroras, Onondagas, Cayugas, Senekas, from the Twelve United Colonies," in *Journal of the Proceedings of the Congress Held at Philadelphia*, May 10, 1775, GLC 05704, 57.

26 Ibid., 158–59.

27 Ibid., 160; "To the People of Ireland," *Journal of the Proceedings of the Congress Held at Philadelphia*, May 10, 1775, GLC 05704, 174.

28 As Barbara Fields writes, "Race . . . came into existence at a discernible historical moment for rationally understandable historical reasons." For example, "during the Revolutionary era, people who favoured slavery and people who opposed it collaborated in identifying the racial incapacity of [the] Afro-American as the explanation for enslavement": see Fields, "Slavery, Race and Ideology in the United States of America," 101. See also Fredrickson, *The Black Image in the White Mind*; Horsman, *Race and Manifest Destiny*; Morgan, *American Slavery, American Freedom*.

29 Jefferson, *Notes on the State of Virginia*, 143.

30 Tucker, *A Dissertation on Slavery*, 87.

31 Morse, *The American Geography*, 463.

32 Warren, *Black and White Strangers*, 12.

33 Otis, *The Rights of British Colonies Asserted and Proved*, 29.

34 Abigail Adams to John Adams, 22 Sept 1774, in Butterfield, *Adams Family Correspondences*, 1:369.

35 Jefferson, *Notes on the State of Virginia*, 162.

36 Hopkins, *A Dialogue Concerning the Slavery of the Africans*, 8; Otis, *The Rights of British Colonies Asserted and Proved*, 29.

37 Sharp, *Law of Liberty*, 49.

38 "Negro Petitions for Freedom," as cited in *Collections of the Massachusetts Historical Society* (1774), repr. ed. (Boston: Massachusetts Historical Society, 1877), 434; "In Behalf of Our Fellow Slaves in This Province and by Order of Their Committee," letter, 20 April 1773, New-York Historical Society, cited in Horton and Horton, *In Hope of Liberty*, 55.

39 Livermore, *An Historical Research Respecting the Opinions of the Founders of the Republic in Negroes as Slaves, as Citizens, and as Soldiers*, 116–17.

40 Wheatley, "To the Right Honorable William Earl of Dartmouth," 69.

41 "Negro Petitions," in *Collections of the Massachusetts Historical Society*, 433, 436.

42 Fredrickson, *The Black Image in the White Mind*, 321.

43 Stowe, *Uncle Tom's Cabin*, 361–62. I focus in Stowe's novel on the child characters, not the "childlike" character of Uncle Tom, precisely because, as I suggested at the beginning of this chapter, the association of African slaves with

childishness has obscured the significance of the child in creating racial differences in the first place. Moreover, although many other texts deploy the child and highlight its racial identity, I focus on *Uncle Tom's Cabin* to show how abolitionist rhetoric relies on the same racial logic that founded the nation and initially justified slavery because of the prominence of Stowe's text to abolitionist rhetoric.

44 As Raymond writes, "The strange and unnatural prejudice against mere color, which is so all prevalent in the American breast" will "nullify the influence" even of Frederick Douglass as "a little slave child" who "stands to-day before this nation" with a "character" full of "the intelligence and refinement and piety of a large proportion of American society," which "label[s] him 'nigger' ": see R. R. Raymond, "Outline of a Man," in Griffiths, *Autographs for Freedom*, 151.

45 See Chesnutt, "What Is a White Man?" For critical commentary on reproduction and racial transmission, see, for example, Pernick, *The Black Stork*; Zack, *Philosophy of Science and Race*.

46 Lincoln, "Notes for Political Speech," 552.

47 Thoreau, "A Plea for Captain John Brown," 25, 65, 170–71, 173.

48 Wilson Armistad, "Letter from Wilson Armistad," in Griffiths, *Autographs for Freedom*, 65.

49 Lowell, "The Prejudice of Color," in Lowell, *Anti-Slavery Papers*, 18.

50 Ibid., 21.

51 Holzer, *The Lincoln–Douglas Debates*, 189.

52 John Jones correspondence, October 3, 1862, GLC 5981.

53 Ibid., March 13, 1863.

54 Thomas Draper correspondence, 1864, GLC 06452.02.

55 Oliver Edwards Collection, January 13, 1863, GLC 02163.

56 George W. Tillotson correspondence, September 4, 1864, GLC 4558.

57 Klein, *The Atlantic Slave Trade*, 130.

58 Gilroy, *The Black Atlantic*, 4. For an account of the materiality of ships in Gilroy's work, see Baker, *Turning South Again*, 84–86.

59 Hawthorne, "Chiefly about War-Matters."

60 For an important account of the slave trade's significance to Hawthorne's work, see Goddu, "Letters Turned to Gold."

61 Hawthorne, "Chiefly about War-Matters."

62 Alert to the tendency of Puritan clergy to read premonitory signs in monstrous births, Hawthorne often deploys his fictional children to critique Puritan practices. Reversing Puritans' understanding of the relation between Puritanism and monstrosity, for example, Hawthorne, in "The Gentle Boy," identifies as "baby-fiends" the Puritan boys who attack a Quaker orphan, by way of commenting on many Puritans' (including his antecedent, Major Hathorne's) oppression of Quakers. For accounts of monstrous births, see Head, *The Life*

and Death of Mother Shipton; E. B., *Strange and Wonderful News of the Birth of a Monstrous Child with Two Heads* (London: John Smith, 1685); *A Letter from an Eminent Merchant: Containing an Account of a Strange and Monstrous Birth* (London: J. Stans, 1682).

63 Du Bois, *The Souls of Black Folk* (1995 ed.), 54.

64 Goodrich, *Peter Parley's Tales about Africa*, unpaginated.

65 Child, *Evenings in New England*, 2.

66 Optic, *Watch and Wait*, 6, 45, 51.

67 *Slave's Friend*, vol. 1, no. 9 (1836), 1–2, 12.

68 Reid, *The Boy Slaves*, 319.

69 Ibid.

70 Anonymous, *The Little Robinson Crusoe*, 21, 94.

71 Goodrich calculated, twenty-nine years after his first volume sold, that he had written or edited about 170 books. For a full account of Goodrich's Peter Parley series, see Branch, *The Sentimental Years, 1836–60*, 307–13.

72 Sherwood, *The Recaptured Negro*, 17.

73 Anonymous, *The Life and Adventures of Olaudah Equiano*, 10.

74 Ibid., 17.

75 Farrar, *Adventures of Congo in Search of His Master*, 26, 86.

76 Ibid., 86, 119.

77 Mills, *Blackness Visible*, 134.

78 Mann, *The One and the Many*.

79 Ibid., 128.

80 Burhans, "Eligibility," 426.

81 For an account of the racial politics of the DAR, see Smith, *American Archives*, 138.

82 Anonymous, *The Child's Anti-Slavery Book*, 14.

83 Lincoln, "Notes for Political Speech."

2 NATIONS ALONG THE MEXICAN BORDER

1 For commentary on Simms's role as spokesperson for the antebellum South, see Warren, *Culture of Eloquence*, 148. For commentary on Simms's use of Revolutionary rhetoric to explain Southern secession, see Welch, "Lorenzo Sabine and the Assault on Sumner." Simms, "An Oration on the Sixty-Ninth Anniversary of American Independence," 24.

2 Simms, "An Oration on the Sixty-Ninth Anniversary of American Independence," 6, 15, 19, 23–24.

3 Ibid., 25.

4 Baker, *Turning South Again*.

5 Smith and Cohn, *Look Away!*

6   Wald, *Constituting Americans*, 2–3.

7   Romero, "Border of Fear, Border of Desire." For additional commentary on border studies, see, for example, Anzaldúa, *Borderlands/La Frontera*; Castillo and Tabuenca Córdoba, *Border Women*; Gutiérrez-Jones, *Rethinking the Borderlands*. For an excellent account of the racial politics of the border, see Saldaña-Portillo, "Wavering on the Horizon of Social Being."

8   Clifford, "Traveling Cultures," 37.

9   Shohat, "Columbus, Palestine and Arab-Jews," 89. Answering José David Saldívar's call (Saldívar, *Border Matters*) for scholars to re-spatialize the field of American studies by way of a knowledge base that is Mexican and Mexican American and that is acutely conscious of the significance of the U.S.-Mexican border to American culture, history, and politics since 1848, scholars have tended to focus either on determining how border disputes like the U.S.-Mexican War affected Anglo-American writing or on uncovering a new literary history of Mexican America. In the first case, see, for example, Rowe, *Literary Culture and U.S. Imperialism*; Streeby, *American Sensations*. Streeby's project attends to the impact of the U.S.-Mexican War on Northeastern cities, arguing that the "scenes of empire-building in the U.S. West, Mexico and the Americas" are inextricable from "class and race formations . . . in Northeastern cities:" Streeby, *American Sensations*, 15. In the second instance, see, for example, Aranda, *When We Arrive*; Gruesz, *Ambassadors of Culture*; Limón, *American Encounters*.

10 Kaplan, *The Anarchy of Empire in the Making of U.S. Culture*, 23–50.

11 Edward O'Sullivan, editor of the *Democratic Review* and the *New York Morning News*, wrote in July 1845 that it was the "manifest destiny" of the United States to overspread the whole of the North American continent. The term was first heard in Congress in January 1846 in connection with debates on Oregon and became the term used to explain the annexation of Texas, as well as the acquisition of lands in Mexico and Central America: see McMillan, "Historical Notes on American Words"; Parish, *The Emergence of the Idea of Manifest Destiny*; Pratt, "The Origin of 'Manifest Destiny.'" See also Weinberg, *Manifest Destiny*; Morton, *The Southern Empire, with Other Papers*, 4, 9.

12 John C. Calhoun to Upshur, letter, August 27, 1843, Calhoun Papers, South Carolina Historical Society, 17:381.

13 Joseph Eve to Southgate, letter, May 5, 1842, in Nance, "A Letter Book of Joseph Eve."

14 Anonymous, *How to Conquer Texas, before Texas Conquers Us*, 4.

15 J. E. Cairnes, "The Slave Power: Its Character, Career, and Probable Designs" (1862), reprinted in Levy and Peart, *The Political Economy of Slavery*, 216–23.

16 Mill, *The Contest in America*, 27.

17 Ibid., 229–30.

18 Olmsted, *A Journey in the Seaboard Slave States in the Years 1853-1854 with Remarks on Their Economy*, 1:201-208, 1:232-36, 2:275-77. See also Olmsted, *The Cotton Kingdom*, xxv-xxvi.

19 The author of *How to Conquer Texas, before Texas Conquers Us* encourages Northerners to undertake the "conquest of Texas" to protect U.S. dominance and to ensure that "free labor and free institutions" are planted "on the virgin soil of a new republic," rather than slavery: anonymous, *How to Conquer Texas, before Texas Conquers Us*, 11.

20 Moss, *Domestic Novelists in the Old South*, 13.

21 Kaplan, *The Anarchy of Empire in the Making of U.S. Empire*, 23.

22 Walker, "South's First Woman Novelist Started Career Here."

23 Evans, *Macaria*, 329.

24 Baym, *Novels, Readers, and Reviewers*, 219.

25 Ryan, "Charity Begins at Home," 751.

26 Brown, "Reading and Children," 93.

27 Hentz, *The Planter's Northern Bride*, 551.

28 Ibid., 509, 579.

29 Ibid., 549.

30 Kennedy, *Texas*, 376.

31 Galt, *Political Essays*, 6.

32 Ibid., 6.

33 Fisher, *Sketches of Texas in 1840*, vi; Kennedy, *Texas*, ix.

34 Kennedy, *Texas*, 560.

35 *Telegraph and Texas Register* (Houston), October 26, 1838.

36 Early Texans of Stephen F. Austin's colony were called Texians. Branch T. Archer, November 3, 1835, in Hans Peter Gammel, *The Laws of Texas, 1822-1897*, 511. Ward, "Pre-Revolutionary Activity in Brazoria County." Stephen F. Austin to Leaming, February 16, 1836, Thomas F. Leaming Papers, 1796-1847.

37 Austin to Leaming, March 1, 1831, Thomas F. Leaming Papers. Smithwick, *The Evolution of a State*, 139. Smithwick describes the Alamo as "a terrible baptism, that of . . . the Lone Star republic."

38 Allen, *Texas in 1840*, 227.

39 Ibid., 264.

40 Ibid., 260.

41 Smith, *Addresses, Etc.* For commentary on Smith, see Haynes, "Anglophobia and the Annexation of Texas," 120.

42 Smith, "Address Delivered in the City of Galveston," in Smith, *Addresses, Etc.*, 11-17. For additional commentary, see Montejano, *Anglos and Mexicans in the Making of Texas, 1836-1986*, 24.

43 Quoted in Nackman, *A Nation Within a Nation*, 107.

44 Ibid., 93.

45 Ibid., 98–99.

46 Leclerc, *Texas and Its Revolution*, 116.

47 Nackman, *A Nation Within a Nation*, 27.

48 Hale, *A Tract for the Day*, 4.

49 Kennedy, *Texas*, 634.

50 North, *Five Years in Texas*, 13. See Smithwick, *The Evolution of a State*, 106. Anonymous, *How to Settle the Texas Question*, 2.

51 McDaniel and Taylor, *The Coming Empire*, 6.

52 Cassius Marcellus Clay, "Speech Delivered in a Mass Meeting of a Portion of the Citizens of the 8th Congressional District, on Saturday, December 30, 1843, at the White Sulphur Springs in Scott County, Kentucky," Newberry Library, Chicago, Graff 4825, 4.

53 Ibid.

54 Ibid., 5.

55 Newell, *History of the Revolution in Texas*, 13.

56 Galt, *Political Essays*, 11.

57 Anonymous, *How to Settle the Texas Question*, 4.

58 Smithwick, *The Evolution of a State*, 101; Elizur Wright Jr., "Circular," Boston, November 3, 1845.

59 Wright, "Circular," 1.

60 Anonymous, *How to Settle the Texas Question*, 6.

61 D. R. Tilden, *Speech of Mr. D. R. Tilden of Ohio, on the Bill to Raise Two Regiments of Riflemen and for Other Purposes, Delivered in the House of Representatives, March 24, 1846* (Washington, D.C.: J. and G. S. Gideon, 1846), 10; Lewis Cass, *Speech of Hon. Lewis Cass of Michigan, on the Bill Providing for the Prosecution of the War against Mexico, Delivered in the Senate of the United States, May 12, 1846* (Washington, D.C.: Blair and Rives, 1846), 6.

62 Cass, *Speech*, 6.

63 R. M. McLane, *Speech of Hon. R. M. McLane of Maryland on the War with Mexico Delivered in the House of Representatives, January 19, 1848* (Washington, D.C.: Congressional Globe Office 1848), 5.

64 Hawthorne, *Life of Franklin Pierce*, 11, 38, 105.

65 Hale, *Twenty-Four Years a Cowboy and Ranchman in Southern Texas and Old Mexico*, 137.

66 See Barnes, *The Antislavery Impulse 1830–1848*; Filler, *The Crusade against Slavery, 1830–1860*; Tutorow, *Texas Annexation and the Mexican War*.

67 Walker "South's First Woman Novelist Started Career Here."

68 Fidler, *Augusta Evans Wilson, 1835–1909*, 157; Augusta J. Evans to L. Virginia French, letter, January 13, 1861, reprinted in *Alabama Historical Quarterly* 3, no. 1 (Spring 1941): 65; Evans, "Southern Literature."

69 Moss, *Domestic Novelists in the Old South*, 181. For commentary on Evans's

correspondence with Southern military leaders, see Holstein, "Offering Up Her Life."

70 Moss, *Domestic Novelists in the Old South*, 155.

71 Mary Forrest, *Women of the South Distinguished in Literature* (New York: Derby and Jackson, 1860), 333.

72 Evans, *Inez*, 12, 18. Posting "Gone To Texas" on their businesses with such frequency that "GTT" became a common acronym throughout the North and the South in the 1840s, many emigrants moved to Texas to relieve their financial embarrassments. As John Adamson claims, "Emigrants [can] speedily become rich, by monopolizing the whole trade of Texas, and securing her great staple of cotton, they [can] add . . . to their own wealth and happiness": see Adamson, *An Account of Texas, with Instructions for Emigrants*, 6. Thomas Hughes collected a variety of correspondence by those who emigrated in *Gone to Texas*.

73 Evans, *Inez*, 294.

74 Ibid., 17, 27–28, 296.

75 Olmsted, *A Journey through Texas*, 150.

76 Ibid., 151–52.

77 Ibid., 160–61, 164. For commentary on the treatment of the Mexican inhabitants of San Antonio after Texas's independence, see Seguín, *A Revolution Remembered*.

78 Olmsted, *A Journey through Texas*, 148–50.

79 Davis, *The West from a Car Window*, 41–45.

80 Speed, "The Hunt for Garza," 103.

81 Paxton, *Stray Yankee in Texas*, x.

82 Evans, *Inez*, 51.

83 Ibid., 31, 33–34.

84 Ibid., 93.

85 Ibid., 94.

86 Ibid., 94, 154. Mexico stipulated that Anglo-Americans who wished to claim territory in Austin's colony had to become Catholic. As Nanna Smithwick Donaldson writes of early settlers like her father, "Austin probably placed a liberal construction on the word 'Catholic' which Webster defines as 'universal,' his colonists as a rule being of no particular opinion on religious matters": Smithwick, *The Evolution of a State*, 81.

87 Evans, *Inez*, 98.

88 Ibid., 115, 147.

89 Ibid., 253–54.

90 Ibid., 162, 257.

91 Ibid., 153.

92 Ibid., 147, 297.

93 Ibid, 295, 297.

94 In this way, Evans contributes to a Southern antebellum literary tradition to which writers like William Gilmore Simms are committed. *Katharine Walton*, for example, was primarily concerned, according to Simms, with "the delineation of the social world of Charleston, during the Revolutionary period": Simms, *Katharine Walton*, 3. For commentary on antebellum Southern literature's depiction of the American Revolution, see, for example, Holman, *The Roots of Southern Writing*.

95 Evans, "Northern Literature" and "Southern Literature."

96 Evans, "The Mutilation of the Hermae."

97 Fidler, *Augusta Evans Wilson, 1835–1909*, 105.

98 Augusta J. Evans to J. L. M. Curry, letter, January 27, 1864, Curry Papers, Division of Manuscripts, Library of Congress, Washington, D.C.

99 . Evans to French, January 13, 1861.

100 Ibid.

101 Fox-Genovese, "Introduction," xxxv.

102 Evans, *Beulah*, 211.

103 Ibid., 5–6, 328.

104 Ibid., 18, 204.

105 Ibid., 19, 28.

106 Ibid., 28.

107 Ibid., 106.

108 "Augusta Evans Wilson," *Guadalupe County Gazette*, 1915, Daughters of the Republic of Texas Library, San Antonio, Texas.

109 Evans, *Macaria*, 299.

110 Ibid., 366.

111 Ibid., 364.

112 Ibid.

113 Ibid., 308.

114 Ibid., 329, 364.

115 Ibid., 367.

116 Ibid., 366–67.

117 Ibid., 329.

118 As Elizabeth Young notes, *Macaria* was considered so incendiary in its support for the Confederacy that it was "literally burned by military leaders in Northern army camps." As such episodes suggest, Evans's final vision of Southern nationhood proved so powerful for those who supported a separate Southern nation that the book took on talismanic powers for many Confederate soldiers, who kept a copy of it in their breast pockets to protect them from enemy fire: Young, *Disarming the Nation*, 5.

119 For commentary on the Confederacy as a separate nation, see, for example, Thomas, *The Confederate Nation, 1861–1865*. The word "filibuster" was first used

in Dutch and English to refer to banditry in the late sixteenth century; by the seventeenth century, it had entered Spanish as the word for pirate. The *Oxford English Dictionary* records the politicization of the word "filibuster" in the late nineteenth century, when it began to connote the "violation of international law, for the purpose of revolutionizing certain states in Central America," particularly Cuba and Puerto Rico. For commentary on filibustering and the South, as well as William Walker's January 18, 1854, proclamation establishing the independent Republic of Sonora, see May, *Manifest Destiny's Underworld*, 42. See also Greenberg, *Manifest Manhood and the Antebellum American Empire*, for an account of gender and empire in Spanish America.

120 William Gilmore Simms, "Treatment of Slaves in the Southern States," *Southern Quarterly Review* 5 (Jan. 1852): 209–20.

121 For commentary on filibusters to Cuba, see, for example, Lazo, *Writing to Cuba*.

122 Pickens, *The Free Flag of Cuba*, 68, 60.

123 Ibid., 67, 117–18, 124.

124 Halstead, *The Story of Cuba*, 110. For commentary on postslave culture in Louisiana and Cuba, see Scott, *Degrees of Freedom*.

125 Canini, *Four Centuries of Spanish Rule in Cuba*, 71.

126 Ibid., 109.

127 Ibid., 75, 191.

128 Ibid., 193.

129 Ibid., 191.

130 For commentary and complete stills of the film, see Cuniberti, *The Birth of a Nation*.

131 Brown, "Child's Play."

3 CONSENTING FICTIONS

1 Dillon, *The Gender of Freedom*, 204.

2 Alryyes, *Original Subjects*, 119. Cindy Weinstein concurs that "novel after novel tells the story of children learning how to feel right about their families, selves, nation, and God": Weinstein, *Family, Kinship, and Sympathy in Nineteenth-Century American Literature*, 1.

3 Fisher, *Hard Facts*, 58.

4 Delbanco, *Required Reading*, 59–61; Hedrick, *Harriet Beecher Stowe*, 191–94.

5 Alryyes, *Original Subjects*; Brown, *Consent of the Governed*, 23; Ferguson, "The Afterlife of the Romantic Child."

6 Shapiro, *The Evolution of Rights in Liberal Theory*.

7 Locke, *Some Thoughts Concerning Education*, 145.

8 Ibid., 207.

9 Story, *A Treatise on the Law of Contracts Not under Seal*, 43.

10 Ibid., 35, 38.

11 Rush, *Of the Mode of Education Proper in a Republic*, 87, 90.

12 For an important account of how literary forms engage with racial formations and slavery, see Levine, "Slavery, Race, and American Literary Genealogies."

13 Franco, "The Nation as Imagined Community," 131.

14 Fahs, *The Imagined Civil War*, 286.

15 Lipsitz, "The Possessive Investment in Whiteness."

16 Sánchez-Eppler, *Dependent States*.

17 Rose, *The Case of Peter Pan*, 10; Sánchez-Eppler, *Dependent States*, 32.

18 Sedgwick, *Epistemology of the Closet*, 154.

19 Heilbrun, "Louisa May Alcott"; Stimpson, "Reading for Love."

20 In her excellent analysis of *The Lamplighter*, Cindy Weinstein offers an important corrective to this trend of interpreting child protagonists as little women: see Weinstein, "A Sort of Adopted Daughter."

21 Nudelman, "Emblem and Product of Sin."

22 An 1856 children's version of the narrative, *The Lamplighter Picture Book*, drew explicit analogies between the plight of Cummins's child protagonist, Gerty Flint, and "the horrors of slavery," encouraging "the reader pitying Gerty" to "extend compassion to Southern chattels." In so doing, this version of the text features the child to perpetuate the same racialized nationalism that chapter 1 of this volume describes: see Williams, "Promoting an Extensive Sale," 187.

23 Wexler is responding to Ann Douglas's critique of sentimental fiction: see Douglas, *The Feminization of American Culture*; Wexler, *Tender Violence*, 124. See also Wexler, "Tender Violence."

24 Lincoln, "Notes for Political Speech," 552.

25 Raymond, "A Plea for Free Speech," 254.

26 Ibid., 170, 254.

27 William Seward, "Being Up and Doing," in Griffiths, *Autographs for Freedom*, 1–4.

28 John Thomas, "Kossuth," in Griffiths, *Autographs for Freedom*, 170.

29 Lowell, "Shall We Ever Be Republican?" 57.

30 The Earl of Carlisle clarifies the importance of whiteness to the sentimental novel when he writes to Harriet Beecher Stowe that, if "slavery is by far the topping question of the world and age we live in, involving all that is most thrilling in heroism and most touching in distress" — if it is, in short, "the real epic of the universe" — "the external appearance of the negro detracts from the romance and sentimentality which might attach to his position and his wrongs." Letter from the Earl of Carlisle to Mrs. Harriet Beecher Stowe, in Griffiths, *Autographs for Freedom*, 7–13.

31 Core, "Getting Good Pictures of Children," 13. As John Tagg notes, by 1850, "There were already two thousand daguerreotypists in the country. . . . [B]y

1853, three million daguerreotypes were being made annually": Tagg, "A Democracy of the Image," 43.

32 Debates about Darwin's theories of natural selection and evolution raged in the United States from the publication of *The Origin of the Species* (1859) on. However, the 1870s was the decade of most intense intellectual discussion: see Poulton, *Charles Darwin and* The Origin of the Species.

33 Fiske, *The Meaning of Infancy*, v.

34 Sulley, *Studies of Childhood*, 5. *Studies of Childhood* was a compilation of essays that Sulley wrote between 1881 and 1884.

35 Darwin, *The Descent of Man*, 144.

36 Lyell, *Travels in North America in the Years 1841–42*, 1:15.

37 Fiske, *The Destiny of Man Viewed in the Light of His Origin*, 15, 56; Sulley, *Studies of Childhood*, 9.

38 As the rest of my argument will make clear, scientists and social commentators read Anglo-American "development" as a process of absorbing indigenous and immigrant cultures.

39 Chamberlain, *The Child*, 462; Fiske, *The Meaning of Infancy*, 51.

40 Chamberlain, *The Child*, 9, 441, 446,

41 Ibid., 290, 464.

42 Ibid., 291; Crafts, *Childhood*, 9.

43 Atkins, *Out of the Cradle into the World of Self Education through Play*, 18.

44 Chamberlain, *The Child*, 320–38; Howells, *A Boy's Town*, 184.

45 Chamberlain, *The Child*, 293.

46 Hall, *Aspects of Child Life and Education*, 298.

47 Chamberlain, *The Child*, 445, 457.

48 Charles Warner, *Being a Boy* (1878), cited in Brown, *The Material Unconscious*, 184. I discuss later the racial affiliations of this savage.

49 Howells, *A Boy's Town*, 67.

50 Johnson, *Rudimentary Society among Boys*, 5.

51 Ibid., 7, 11, 13, 15.

52 Atkins, *Out of the Cradle into the World of Self Education through Play*, 27.

53 Spencer, *Education*, 23, 125. Herbert Spencer was one of the most popular men of letters in the United States in the second half of the nineteenth century. As Malcolm Cowley notes in "Naturalism in American Literature," Spencer's "popularity . . . is something without parallel in the history of philosophic writing. From 1860–1903 his books had a sale of 368,755 copies. . . . [I]n the memoirs of many famous Americans one finds the reading of Spencer mentioned as an event that changed their lives": as quoted in Person, *Evolutionary Thought in America*, 302.

54 Spencer, *Education*, 62, 107.

55 Atkins, *Out of the Cradle into the World of Self Education through Play*, 20.

56 Ibid., 42.

57 Fiske, *The Meaning of Infancy*, vii.

58 See, for example, Baym, *Novels, Readers, and Reviewers*; Carby, *Reconstructing Womanhood*; Samuels, *The Culture of Sentiment*; Tompkins, *Sensational Designs*; Yellin, *Women and Sisters*.

59 Donald Pizer, "Introduction: The Problem of Definition," in Pizer, *The Cambridge Companion to American Realism and Naturalism*, 6, 10.

60 Shi, *Facing Facts*, 9.

61 Fiske, *The Destiny of Man Viewed in the Light of His Origin*, 100. For discussion of Fiske's role in increasing awareness of social evolution in the United States, see Pyne, *Art and the Higher Life*. As Pyne notes, Fiske was endorsed by Spencer as his "American mouthpiece," so "from the 1870s on Fiske was the most important conduit of Spencer's evolution to the upper middle-class, anglo-American populace": Pyne, *Art and the Higher Life*, 22. Fiske's success on the lecture circuit was second only to Ralph Waldo Emerson's. See also Poulton, *Charles Darwin and* The Origin of the Species.

62 For discussion of sentiment, see Samuels, *The Culture of Sentiment*; Tompkins, *Sensational Designs*.

63 Darwin, *The Expression of the Emotions in Man and Animals*, 358.

64 Foucault, *The Order of Things*, 234.

65 See, most recently, Clark, "Domesticating the School Story, Regendering a Genre"; Hendler, "The Limits of Sympathy."

66 For an account of the impact of evolutionary theory on American culture, see, for example, Person, *Evolutionary Thought in America*.

67 Both books had record sales: *The Lamplighter* was the second most popular book of the 1850s after *Uncle Tom's Cabin* and remained in print through the 1920s, while *Little Lord Fauntleroy* sold well over 1 million copies during the six decades it was constantly in print. In addition, dramatic adaptations, imitative clothing, and popular cultural artifacts were produced around the books. All of this attests to their important instructional role for an American readership eager to identify themselves with an increasingly powerful middle class.

68 Alcott, *Little Men*, 366.

69 Ibid., 15.

70 Ibid., 128.

71 Ibid., 28.

72 Ibid, 283.

73 Ibid., 2.

74 Ibid., 27, 40.

75 Ibid., 22.

76 Ibid., 260.

77 Ibid., 39, 111, 116.

78 Ibid., 208.

79 Ibid., 108.

80 Ibid, 160, 166–67.

81 Ibid., 119.

82 Ibid., 126.

83 Ibid., 124–25.

84 My discussion of whiteness is indebted to the wealth of recent critical analyses of the category. Motivated by Toni Morrison's *Playing in the Dark*, such works include, but are not limited, to Dyer, *White*; Frankenberg, *Displacing Whiteness*; Hodes, *White Women, Black Men*; Lazarre, *Beyond the Whiteness of Whiteness*.

85 Alcott, *Little Men*, 214.

86 One of the appeals of middle-class ideology, as Goldilocks illustrates, is the strict gendering of public and privates spheres and the heterosexual culture such gendering helps to consolidate.

87 Alcott, *Little Men*, 282.

88 Ibid., 360.

89 Ibid., 6, 11, 14–15, 52.

90 Ibid., 152, 158–59, 173.

91 Ibid., 156, 165, 175.

92 Frederic De Peyster, cited in Orsosz, *Curators and Culture*, 220.

93 Ibid., 224.

94 Kevin Walsh discusses how "museum displays of the nineteenth century" strategically represented the past in order to contribute to the notions of progress resulting from industrialization: see Walsh, *The Representation of the Past*, 8, 22.

95 Alcott, *Little Men*, 220, 306.

96 Eileen Hooper draws on Foucault's description, in *The Order of Things*, of the nomination of the visible in modern culture: see Hooper, *Museums and the Shaping of Knowledge*, 138.

97 See Bennet, *The Birth of the Museum*, 186.

98 Alcott, *Little Men*, 180, 185.

99 For an extended account of the enduring popularity of Cummins's novel, see Baym, "Introduction."

100 See Kaplan, *The Anarchy of Empire in the Making of U.S. Culture*, 46–47; Lang, *The Syntax of Class*, 14–29.

101 Cummins, *The Lamplighter*, 6.

102 Ibid., 42.

103 Ibid., 61.

104 Lynes, *The Domesticated Americans*, 139.

105 Rush, *Of the Mode of Education Proper in a Republic*, 88, 90.

106 Kerber, "The Revolutionary Generation," 36f.

107 Larcom, *A New England Girlhood Outlined from Memory*, 99.

108 Stowe, *Household Papers and Stories*, 15. For commentary on the parlor and separate spheres, see Halttunen, *Confidence Men and Painted Women*, 59.

109 Cummins, *The Lamplighter*, 60; Sedgwick, *Home*, 27.

110 Cummins, *The Lamplighter*, 61.

111 Ibid., 42, 138.

112 Ibid., 55.

113 Ibid., 82.

114 Ibid., 55, 392.

115 Ibid., 87, 89.

116 Ibid., 111, 150. Teresa Goddu argues that the metaphorical use of the term "dark" carries racial significance throughout nineteenth-century U.S. narrative: see Goddu, *Gothic America*.

117 Cummins, *The Lamplighter*, 97.

118 Ibid., 35.

119 Ibid., 245, 249–50.

120 For an account of the history of Anglo-Americans' resistance to the increase in immigration from the 1880s through the turn of the twentieth century, see Bederman, *Manliness and Civilization*; Gerstle, *American Crucible*, chaps. 1–2; Guterl, *The Color of Race in America*; Mann, *The One and the Many*, 128.

121 Freedman, "The History of the Family and the History of Sexuality," 300. See also Guterl, *The Color of Race in America*; Mann, *The One and the Many*.

122 For an account of the Burnett family and Vivian's influence on the creation of Cedric Fauntleroy, see Tom McCarthy, "The Real Little Lord Fauntleroy." Wilson, "*Little Lord Fauntleroy*."

123 Burnett, *Little Lord Fauntleroy*, 5–6.

124 Ibid., 5, 25.

125 Ibid., 8.

126 Ibid., 7, 31, 60, 78.

127 Ibid., 3.

128 Ibid., 25, 61, 205.

129 Ibid., 122.

130 Ibid., 61, 76–77, 84, 92, 99, 108–9, 132, 138, 142.

131 Ibid., 160, 164, 172, 181–82, 184, 206.

132 Wexler, 98.

133 Ivy, "Have You Seen Me?"

134 Hacking, "The Making and Molding of Child Abuse," 262, 285.

135 Whitman, "Democratic Vistas," 424–25. Brown, "Child's Play"; Douglas, *The Feminization of American Culture*.

136 Louise Rockford Wardner, "Girls in Reformatories," *Proceedings of the Annual Conference of Charities*, 1879, 188.

137 Addams, *The Spirit of Youth and the City Streets*, 5.

138 Altgeld, *Our Penal Machinery and Its Victims*, 38–40.

139 John P. Altgeld, "Biennial Message," *Journal of the House of Representatives of Illinois* (1897), unpaginated.

4 TRANSNATIONAL TWAIN

1 Allen, *The Invention of the White Race*; Horsman, *Race and Manifest Destiny*. See Love, *Race over Empire*.

2 Parker, *Collected Works*, 270.

3 Stone, *The Innocent Eye*, 44; Mintz, *Huck's Raft*, 5.

4 Kaplan, *The Anarchy of Empire in the Making of U.S. Empire*, 64. See also Kaplan, "Imperial Triangles."

5 Kaplan, *The Anarchy of Empire in the Making of U.S. Empire*, 64; Fishkin, *Was Huck Black?*

6 Webster, *A Grammatical Institute of the English Language*, 14.

7 Alryyes, *Original Subjects*; Berlant, *The Queen of America Goes to Washington City*; Brown, "Child's Play"; Castronovo, "Radical Configurations of History"; Takaki, *Iron Cages*, 5–11.

8 Balibar, "Racism and Nationalism," and "Racism as Universalism"; Kohn, *American Nationalism*, 29; Mommsen, "The Renaissance of the Nation-State and the Historians"; Renan, "What Is a Nation?"

9 Linke, *Blood and Nation*; Marx, *Making Race and Nation*; Rowe, *The New American Studies*, 53.

10 West, "The Dilemma of the Black Intellectual."

11 For an excellent commentary on the novel's development of black revolutionary perspectives, see Levine, "Introduction."

12 Crozier, *The Novels of Harriet Beecher Stowe*; Newman, "Was Tom White?"

13 Stowe, *Dred*, 30, 79.

14 Ibid., 131.

15 Ibid., 376.

16 Ibid., 546.

17 See Banet-Weiser, "Elián González and 'The Purpose of America.'" For additional commentary on Elián González, see Rowe, *The New American Studies*, 204.

18 Ala Alryyes, *Original Subjects*, 76, 87.

19 As Thomas Paine wrote in 1791, if "Britain is the parent country . . . then the more shame upon her conduct. Even brutes do not devour their young, nor savages make war upon their families. . . . The infant state of the colonies. . so far from being against, is an argument in favor of independence, [for] youth is the seed time of good habits, as well in nations as individuals": see Paine, *Rights of Man*, 135.

20 Adams, "We Won't Be Their Negroes."

21 Grund, *The Americans, in their Moral, Social, and Political Relations*, 150–51.

22 Chamberlain, *Foundations of the Nineteenth Century*, 565.

23 Ibid., 518, 558.

24 Hemminghaus, *Mark Twain in Germany*, 1.

25 Fiske, *American Political Ideals Viewed from the Standpoint of Universal History*, 6–7, 87.

26 Ibid., 7, 87.

27 Knox, *Races of Men*, 59, 54.

28 Fiske, *American Political Ideals Viewed from the Standpoint of Universal History*, 7.

29 Nourse, *Remarks on the Past and Its Legacies to American Society*, 39, 71–72, 206–7.

30 Fiske, *American Political Ideals Viewed from the Standpoint of Universal History*, 138.

31 See Burg, "Monarchism as a National Ideology," 84; vom Bruch, "Culture as an Expression of Nationalist Values in Germany," 167.

32 Vom Bruch notes the evolving definition of Germany from the 1885 *Brockhaus* definition to an 1896 definition of the "German nation-state as a prospective vehicle of consensus" that bases "the cultural superiority of German nationality and of the German nation-state on the principles of Social Darwinism," finally, to the emergence in 1907 of the term 'national sentiment' that connotes "a "vivid awareness of belonging to a larger whole, to a national characterized by . . . a distinct national identity (*Volkstum*)": vom Bruch, "Culture as an Expression of Nationalist Values in Germany," 168.

33 Chamberlain, *Foundations of the Nineteenth Century*, 269.

34 Ibid., 327, 519, 543.

35 *Handbuch des Alldeutschen Verbandes*, 17th ed, (Munich, 1914), 7, cited in Chickering, *We Men Who Feel Most German*, 4. For additional commentary on the Pan-German League and other German nationalist associations, see Coetzee, *The Germany Army League*, 4. For additional commentary on the racial politics of post-Bismarkian Germany, see Eley, *Reshaping the German Right*.

36 For commentary on the racial basis of Germany's imperialism, see, for example, Eley, *Society, Culture, and the State in Germany, 1870–1930*; Geiss, *German Foreign Policy, 1871–1914*; Schöllgen, *Escape into War*.

37 Fiske, *American Political Ideals Viewed from the Standpoint of Universal History*, 46; Poesche and Goepp, *The New Rome*, 48–55, iv.

38 Fiedler, *Freaks*, 347. For critical commentary on Fiedler's work, see Adams, *Sideshow U.S.A.*, 139–57.

39 Cook, "Of Men, Missing Links, and Nondescripts," 147–55; Dennett, *Weird and Wonderful*; Rothfels, "Aztecs, Aborigines, and Ape-People," 162.

40 Rothfels, *Savages and Beasts*, 90–91.

41 Gould and Pyle, *Anomalies and Curiosities of Medicine*, 231; Lerman, "Wilhelmine Germany," 207.

42 Kersten, "When You Don't Get What You See," 78.

43 According to Henry Pochmann, the "most important" literary outcome of Twain's 1891 summer in Berlin was his discovery of Hoffman's nursery book and his decision to "set to translating it for the edification of his children": see Pochmann, *German Culture in America*, 479.

44 Twain, *Pudd'nhead Wilson and Those Extraordinary Twins*, 230.

45 Ibid., 91.

46 For extended commentary on the significance of illustration to Twain's writing, see Beverly, *Mark Twain and His Illustrators*. As David Beverly notes, "Mark Twain knew the language and power of pictures," and he used illustration throughout his career to "dictat[e] his reader's response" to his prose: ibid., 2.

47 Hoffman, *Der Struwwelpeter oder lustige Geschichten und drollige Bilder*.

48 Renan, "What Is a Nation?" 170.

49 For commentary on U.S.-German relations, see, for example, Kusmer, "Toward a Comparative History of Racism and Xenophobia in the United States and Germany, 1865–1933," 146. See also Finzsch and Schirmer, *Identity and Intolerance*; Silber, "The Romance of Reunion."

50 Stahl, "Mark Twain's 'Slovenly Peter' in the Context of Twain and German Culture," 168.

51 Chesnutt, "What Is a White Man?" 837.

52 For an account of Twain's visit to the Chicago Exposition, see Larson, *The Devil in the White City*, 285. See also *The Story of Columbus and the World's Columbian Exposition*, 316–17.

53 Blight, *Race and Reunion*, 9. See also Fahs, *The Imagined Civil War*.

54 "Germany at the World's Fair: The Most Complete Exhibit of all Foreign Nations," *New York Times*, July 2, 1893, 17; "Germany Is Easily in the Lead: Its Exhibit Will Be Better Than That of Other Foreign Nations," *Chicago Tribune*, March 29, 1893, 11. See also Appelbaum, *The Chicago World's Fair of 1893*, 77.

55 Du Bois et al., *The Reason Why the Colored American Is Not in the World's Columbian Exposition*, 77. My thanks to Bob Levine for alerting me to this text.

56 For commentary on the Krupps gun and the child's role in illustrating Germany's power during the period of world imperialism in which Germany was the supreme force, see Bertuca, *The World's Columbian Exposition*, 121.

57 Ibid., 344. Shepp and Shepp, *Shepp's World's Fair Photographed*, 460, 494; *The Story of Columbus and the World's Columbian Exposition*, 346.

58 *The Story of Columbus and the World's Columbian Exposition*, 344.

59 Twain, "The German Chicago," 246, 250.

60 Heber De Long, "The Children's Home: The Children's Building," *Memories of the World's Columbian Exposition*, pamphlet, case R 1832.222, Newberry Library, Chicago.

61 Twain, *Pudd'nhead Wilson and Those Extraordinary Twins*, 343.

62 Ibid., 349.

63 See Gillman, *Dark Twins*.

64 For commentary on the exhibition route of the Tocci brothers, see Bondeson, *The Two-Headed Boy and Other Medical Marvels*, 176–81.

65 Sundquist, "Mark Twain and Homer Plessy," 102–28; Boeckmann, *A Question of Character*, 117; Thomas, "Tragedies of Race, Training, Birth and Communities of Competent Pudd'nheads." See also Ladd, *Nationalism and the Color Line in George Cable, Mark Twain and William Faulkner*, 85–138, for an important commentary on racial science for Twain's work.

66 Twain, *Pudd'nhead Wilson and Those Extraordinary Twins*, 230.

67 As Sterling Fishman and Lothar Martin write, "A twin study of the two Germanys offers even more possibilities than one might expect. . . . [T[his is a study of society and education in those estranged twins, East and West Germany": see Fishman and Martin, *Estranged Twins*, 2.

68 See Bondeson, *The Two-Headed Boy and Other Medical Marvels*; Fredricks, "Twain's Indelible Twins," 498.

69 Gould and Pyle, *Anomalies and Curiosities of Medicine*, 222. The "life history of twins," as Sir Francis Galton notes in "The History of Twins, as a Criterion of the Relative Powers of Nature and Nurture" (1875), the first scientific study of twins ever published, offers "a veritable treasure house of information" for the keen observer not only on the question of whether "nature prevails enormously over nurture" but on the question of what constitutes the individual and distinguishes it from others: see Galton, "The History of Twins as a Criterion of the Relative Powers of Nature and Nurture."

70 "The Tocci Twins," *Scientific American*, December 12, 1891.

71 Harris, "The Blended Tocci Brothers and Their Historical Analogues," 460.

72 Gould and Pyle, *Anomalies and Curiosities of Medicine*, 186.

73 Twain, *Pudd'nhead Wilson and Those Extraordinary Twins*, 88, 178.

74 Ibid., 88.

75 Ibid., 278, 294.

76 Ibid., 138.

77 Ibid., 57–58.

78 Ibid., 158.

79 Davis, *Who Is Black?* 5, 8, 15.

80 Martí, "Our America" (1891), reprinted in Pecora, *Nations and Identities*, 178, 184. Walter Michaels takes his title from Waldo Frank's *Our America* (1919) to argue for race's irrelevance, but turning to the Martí text from which Michaels's title might also derive reveals that the child functions as a primary mechanism through which race endures as a powerful conceptual premise of U.S. society: Michaels, *Our America*.

81 Renan, "What Is a Nation?" 169–70.

82 Bourne, "Trans-National America," *Atlantic Monthly* (1916), reprinted in Hollinger and Capper, *The American Intellectual Tradition*, 174, 180.

83 Du Bois, "The Souls of White Folk," in Du Bois, *Darkwater*, 46, 49.

84 Ibid., 41.

5 PSYCHOLOGIES OF RACE

1 Freud, "A Child Is Being Beaten," 108.

2 Ibid.

3 James, *A Small Boy and Others*, 159.

4 Heinze, "*Schizophrenia Americana*," 251.

5 Gilman, *Freud, Race, and Gender*.

6 See, for example, Blair, *Henry James and the Writing of Race and Nation*; Davis, "Solid, Liquid, or Gas?"; McKee, *Producing American Races*; Michaels, "Jim Crow Henry James?"; Warren, *Black and White Strangers*.

7 For accounts of the child's importance to Henry James's writing, see, for example, Moon, *A Small Boy and Others*; Rowe, *The Other Henry James*. During the 1890s, as Tessa Hadley writes, James "produced a series of fictions centred on studies of childhood": Hadley, *Henry James and the Imagination of Pleasure*, 41.

8 James, *The Turn of the Screw*, 10, and *The American Scene*, 131. Warren, *Black and White Strangers*, 12.

9 Baldwin, *The Mental Development in the Child and the Race*, 4.

10 Haygood, *Our Brother in Black*, 42.

11 See, for example, Blight, *Race and Reunion*; Silber, *Romance of Reunion*.

12 Haygood, *Our Brother in Black*, 23, 48, 57, 91.

13 Baldwin, *The Mental Development in the Child and the Race*, 521.

14 Many scientists believed, as Alexander Chamberlain writes, that "the child is a little compressed, synthetic picture of all the stages of man's evolution": Chamberlain, *The Child*, 291. Hall, "Pedagogical Methods in Sunday School Work," 719.

15 For an account of American psychology's reliance on evolutionary theory, see Person, *Evolutionary Thought in America*; Pyne, *Art and the Higher Life*.

16 Smith, "A Study in Race Psychology," *Popular Science Monthly* (New York: Appleton, 1897), 360, 362.

17 Odum, *Social and Mental Traits of the Negro*, 165.

18 Morse, "A Comparison of White and Colored Children," 78.

19 Mayo, "The Mental Capacity of the American Negro."

20 Garth, *Race Psychology*, 38.

21 Baldwin, *The Mental Development in the Child and the Race*, 25–26, 28.

22 Hall, *Adolescence*.

23 Ibid., 714.

24 Ibid., 334.

25 Ibid., 675.

26 For commentary on late-nineteenth-century fascination with the non-visible, see Beer, "Authentic Tidings of Invisible Things"; Krasner, *The Entangled Eye*.

27 Bardin, "The Psychological Factor in Southern Race Problems," 372.

28 Ibid., 372–74.

29 Garth, *Race Psychology*, 5.

30 Hall, "The Negro in Africa and America," 358.

31 Ibid., 367, 350–51, 355. Bean, "Some Racial Peculiarities of the Negro Brain."

32 William James to Henry James, letter, April 11, 1892, William James correspondence, Houghton Library, Harvard University, Cambridge, Mass; "Mr. James's New Book," *Bookman* (November 1898).

33 Hayes, *Henry James*, 302–12.

34 James, *Talks to Teachers on Psychology and to Students on Some of Life's Ideals*.

35 Hall, *Adolescence*, 283.

36 James, *The Turn of the Screw*, 11; James, *What Maisie Knew*, 53.

37 James, *What Maisie Knew*, 6, 52.

38 Ibid., 18, 120.

39 Ibid., 79. For accounts of the significance of race in James's depiction of the Countess, see Michaels, "Jim Crow Henry James?"; Morrison, *Playing in the Dark*.

40 James, *What Maisie Knew*, 137.

41 James, *The American Scene*, 196. Renner, "Red Hair, Very Red, Close-Curling." Ignatiev, *How the Irish Became White*.

42 James, *The Turn of the Screw*, 28.

43 James, *What Maisie Knew*, 22. Sara Blair notes the importance of "phantasmagoria" to James's consideration of racial otherness in *The American Scene*: Blair, "Documenting American."

44 James, *What Maisie Knew*, 5; James, *The Turn of the Screw*, 87.

45 James, *The American Scene*, 124.

46 James, *What Maisie Knew*, 6, 9.

47 Ibid., 9.

48 James, "The Hidden Self," 369.

49 See, for example, Carby, *Reconstructing Womanhood*; Gillman, "Pauline Hopkins and the Occult"; Horvitz, "Hysteria and Trauma in Pauline Hopkins's *Of One Blood; or, the Hidden Self*"; Otten, "Pauline Hopkins and the Hidden Self of Race"; Schrager, "Pauline Hopkins and William James."

50 Du Bois, "Strivings of the Negro People," 194. He makes a similar claim when he states that the "Negro" inherits a "double-consciousness" and "ever feels his two-ness": Du Bois, *The Souls of Black Folk* (1995), 45. Many scholars have documented the relationship between James and Du Bois, which will be explored in the next chapter.

51 James, "The Hidden Self," 369.

52 Ibid., 363, 367.

53 Ibid., 361.

54 Ibid., 362.

55 Brown, *Clotel*, 184.

56 Ibid. Clarke, *Anti-Slavery Days*, 11.

57 Clarke, *Anti-Slavery Days*, 11; James, "The Hidden Self," 373.

58 James, "The Hidden Self," 372.

59 Baldwin, *Social and Ethical Interpretations in Mental Development*, 491.

60 Ibid., 491–92.

61 McKie, "A Brief History of Insanity and Tuberculosis in the Southern Negro," *Journal of the American Medical Association* March 20, 1888: 538.

62 Ray, "Observations upon Eye Diseases and Blindness in the Colored Race," 88.

63 Nordeau, *Degeneration* (New York: D. Appleton, 1895), 27.

64 Ibid., 27, 55, 57.

65 James, "The Hidden Self," 371.

66 Ibid., 369, 371.

67 See Schrager, "Pauline Hopkins and William James," article for an extended and conclusive account of Hopkins's knowledge of William James's work.

68 Hopkins, *A Primer of Facts*, title page.

69 Ibid., 7–8.

70 Ibid., 9.

71 Ibid., 8.

72 For an interesting commentary on the imperialist dimensions of Hopkins's novel, see Gaines "Black Americans' Racial Uplift Ideology as 'Civilizing Mission.'"

73 Hopkins, *A Primer of Facts*, 7–9.

74 Ibid., 21, 27.

75 Ibid., 15, 20, 29.

76 Scott, "Fantasy Echo."

77 Hopkins, *Of One Blood*, 532.

78 Ibid., 442.

79 Ibid., 361, 442–44.

80 Ibid., 449.

81 Hopkins, *A Primer of Facts*, 27.

82 Hopkins, *Of One Blood*, 445, 449, 454, 459, 469–70.

83 Ibid., 472.

84 Ibid., 495, 516, 520, 526, 532, 534, 536, 584.

85 Ibid., 547, 560, 570, 572–73, 576.

86 Baldwin, *Social and Ethical Interpretations in Mental Development*, 491.

6 RACELESS STATES

1   Du Bois, *Darkwater*, 202.

2   Ibid., 213.

3   Du Bois, *The Souls of Black Folk*.

4   Posnock, *Color and Culture*, 12.

5   Eric Foner describes Du Bois's career-long interest in racelessness and equal racial representation: see Foner, *A Short History of Reconstruction*, 122, 127.

6   Tomasi, *Liberalism beyond Justice*, 28. Callan, *Autonomy and Schooling*, 21.

7   For additional commentary on Cuba's national history, see Fernández and Betancourt, *Cuba, the Elusive Nation*, 3.

8   Martí, "My Race," 319.

9   Logan, *Betrayal of the Negro*, 62.

10 Quoted in Logan, *Betrayal*, 62.

11 Juguo, *W. E. B. Du Bois*, 15.

12 Du Bois, *The Autobiography of W. E. B. Du Bois*, 125.

13 Hamilton, *The Writings of W. E. B. Du Bois*, 14–15.

14 Du Bois, *The Negro American Family*.

15 See Du Bois, "My Evolving Program for Negro Freedom," 49, 54, 70, and "The Atlanta Conference," 57.

16 Du Bois, 822, 825–26.

17 Du Bois, "The Study of the Negro Problem, in Aptheker, *Writings by W. E. B. Du Bois in Periodicals Edited by Others*, 1:182.

18 Du Bois, *The Souls of Black Folk* (1995), 52. Reed, *W. E. B. Du Bois and American Political Thought*, 123.

19 Du Bois, "The Atlanta Conferences," 55.

20 Du Bois, "The Negro Voter," 6.

21 Maceo, quoted in Jorge Ibarra, *Ideología Mambisa*, 52.

22 Maceo, *Antonio Maceo*, 64–5.

23 Carlos de Manuel Céspedes, January 3, 1869, "Diplomatic Communication," in Portuondo and Picardo, *Letters*, 1:142–46.

24 "October 10," in *La Revolución*, National Historical Archive, Madrid, cited in Ferrer, *Insurgent Cuba*, 39. I am indebted to Ferrer's work for a number of this paragraph's references.

25 Quoted in Ferrer, *Insurgent Cuba*, 39.

26 Halstead, *The Story of Cuba*, 110.

27 José Martí, "My Race," 318–20.

28 Martí, "Plato de Lentejas," *Patria*, January 6, 1894, and "My Race," *Patria*, April 16, 1893, reprinted in *José Martí: Selected Writings*, ed. Esther Allen (New York: Penguin Classics, 2002), 489, 319.

29 Ibid.

30 Hassan, "The Figuration of Martí." See also Rotker, *The American Chronicles of José Mart*.

31 Oviedo, *Para la Historia*, 3–4, 166.

32 Dana, *To Cuba and Back*, 205, 268.

33 Ibid., 19.

34 Manners, "Cuba," 15, 44.

35 Canini, *Four Centuries of Spanish Rule in Cuba*, 189.

36 Roosevelt, *The Rough Riders*.

37 Canini, *Four Centuries of Spanish Rule in Cuba*, 189–90.

38 Blanco, "Bastards of the Unfinished Revolution."

39 Cabrera, *Cuba and the Cubans*, 272–73.

40 Quesada, *War in Cuba*, 42.

41 Ibid., ii.

42 Ibid., 60.

43 Martí, "The Truth About the United States," 332.

44 Martí, "Our America," 293.

45 Martí, "Classical and Scientific Education." Cited in Randall, *On Education*, 24.

46 Martí, "A False Conception of Public Education," *La Nación*, Nov. 14, 1886, cited in Randall, *On Education*, 77.

47 Martí, *Tropico Edition*, vol. 39, 109, cited in Randall, *On Education*, 14.

48 Du Bois, *The Souls of Black Folk* (1995), 78; Martí, "A Vindication of Cuba," in Allen, ed., *José Martí: Selected Writings*, 266–67.

49 Shafter, quoted in Foner, *Spanish–Cuban–American War and the Birth of American Imperialism*, 1895–1902, 2:394–95. Fisher, *Principles of Colonial Government Adapted to the Present Needs of Cuba and Porto Rico and the Philippines*, 19.

50 Polavieja, quoted in Ferrer, *Insurgent Cuba*, 78; Halstead, *The Story of Cuba*, 110.

51 Musgrave, *Under Three Flags in Cuba*, 358.

52 Leonard Wood to President of the United States, November 27, 1898, Leonard Wood Papers, Library of Congress, Washington, D.C., mss. box 26; Musgrave, *Under Three Flags in Cuba*, 355.

53· Fisher, *Principles of Colonial Government Adapted to the Present Needs of Cuba and Porto Rico and the Philippines*, 28; Musgrave, *Under Three Flags in Cuba*, 365.

54 Fisher, *Principles of Colonial Government Adapted to the Present Needs of Cuba and Porto Rico and the Philippines*, 50.

55 Wheeler et al., *Under Fire with the 10th U.S. Cavalry*, 120–21.

56 Ibid., 50.

57 Ibid., 49, 208.

58 *Under Fire with the 10th U.S. Calvary*, 177.

59 Ibid., 270.

60 "Slavery Question in Another Form," Springfield *Republican* September 7, 1900, reprinted in Foner and Winchester, *The Anti-Imperialist Reader*, 168.

61 Charles Baylor, "Hanna, Irelandism and the Color Line in Cuba," *Planet* (Richmond), July 30, 1898, reprinted ibid., 149.

62 "Immortal Doctrines of Liberty Ably Set Out by a Colored Man: The Effect of Imperialism upon the Negro Race," *Springfield Republican*, September 7, 1900, reprinted ibid., 177–80.

63 "The Insurgents and the Government," *Planet* (Richmond.), July 30, 1898, reprinted ibid., 146.

64 Baylor, "Hanna, Irelandism, and the Color Line in Cuba," reprinted ibid., 149.

65 "McKinley's Inconsistencies," *Planet* (Richmond), July 22, 1899, reprinted ibid., 163.

66 "Open Letter to President McKinley," *Bee* (Washington, D.C.), October 23, 1899, reprinted ibid., 144.

67 Financed by the W. E. B. Du Bois Foundation, Inc., and the Fernando Ortiz Foundation, *The Souls of Black Folk* was recently published in Cuba.

68 Du Bois, "Dusk of Dawn: An Essay toward an Autobiography of a Race Concept" (1940), in Du Bois, *Writings*, 651.

69 Du Bois, "From McKinley to Wallace: My Fifty Years as an Independent" (1948), in Lewis, *W. E. B. Du Bois*, 483.

70 "New York City, August 3, 1915, to the President of the United States," in Aptheker, *The Correspondence of W. E. B. Du Bois*, 1:211.

71 "The Enforcement of the Slave Trade Laws," in Aptheker, *Writings by W. E. B. Du Bois in Periodicals Edited by Others*, 24.

72 "The Future of the Negro Race in America," ibid., 190.

73 "The Present Outlook for the Dark Races of Mankind," *Church Review*, October 17, 1900, reprinted in Aptheker, *Writings by W. E. B. Du Bois in Periodicals Edited by Others*, 77.

74 Ibid.

75 Aptheker, *The Correspondence of W. E .B. Du Bois*, 1:304.

76 Hughes, *I Wonder as I Wander*, 11, 14.

77 Washington, "Signs of Progress among the Negroes."

78 Aptheker, *The Correspondence of W. E. B. Du Bois*, 1:415.

79 Ibid., 1:403. Raymond Buell's letter of May 25, 1929, to Du Bois reads: "We are planning to publish a report on Haiti . . . similar to our reports on Puerto Rico and Cuba . . . and welcome any information and suggestions." Du Bois writes to Mrs. Alexander on January 10, 1930, "I think I can get to your home Jan[uary] 18 and talk very sketchily about Haiti and Cuba": Du Bois, *The Souls of Black Folk* (1995), 45.

80 W. E. B. Dubois to President of the United States, New York City, August 3, 1915, in Aptheker, *The Correspondence of W. E. B. Du Bois*, 1:211.

81 Du Bois, *Writings*, 1194.

82 Du Bois, "The Dilemma of the Negro," 181.

83 The points of convergence between the two movements can be seen not only in Du Bois's interest in Cuba, but also in Martí's interest in, and 1893 visit to, Haiti, where he and Joseph-Antenor Firmin, Haiti's minister of foreign affairs, recognized in each other the drive to be "like Du Bois creating the foundations of a new science, philosophy, and literature": see, Plummer, "Firmin and Martí at the Intersection of Pan-Americanism and Pan-Africanism," 214.

84 Du Bois, *The Negro American Family*, 23.

85 Ibid., 37.

86 Du Bois, *Mortality among Negroes in Cities*, 26.

87 Du Bois, *The Negro American Family*, 39–41.

88 Du Bois, *Darkwater*, 204, 209.

89 Du Bois, *Dark Princess*, 311.

90 Posnock, *Color and Culture*, 147.

91 Dewey, *The Later Works, 1925–1953*, 11:272, 11:280–81.

92 Faulkner, *Intruder in the Dust*, 48–49. My gratitude to Ken Warren for alerting me to this text.

93 Ibid., 71–72, 89.

94 Ibid., 138.

95 Ibid., 18.

96 Ibid., 32, 96.

97 Mills, *From Class to Race*, 217.

98 Martha Nussbaum, *Hiding From Humanity: Disgust, Shame and the Law* (Princeton: Princeton University Press, 2004), 319.

BIBLIOGRAPHY

Adams, John (Humphrey Ploughjogger). "We Won't Be Their Negroes." *Boston Gazette*, October 14, 1765.

Adams, Michael Vannoy. *The Multicultural Imagination: "Race," Color, and the Unconscious*. New York: Routledge, 1996.

Adams, Rachel. *Sideshow U.S.A.: Freaks and the American Cultural Imagination*. Chicago: University of Chicago Press, 2001.

Adamson, John. *An Account of Texas, with Instructions for Emigrants*. London: J. Eames, 1839.

Addams, Jane. *The Spirit of Youth and the City Streets* (1909), reprint. ed. Chicago: University of Illinois Press, 1972.

Alcott, Louisa May. *Little Men: Life at Plumfield with Jo's Boys* (1871), reprint. ed. London: Puffin Books, 1994.

Allen, Theodore. *The Invention of the White Race: The Origin of Racial Oppression in Anglo America*. London: Verso, 1997.

Allen, William. *Texas in 1840; or, The Emigrant's Guide to the New Republic*. New York: William W. Allen, 1840.

Alryyes, Ala. *Original Subjects: The Child, the Novel and the Nation*. Cambridge, Mass.: Harvard University Press, 2001.

Altgeld, John P. *Our Penal Machinery and Its Victims*. Chicago: Jansen, McClurg, 1884.

Anderson, Benedict. *Imagined Communities: Reflections on the Origin and Spread of Nationalism*. London: Verso, 1983 (reprint. 1991).

Anonymous. *The Child's Anti-Slavery Book*. Boston: American Tract Society, 1859.

————. *How to Conquer Texas, before Texas Conquers Us*. Boston: Redding, 1845.

————. *The Life and Adventures of Olaudah Equiano; or, Gustavus Vass, the African*. New York: Wood and Sons, 1829.

Anonymous. *How to Settle the Texas Question: Address to the Friends of Free Institutions in Massachusetts and Other Free States*, October 21, 1845. Government pamphlet, Newberry Library, Chicago.

———. *The Little Robinson Crusoe*. Philadelphia: Theodore Bliss, 1855.

———. *The Story of Columbus and the World's Columbian Exposition*. Detroit: F. B. Dickerson, 1892.

Anzaldúa, Gloria. *Borderlands/La Frontera: The New Mestiza*. San Francisco: Spinsters/Aunt Lute, 1987.

Appelbaum, Nancy, Anne Macpherson, and Karin Rosenblatt. *Race and Nation in Modern Latin America*. Chapel Hill: University of North Carolina Press, 2003.

Appelbaum, Stanley. *The Chicago World's Fair of 1893: A Photographic Record*. New York: Dover, 1980.

Appiah, Kwame Anthony. *The Ethics of Identity*. Princeton: Princeton University Press, 2005.

———. "Liberalism, Individuality, and Identity." *Critical Inquiry* 27 (2001): 305–32.

Aptheker, Herbert, ed. *The Correspondence of W. E. B. Du Bois*, vol. 1 (1877–1934). Boston: University of Massachusetts Press, 1973.

———. *The Correspondence of W. E. B. Du Bois*, vol. 2 (1934–44). Boston: University of Massachusetts Press, 1976.

———. *Writings by W. E. B. Du Bois in Periodicals Edited by Others*, vol. 1 (1891–1909). New York: Kraus-Thomson Organization, 1982.

Arac, Jonathan. "Toward a Critical Genealogy of the U.S. Discourse of Identity." *boundary 2* 30, no. 2 (2003): 194–205.

Aranda, José. *When We Arrive: A New Literary History of Mexican America*. Tucson: University of Arizona Press, 2003.

Argument of Charles Sumner, Esq., against the Constitutionality of Separate Colored Schools in the Case of Sarah C. Roberts vs. the City of Boston. Boston: B. F. Roberts, 1849.

Ariès, Philippe. *Centuries of Childhood: A Social History of Family Life*, trans. Robert Baldick. New York: Vintage Press, 1962.

Ashby, Leroy. *Endangered Children: Dependency, Neglect and Abuse in America*. New York: Twayne Publishers, 1997.

Atkins, Thomas Benjamin. *Out of the Cradle into the World of Self Education through Play*. Boston: Sterling, 1895.

Avery, Gillian. *Behold the Child: American Children and Their Books, 1621–1922*. Baltimore: Johns Hopkins University Press, 1994.

Backus, Isaac. "A Discourse Showing the Nature and Necessity of an Internal Call to Preach the Everlasting Gospel." Pp. 65–129 in *Isaac Backus on Church, State, and Calvinism: Pamphlets, 1754–1789*, ed. William McLoughlin. Cambridge, Mass.: Harvard University Press, 1968.

Baker Jr., Houston A. *Turning South Again: Re-Thinking Modernism/Re-Reading Booker T.* Durham: Duke University Press, 2001.

Baldwin, James Mark. *The Mental Development in the Child and the Race*. New York: Macmillan, 1894.

————. *Social and Ethical Interpretations in Mental Development*. New York: Macmillan, 1897.

Balibar, Etienne. "Racism and Nationalism." Pp. 37–69 in *Race, Nation, Class: Ambiguous Identities*, eds. Etienne Balibar and Immanuel Wallerstein. London: Verso, 1991.

————. "Racism as Universalism." *New Political Science* no. 16–17 (Fall–Winter) 1989: 9–22.

Bancroft, George. *Literary and Historical Miscellanies*. New York: Harper and Brothers, 1855.

Banet-Weiser, Sarah. "Elián González and 'The Purpose of America': Nation, Family, and the Child-Citizen." *American Quarterly* 55, no. 2 (June 2003): 149–78.

Bardin, James. "The Psychological Factor in Southern Race Problems." *Popular Science Monthly* (1913).

Barnes, Gilbert. *The Antislavery Impulse 1830–1848*. New York: Harcourt, Brace, and World, 1974.

Basler, Roy, ed. *The Collected Works of Abraham Lincoln*. New Brunswick, N.J.: Rutgers University Press, 1953.

Baym, Nina. "Introduction." Pp. ix–xxxiv in Maria Susanna Cummins, *The Lamplighter* (1854), reprint. ed. New Brunswick, N.J.: Rutgers University Press, 1988.

————. *Novels, Readers, and Reviewers: Responses to Fiction in Antebellum America*. Ithaca: Cornell University Press, 1985.

————. Unsigned review of *Inez* in *Godey's* in *Novels, Readers, and Reviewers: Responses to Fiction in Antebellum America*. Ithaca: Cornell University Press, 1984, 219.

Bean, Robert. "Some Racial Peculiarities of the Negro Brain." *American Journal of Anatomy* 5 (1906): 333–43, 379.

Bederman, Gail. *Manliness and Civilization: A Cultural History of Gender and Race in the United States, 1880–1917*. Chicago: University of Chicago Press, 1995.

Beer, Gillian. "'Authentic Tidings of Invisible Things': Vision and the Invisible in the Later Nineteenth Century." Pp. 83–100 in *Vision in Context: Historical and Contemporary Perspectives on Sight*, eds. Teresa Brennan and Martin Jay. New York: Routledge, 1996.

Belnap, Jeffrey, and Raul Fernandez, eds. *José Martí's "Our America": From National to Hemispheric Cultural Studies*. Durham: Duke University Press, 1998.

Bennet, Tony. *The Birth of the Museum: History, Theory, Politics*. London: Routledge, 1995.

Bergner, Gwen. *Taboo Subjects: Race, Sex, and Psychoanalysis*. Minneapolis: University of Minnesota Press, 2005.

Berlant, Lauren. *The Queen of America Goes to Washington City: Essays on Sex and Citizenship*. Durham: Duke University Press, 1997.

Berrol, Selma Cantor. *Growing Up American: Immigrant Children in America Then and Now*. New York: Twayne Publishers, 1995.

Bertuca, David. *The World's Columbian Exposition: A Centennial Bibliographic Guide*. New York: Greenwood Press, 1996.

Beverly, David. *Mark Twain and His Illustrators*. Albany, N.Y.: Whitston Publishing, 2001.

Blair, Sara. "Documenting American: Racial Theater in *The American Scene*." *Henry James Review* 16 (1995): 264–72.

————. *Henry James and the Writing of Race and Nation*. New York: Cambridge University Press, 1996.

Blake, William. "The Little Black Boy." P. 23 in *Songs of Innocence* (1789), reprint. ed. London: J. Pearson, 1884.

Blanco, John D. "Bastards of the Unfinished Revolution: Bolívar's Ismael and Rizal's Martí at the Turn of the Twentieth Century." *Radical History Review* 89 (Summer 2004): 92–114.

Blight, David W. *Race and Reunion: The Civil War in American Memory*. Cambridge, Mass.: Harvard University Press, 2001.

Blumin, Stuart. *The Emergence of the Middle Class: Social Experience in the American City, 1760–1900*. New York: Cambridge University Press, 1989.

Brodhead, Richard. "Sparing the Rod: Discipline and Fiction in Antebellum America." *Representations* 21 (Winter 1988): 67–96.

Boeckmann, Cathy. *A Question of Character: Scientific Racism and the Genres of American Fiction, 1892–1912*. Tuscaloosa: University of Alabama Press, 2000.

Bondeson, Jan. *The Two-Headed Boy and Other Medical Marvels*. Ithaca: Cornell University Press, 2000.

Bourne, Randolph. "Trans-National America" (1916). Pp. 171–81 in *The American Intellectual Tradition: A Sourcebook*, eds. David Hollinger and Charles Capper. New York: Oxford University Press, 2006.

Brickman, Celia. *Aboriginal Populations in the Mind: Race and Primitivity in Psychoanalysis*. New York: Columbia University Press, 2003.

Brown, Bill. *The Material Unconscious: American Amusement, Stephen Crane and the Economics of Play*. Cambridge, Mass.: Harvard University Press, 1996.

Brown, Gillian. "Child's Play." *differences* 11 (Fall 2000): 75–106.

————. *Consent of the Governed: The Lockean Legacy in Early American Culture*. Cambridge, Mass.: Harvard University Press, 2001.

————. "Reading and Children: *Uncle Tom's Cabin* and *The Pearl of Orr's Island*." Pp. 77–96 in *The Cambridge Companion to Harriet Beecher Stowe*, ed. Cindy Weinstein. New York: Cambridge University Press, 2004.

Brown, William Wells. *Clotel; or, The President's Daughter* (1853), reprint. ed. Salem, N.H.: Ayer, 1988.

Burg, Peter. "Monarchism as a National Ideology." Pp. 71–97 in *German and American Nationalism: A Comparative Perspective*, eds. Harmut Lehmann and Hermann Wellenreuther. Oxford: Berg, 1999.

Burnett, Frances Hodgson. *Little Lord Fauntleroy*. New York: Scribner's Sons, 1889.

Butterfield, Lyman. *Adams Family Correspondences*. Cambridge, Mass.: Harvard University Press, 1963.

Cabrera, Raimondo. *Cuba and the Cubans*, trans. Laura Guitéras. Philadelphia: Levytype, 1896.

Callan, Eamonn. *Autonomy and Schooling.* Kingston, Ont.: McGill-Queen's University Press, 1988.

Calvert, Karin. *Children in the House: The Material Culture of Early Childhood, 1600–1900.* Boston: Northeastern University Press, 1992.

Canini, Italo Emilio. *Four Centuries of Spanish Rule in Cuba; or, Why We Went to War with Spain.* Chicago: Laird and Lee, 1898.

Carby, Hazel. *Reconstructing Womanhood: The Emergence of the Afro-American Woman Novelist.* New York: Oxford University Press, 1987.

Castillo, Debra, and Maria Socorro Tabuenca Córdoba. *Border Women: Writing from La Frontera.* Minneapolis: University of Minnesota Press, 2002.

Castro-Klarén, Sara, and John Charles Chasteen, eds. *Beyond Imagined Communities: Reading and Writing the Nation in Nineteenth-Century Latin America.* Baltimore: Johns Hopkins University Press, 2003.

Castronovo, Russ. *Fathering the Nation: American Genealogies of Slavery and Freedom* Berkeley: University of California Press, 1995.

————. "Radical Configurations of History." Pp. 523–47 in *Subjects and Citizens: Nation, Race, and Gender from Oroonoko to Anita Hill,* eds. Michael Moon and Cathy Davidson. Durham: Duke University Press, 1995.

Chafe, William. "Race in America: The Ultimate Test of Liberalism." Pp. 161–81 in *The Achievement of American Liberalism: The New Deal and Its Legacies,* ed. William Chafe. New York: Columbia University Press, 2003.

Chamberlain, Alexander. *The Child: A Study in the Evolution of Man.* London: Walter Scott Publishing, 1900.

Chamberlain, Houston Stewart. *Foundations of the Nineteenth Century.* New York: John Lane, 1914.

Chesnutt, Charles. "What Is a White Man?" *Independent* (May 30, 1889): 837–41.

Chickering, Roger. *We Men Who Feel Most German: A Cultural Study of the Pan-German League, 1886–1914.* Boston: Allen and Unwin, 1984.

Child, Lydia Maria. *Evenings in New England.* Boston: Cummings, Hilliard, 1824.

Clark, Beverly Lyon. "Domesticating the School Story, Regendering a Genre: Alcott's *Little Men.*" *New Literary History* 26 (1995): 323–42.

Clarke, James. *Anti-Slavery Days: A Sketch of the Struggle Which Ended in the Abolition of Slavery in the United States.* New York: R. Worthington, 1884.

Clement, Priscilla Ferguson. *Growing Pains: Children in the Industrial Age, 1850–1890.* New York: Twayne Publishers, 1997.

Clifford, James. "Traveling Cultures." Pp. 17–47 in *Routes: Travel and Translation in the Late Twentieth Century.* Cambridge, Mass.: Harvard University Press, 1997.

Clinton, David. *Tocqueville, Lieber, and Bagehot: Liberalism Confronts the World.* New York: Macmillan, 2003.

Coetzee, Marilyn Shevin. *The Germany Army League: Popular Nationalism in Wilhelmine Germany.* New York: Oxford University Press, 1990.

Cohen, Nancy. *The Reconstruction of American Liberalism, 1865–1914.* Chapel Hill: University of North Carolina Press, 2002.

Coleman, Michael. *American Indian Children at School, 1850–1930*. Jackson: University Press of Mississippi, 1993.

Cooper, Frederick, and Ann Laura Stoler, eds. *Tensions of Empire: Colonial Cultures in a Bourgeois World*. Berkeley: University of California Press, 1997.

Core, E. B. "Getting Good Pictures of Children." *Ladies Home Journal* (February 1898).

Crafts, W. F. (Rev.). *Childhood: The Text-Book of the Age, for Parents, Pastors, and Teachers, and All Lovers of Childhood*. Boston: Lee and Shepard, 1875.

Cross, Gary. *Kids' Stuff: Toys and the Changing World of American Childhood*. Cambridge, Mass.: Harvard University Press, 1997.

Crozier, Alice. *The Novels of Harriet Beecher Stowe*. New York: Oxford University Press, 1969.

Cummins, Maria Susanna. *The Lamplighter*. Boston: Jewett, 1854.

Cuniberti, John. *The Birth of a Nation: A Formal Shot-by-Shot Analysis Together with Microfiche*. Woodbridge, Conn.: Research Publications, 1979.

Dain, Bruce. *A Hideous Monster of the Mind: American Race Theory in the Early Republic*. Cambridge, Mass.: Harvard University Press, 2002.

Dana, Richard Henry. *To Cuba and Back: A Vacation Voyage*. Boston: Ticknor and Fields, 1859.

Darwin, Charles. *The Descent of Man*. Chicago: Encyclopaedia Britannica, 1955.

———. *The Expression of the Emotions in Man and Animals*. New York: Appleton, 1897.

Davis, F. James. *Who is Black? One Nation's Definition* (1991), reprint. ed. University Park: Pennsylvania State University Press, 2001.

Davis, James. "Solid, Liquid, or Gas? Race as a State of Matter." *Henry James Review* 21 (2000): 261–69.

Davis, Richard Harding. *The West from a Car Window*. New York: Harper and Brothers, 1892.

Degler, Carl. *At Odds: Women and the Family in America from the Revolution to the Present*. New York: Oxford University Press, 1980.

Delbanco, Andrew. *Required Reading: Why Our American Classics Matter Now*. New York: Farrar, Straus, and Giroux, 1996.

Demos, John. *Past, Present, and Personal: The Family and the Life Course in American History*. New York: Oxford University Press, 1986.

Dewey, John. *The Later Works, 1925–1953*, ed. Jo-Ann Boydston, vols. 1–17. Carbondale: Southern Illinois University Press, 1986.

———. *Liberalism and Social Action* (1935), reprint. ed. New York: Prometheus Books, 2000.

Dillon, Elizabeth. *The Gender of Freedom: Fictions of Liberalism and the Literary Public Sphere*. Stanford, Calif.: Stanford University Press, 2004.

Douglas, Ann. *The Feminization of American Culture*. New York: Alfred A. Knopf, 1977.

Douglass, Frederick. "What To the Slave Is the Fourth of July?" Pp. 108–31 in *The*

Oxford Frederick Douglass Reader, ed. William L. Andrews. New York: Oxford University Press, 1996.

Du Bois, W. E. B. "The Atlanta Conference." Pp. 53–61 in *W. E. B. Du Bois on Sociology and Black Community*, eds. Dan S. Green and Edwin D. Driver. Chicago: University of Chicago Press, 1978.

————. *The Autobiography of W. E. B. Du Bois: A Soliloquy on Viewing My Life from the Last Decade of Its First Century*. New York: International Publishers, 1968.

————. "The Conservation of Races" (1897). Pp. 38–47 in *The Oxford W. E. B. Du Bois Reader*, ed. Eric Sundquist. New York: Oxford University Press, 1996.

————. *Dark Princess: A Romance*. Jackson: University Press of Mississippi, 1995.

————. *Darkwater: Voices from Within the Veil*. New York: Scrivener's, 1919.

————. "The Dilemma of the Negro." *American Mercury* (October 1924): 179–85.

————. "My Evolving Program for Negro Freedom." In *What the Negro Wants*, ed. Rayford Logan. Notre Dame, Ind.: University of Notre Dame Press, 2001.

————. "The Negro Voter." *Horizon* 4, no. 1 (July 1908).

————. *The Souls of Black Folk* (1903), reprint. ed. New York: Penguin, 1983.

————. *The Souls of Black Folk* (1903), reprint. ed. New York: Signet, 1995.

————. "Strivings of the Negro People." *Atlantic Monthly* 80 (1897), 194–98.

————. *Writings*. New York: Library of America, 1986.

Du Bois, W. E. B., ed. *Mortality among Negroes in Cities, May 26–27, 1896*. Atlanta: Atlanta University Press, 1903.

————. *The Negro American Family: A Social Study Made by Atlanta University*. Atlanta: Atlanta University Press, 1908.

Du Bois, W. E. B., Ida B. Wells, et al. *The Reason Why the Colored American Is Not in the World's Columbian Exposition: The African American's Contribution to Columbian Literature* (1893), reprint. ed., ed. Robert W. Rydell. Urbana: University of Illinois Press, 1999.

Dyer, Richard. *White*. New York: Routledge, 1997.

Edelman, Lee. "The Future Is Kid Stuff: Queer Theory, Disidentification, and the Death Drive." *Narrative* 6 (January 1998): 18–30.

————. *No Future: Queer Theory and the Death Drive*. Durham: Duke University Press, 2004.

Eley, Geoff. *Reshaping the German Right: Radical Nationalism and Political Change after Bismarck*. New Haven, Conn.: Yale University Press, 1980.

Eley, Geoff, ed. *Society, Culture, and the State in Germany, 1870–1930*. Ann Arbor: University of Michigan Press, 1996.

Emerson, Ralph Waldo. *English Traits*. London: Routledge, 1856.

————. "Nature" (1836). Pp. 3–49 in *The Collected Works of Ralph Waldo Emerson*, vol. 1, eds. R. E. Spiller and A. R. Ferguson. Cambridge: Belknap Press of Harvard University Press, 1971.

————. "Self-Reliance" (1841). Pp. 25–53 in *The Collected Works of Ralph Waldo Emerson*, vol. 2, eds. R. E. Spiller and A. R. Ferguson. Cambridge, Mass.: Belknap Press of Harvard University Press, 1971.

Evans, Augusta J. *Beulah* (1859), reprint. ed. Baton Rouge: Louisiana State University Press, 1992.

———. *Inez: A Tale of the Alamo*. New York: John Bradburn, 1864.

———. *Macaria; or, Altars of Sacrifice* (1864), reprint. ed. Baton Rouge: Louisiana State University Press, 1992.

———. "The Mutilation of the Hermae." *Gulf City Home Journal*, November 9, 1862.

———. "Northern Literature." *Daily Advertiser* (Mobile), October 10, 1859.

———. "Southern Literature." *Daily Advertiser* (Mobile), November 6, 1859.

Fahs, Alice. *The Imagined Civil War: Popular Literature of the North and South, 1861–1865*. Chapel Hill: University of North Carolina Press, 2001.

Farrar, Mrs. John. *Adventures of Congo in Search of His Master: An American Tale*. Boston: Munroe and Francis, 1825.

Fass, Paula, and Mary Ann Mason, eds. *Childhood and America*. New York: New York University Press, 2000.

Faulkner, William. *Intruder in the Dust*. New York: Random House, 1948.

Fenton, Norman. *Mental Hygiene in School Practice*. Stanford, Calif.: Stanford University Press, 1949.

Ferguson, Frances. "The Afterlife of the Romantic Child: Rousseau and Kant Meet Deleuze and Guattari." *South Atlantic Quarterly* 102, no. 1 (2003): 215–34.

Fernández, Damiân, and Madeline Betancourt, eds. *Cuba, the Elusive Nation: Interpretations of National Identity*. Gainesville: University Press of Florida, 2000.

Ferrer, Ada. *Insurgent Cuba: Race Nation, and Revolution, 1868–1898*. Chapel Hill: University of North Carolina Press, 1999.

Ficker, Douglas. "From Roberts to Plessy: Educational Segregation and the 'Separate but Equal' Doctrine." *Journal of Negro History* 84, no. 4 (Fall 1999): 301–14.

Fidler, William. *Augusta Evans Wilson, 1835–1909: A Biography*. Birmingham: University of Alabama Press, 1951.

Fiedler, Leslie. *Freaks: Myths and Images of the Secret Self* (1978), reprint. ed. New York: Anchor, 1993.

Fields, Barbara. "Slavery, Race and Ideology in the United States of America." *New Left Review* 181 (May–June 1990): 95–118.

Filler, Louis. *The Crusade against Slavery, 1830–1860*. New York: Harper, 1986.

Finzsch, Norbert, and Dietmar Schirmer, eds. *Identity and Intolerance: Nationalism, Racism, and Xenophobia in Germany and the United States*. Cambridge: Cambridge University Press, 1998.

Fisher, Horace. *Principles of Colonial Government Adapted to the Present Needs of Cuba and Porto Rico and the Philippines*. Boston: L. C. Page, 1899.

Fisher, Orceneth. *Sketches of Texas in 1840*. Springfield, Ill.: Walters and Weber, 1841.

Fisher, Philip. *Hard Facts: Setting and Form in the American Novel*. New York: Oxford University Press, 1985.

Fishkin, Shelley Fisher. *Was Huck Black? Mark Twain and African-American Voices*. New York: Oxford University Press, 1993.

Fishman, Sterling. and Lothar Martin. *Estranged Twins: Education and Society in the Two Germanys*. New York: Praeger, 1987.

Fiske, John. *American Political Ideals Viewed from the Standpoint of Universal History.* New York: Harper and Brothers, 1885.

———. *The Destiny of Man Viewed in the Light of His Origin* (1884), reprint. ed. Boston: Houghton Mifflin, 1899.

———. *The Meaning of Infancy* (1883), reprint. ed. Boston: Houghton Mifflin, 1909.

Fliegelman, Jay. *Prodigals and Pilgrims: The American Revolution against Patriarchal Authority, 1750–1800.* New York: Cambridge University Press, 1982.

Foner, Eric. *A Short History of Reconstruction: 1863–1877.* New York: Harper, 1990.

Foner, Philip. *Spanish–Cuban–American War and the Birth of American Imperialism, 1895–1902,* 2 vols. New York: Monthly Review Press, 1972.

Foner, Philip, and Richard Winchester, eds. *The Anti-Imperialist Reader: A Documentary History of Anti-Imperialism in the United States,* vol. 1. New York: Homes and Meier, 1984.

Forrest, Mary. *Women of the South Distinguished in Literature.* New York: Derby and Jackson, 1860.

Foucault, Michel. *The Order of Things: An Archaeology of the Human Sciences.* New York: Vintage, 1973.

Fox-Genovese, Elizabeth. "Introduction." Pp. xi–xxxvi in Augusta J. Evans, *Beulah* (1859), reprint. ed. Baton Rouge: Louisiana State University Press, 1992.

Franco, Jean. "The Nation as Imagined Community." Pp. 130–73 in *Dangerous Liaisons: Gender, Nation, and Postcolonial Perspectives,* eds. Anne McClintock, Aamir Mufti, and Ella Shohat. Minneapolis: University of Minnesota Press, 1997.

Frankenberg, Ruth, ed. *Displacing Whiteness: Essays in Social and Cultural Criticism.* Durham: Duke University Press, 1998.

Fredricks, Nancy. "Twain's Indelible Twins." *Nineteenth-Century Literature* 43, no. 3 (March 1989): 484–500.

Fredrickson, George. *The Black Image in the White Mind.* New York: Harper and Row, 1971.

Freedman, Estelle. "The History of the Family and the History of Sexuality." Pp. 285–310 in *The New American History: Revised and Expanded Edition,* ed. Eric Foner. Philadelphia: Temple University Press, 1997.

Freud, Sigmund. "A Child Is Being Beaten: A Contribution to the Origin of Sexual Perversions" (1919). Pp. 107–33 in *Sexuality and the Psychology of Love,* trans. James Strachey. New York: Macmillan, 1963.

Gaines, Kevin. "Black Americans' Racial Uplift Ideology as 'Civilizing Mission': Pauline E. Hopkins on Race and Imperialism." Pp. 433–56 in *Cultures of United States Imperialism,* eds. Amy Kaplan and Donald Pease. Durham: Duke University Press, 1993.

Galt, James. *Political Essays.* Williamsburg, Va., 1844.

Gammel, Hans Peter. *The Laws of Texas, 1822–1897,* vol. 1. Austin: Gammel Book Company, 1898.

Garth, Thomas. *Race Psychology: A Study of Racial Mental Differences.* New York: McGraw-Hill, 1913.

Geiss, Imanuel. *German Foreign Policy, 1871–1914.* London: Routledge, 1976.

Gellner, Ernest. *Nations and Nationalism*. Ithaca: Cornell University Press, 1983.

Gerstle, Gary. *American Crucible: Race and Nation in the Twentieth Century*. Princeton: Princeton University Press, 2001.

Gikandi, Simon. "Race and Cosmopolitanism," *American Literary History* 14, no. 3 (2002): 593–614.

Gillman, Susan. *Dark Twins: Imposture and Identity in Mark Twain's America*. Chicago: University of Chicago Press, 1989.

———. "Pauline Hopkins and the Occult: African-American Revisions of Nineteenth-Century Sciences." *American Literary History* 8 (1996): 57–83.

Gilman, Sander. *Freud, Race, and Gender*. Princeton: Princeton University Press, 1993.

Gilroy, Paul. *The Black Atlantic: Modernity and Double Consciousness*. Cambridge, Mass.: Harvard University Press, 1993.

Goddu, Teresa. *Gothic America: Narrative, History, and Nation*. New York: Columbia University Press, 1997.

———. "Letters Turned to Gold: Hawthorne, Authorship, and Slavery." *Studies in American Fiction* (2001): 49–76.

Goldberg, David Theo. *The Racial State*. New York: Blackwell, 2002.

Goodenough, Elizabeth. "Demons of Wickedness, Angels of Delight: Hawthorne, Woolf, and the Child." Pp. 226–36 in *Hawthorne and Women: Engendering and Expanding the Hawthorne Tradition*, eds. John Idol Jr. and Melinda M. Ponder. Amherst: University of Massachusetts Press, 1995–99.

Goodenough, Elizabeth, Mark Heberle, and Naomi Sokoloff, eds. *Infant Tongues: The Voice of the Child in Literature*. Detroit: Wayne State University Press, 1994.

Goodrich, Samuel. *Peter Parley's Tales about Africa*. Boston: Gray and Bowen, 1830.

Goshgarian, G. M. *To Kiss the Chastening Rod: Domestic Fiction and Sexual Ideology in the American Renaissance*. Ithaca: Cornell University Press, 1992.

Gould, Gerald, and Walter Pyle. *Anomalies and Curiosities of Medicine*. New York: Julian Press, 1896.

Gould, Stephen Jay. "The Geometer of Race." P. 1 in *The Concept of "Race" in Natural and Social Science*, ed. E. Nathaniel Gates. New York: Garland Publishing, 1997.

Graff, Harvey. *Conflicting Paths: Growing Up in America*. Cambridge, Mass.: Harvard University Press, 1995.

Greenberg, Amy. *Manifest Manhood and the Antebellum American Empire*. New York: Cambridge University Press, 2005.

Griffiths, Julia, ed. *Autographs for Freedom*. Boston: Jewett, 1853.

Grob, Gerald, ed. *Mental Hygiene in Twentieth Century America: Four Studies, 1921–1924*. New York: Arno Press, 1980.

Gruesz, Kirsten Silva. *Ambassadors of Culture: The Transamerican Origins of Latino Writing*. Princeton: Princeton University Press, 2001.

Grund, Francis. *The Americans, in Their Moral, Social, and Political Relations*. Boston: Marsh, Capen, and Lyon, 1837.

Gubar, Susan. *Racechanges: White Skin, Black Face in American Culture*. New York: Oxford University Press, 1997.

Guterl, Matthew Pratt. *The Color of Race in America: 1900–1940*. Cambridge, Mass.: Harvard University Press, 2001.

Gutiérrez-Jones, Carl. *Rethinking the Borderlands: Between Chicano Culture and Legal Discourse*. Berkeley: University of California Press, 1995.

Gutmann, Amy. "Children, Paternalism, and Education: A Liberal Argument." *Philosophy and Public Affairs* 9, no. 4 (1980): 338–58.

Habermas, Jürgen. *The Postnational Constellation: Political Essays*, trans. Max Pensky. Cambridge, Mass.: MIT Press, 2001.

Hacking, Ian. "The Making and Molding of Child Abuse." *Critical Inquiry* 17 (1991): 253–88.

Hadley, Tessa. *Henry James and the Imagination of Pleasure*. New York: Cambridge University Press, 2002.

Hale, Edward Everett. *A Tract for the Day*. Boston: Redding, 1845.

Hale, William. *Twenty-Four Years a Cowboy and Ranchman in Southern Texas and Old Mexico*. Norman: University of Oklahoma Press, 1959.

Hall, Granville Stanley. *Adolescence: Its Psychology and Its Relations to Physiology, Anthropology, Sociology, Sex, Crime and Religion*. New York: Appleton, 1904.

———. "The Negro in Africa and America." *Pedagogical Seminary* 12 (1905): 350–68.

———. "Pedagogical Methods in Sunday School Work." *Christian Register* 74 (1895): 719–20.

Hall, Granville Stanley, ed. *Aspects of Child Life and Education*. Boston: Atheneum Press, 1907.

Halstead, Murat. *The Story of Cuba: Her Struggles for Liberty*. Akron, Ohio: Werner, 1896.

Halttunen, Karen. *Confidence Men and Painted Women: A Study of Middle-Class Culture in America, 1830–70*. New Haven, Conn.: Yale University Press, 1982.

Hamilton, Virginia, ed. *The Writings of W. E. B. Du Bois*. New York: Thomas Crowell, 1975.

Harris, Robert. "The Blended Tocci Brothers and their Historical Analogues." *American Journal of Obstetrics and Diseases of Women and Children* 25 (1892): 460–73.

Hassan, Salah D. "The Figuration of Martí: Before and after the Revolution." *Radical History Review* 89 (Summer 2004): 191–205.

Hawes, Joseph, and Ray Hiner, eds. *American Childhood: A Research Guide and Historical Handbook*. Westport, Conn.: Greenwood Press, 1985.

Hawthorne, Nathaniel. *American Notebooks, Centenary Edition* 7 : 4, ed. Randall Stewart. New Haven: Yale University Press, 1932.

———. "Chiefly about War-Matters." *Atlantic Monthly*, July 1862, 50.

———. *The Life of Franklin Pierce*. Boston: Ticknor, Reed, and Fields, 1852.

———. "A Wonder Book" and "Tanglewood Tales." In *The Complete Works of Nathaniel Hawthorne*, vol. 4, ed. George Parsons Lathrop. Boston: Houghton Mifflin, 1909.

Hayden, Patrick. *John Rawls: Towards a Just World Order*. Cardiff: University of Wales Press, 2002.

Hayes, Kevin, ed. *Henry James: The Contemporary Reviews*. New York: Cambridge University Press, 1996.

Haygood, Atticus. *Our Brother in Black: His Freedom and His Future*. New York: Phillips and Hunt, 1892.

Haynes, Sam. "Anglophobia and the Annexation of Texas: The Quest for National Security." Pp. 115–46 in *Manifest Destiny and Empire: American Antebellum Expansion*, eds. Sam Haynes and Christopher Morris. College Station: Texas A&M University Press, 1997.

Head, Richard. *The Life and Death of Mother Shipton: Giving a Wonderful Account of her Strange and Monstrous Birth*. London: J. Back, 1694.

Hedrick, Joan. *Harriet Beecher Stowe: A Life*. New York: Oxford University Press, 1994.

Heilbrun, Carolyn. "Louisa May Alcott: The Influence of *Little Women*." Pp. 20–26 in *Women, the Arts, and the 1920s in Paris and New York*, eds. Kenneth Wheeler and Virginia Lussier. New Brunswick, N.J.: Transaction Books, 1982.

Heininger, Mary Lynn Stevens. "Children, Childhood, and Change in America, 1820–1920." Pp.1–33 in *A Century of Childhood: 1820–1920*. Rochester, N.Y.: Margaret Woodbury Strong Museum, 1984.

Heinze, Andrew. "*Schizophrenia Americana*: Aliens, Alienists and the 'Personality Shift' of Twentieth-Century Culture." *American Quarterly* 55 (June 2003): 227–56.

Hemminghaus, Edgar. *Mark Twain in Germany*. New York: Columbia University Press, 1939.

Hendler, Glen. "The Limits of Sympathy: Louisa May Alcott and the Sentimental Novel." *American Literary History* 23 (1995): 685–706.

Hentz, Caroline Lee. *The Planter's Northern Bride*. Philadelphia: T. B. Peterson and Brothers, 1854.

Hiner, Ray, and Joseph Hawes, eds. *Growing Up in America: Children in Historical Perspective*. Urbana: University of Illinois Press, 1985.

Hobbes, Thomas. *Leviathan* (1651), reprint. ed. New York: Dutton, 1950.

Hobsbawm, E. J. *Nations and Nationalism since 1780*. New York: Cambridge University Press, 1990.

Hodes, Martha. *White Women, Black Men: Illicit Sex in the Nineteenth-Century South*. New Haven, Conn.: Yale University Press, 1997.

Hoffman, Heinrich. *Der Struwwelpeter oder lustige Geschichten und drollige Bilder*, trans. Mark Twain. Frankfurt am Main: Struwwelpeter Museum, 1996.

Holman, C. Hugh. *The Roots of Southern Writing: Essays on the Literature of the American South*. Athens: University of Georgia Press, 1970.

Holstein, Suzy Clarkson. "Offering Up Her Life: Confederate Women on the Altars of Sacrifice." *Southern Studies* 2, no. 2 (1991): 113–31.

Holzer, Harold. ed. *The Lincoln–Douglas Debates*. New York: Harper Collins, 1993.

Honeyman, Susan. *Elusive Childhood: Impossible Representations in Modern Fiction*. Columbus: Ohio State University Press, 2005.

Hooper, Eilean. *Museums and the Shaping of Knowledge*. London: Routledge, 1992.

Hopkins, Pauline. *Of One Blood; or, The Hidden Self* (1902), reprint. ed. New York: Oxford University Press, 1988.

———. *A Primer of Facts: Pertaining to the Early Greatness of the African Race and the Possibility of Restoration by Its Descendants—with Epilogue.* Cambridge: P. E. Hopkins, 1905.

Hopkins, Samuel. *A Dialogue Concerning the Slavery of the Africans.* New York: Robert Hodes, 1776.

Horsman, Reginald. *Race and Manifest Destiny: The Origins of American Racial Anglo-Saxonism.* Cambridge, Mass.: Harvard University Press, 1981.

Horton, James Oliver, and Lois E. Horton. *In Hope of Liberty: Culture, Community, and Protest among Northern Free Blacks, 1700–1860.* New York: Oxford University Press, 1997.

Horvitz, Deborah. "Hysteria and Trauma in Pauline Hopkins's *Of One Blood; or, The Hidden Self.*" *African American Review* 33 (1999): 245–60.

Howells, William Dean. *A Boy's Town* (1890), reprint. ed. Hartford, Conn.: Greenwood Press, 1970.

Hughes, Langston. *I Wonder as I Wander: An Autobiographical Journey.* New York: Farrar, Straus and Giroux, 1956.

Hughes, Thomas. *Gone to Texas: Letters from our Boys.* London: Macmillan, 1884.

Ibarra, Jorge. *Ideología Mambisa.* Havana: Instituto Cubano del Libro, 1967.

Ignatiev, Noel. *How the Irish Became White.* New York: Routledge, 1995.

Ivy, Marilyn. "Have You Seen Me? Recovering the Inner Child in Late Twentieth-Century America." Pp. 79–104 in *Children and the Politics of Culture,* ed. Sharon Stephens. Princeton: Princeton University Press, 1995.

James, Henry. *The American Scene.* New York: Scribner's, 1946.

———. *A Small Boy and Others.* New York: Charles Scribner's Sons, 1913.

———. *The Turn of the Screw.* New York: Norton, 1966.

———. *What Maisie Knew.* New York: Oxford University Press, 1996.

James, William. "The Hidden Self." *Scribner's Magazine* 7 (1890): 361–72.

———. *Talks to Teachers on Psychology and to Students on Some of Life's Ideals.* New York: Henry Holt, 1899.

Jefferson, Thomas. *Notes on the State of Virginia* (1787), ed. William Peden, reprint. ed. Chapel Hill: University of North Carolina Press, 1955.

Johnson, John. *Rudimentary Society among Boys.* Baltimore: N. Murray, 1884.

Juguo, Zhang. *W. E. B. Du Bois: The Quest for the Abolition of the Color Line.* New York: Routledge, 2001.

Kaplan, Amy. *The Anarchy of Empire in the Making of U.S. Empire.* Cambridge, Mass.: Harvard University Press, 2002.

———. "Imperial Triangles: Mark Twain's Foreign Affairs." Pp. 330–47 in *Negotiations of America's National Identity,* vol. 2, eds. Roland Hegenbuchle and Josef Raab. Rubingen: Staseffenberg Verlag, 2000.

Kazanjian, David. *The Colonizing Trick: National Culture and Imperial Citizenship in Early America.* Minneapolis: University of Minnesota Press, 2003.

Kelley, Blair. "*Plessy* and Early Challenges to the Doctrine of 'Separate, but Equal.' "

Pp. 19–44 in *From the Grassroots to the Supreme Court: Brown v. Board of Education and American Democracy*, ed. Peter Lau. Durham: Duke University Press, 2004.

Kennedy, William. *Texas: The Rise, Progress, and Prospects of the Republic of Texas* (1841), reprint. ed. Fort Worth: Molyneaux Craftsmen, 1925.

Kerber, Linda. "The Revolutionary Generation: Ideology, Politics, and Culture in the Early Republic." Pp. 31–60 in *The New American History: Revised and Expanded Edition*, ed. Eric Foner. Philadelphia: Temple University Press, 1997.

———. *Women of the Republic: Intellect and Ideology in Revolutionary America*. Chapel Hill: University of North Carolina Press, 1980.

Kerkering, Jack. *The Poetics of National and Racial Identity in Nineteenth-Century American Literature*. New York: Cambridge University Press, 2003.

Kersten, Holger. "When You Don't Get What You See: What Mark Twain Knew about Germany before He Visited the Country." Pp. 77–87 in *Images of Central Europe in Travelogues and Fiction by North American Writers*, ed. Waldemar Zacharasiewicz. New York: Stauffenburg Verlag, 1995.

Kincaid, James. *Child-Loving: The Erotic Child and Victorian Culture*. New York: Routledge, 1992.

———. *Erotic Innocence: The Culture of Child Molesting*. Durham: Duke University Press, 1998.

King, Wilma. *Stolen Childhood: Slave Youth in Nineteenth-Century America*. Bloomington: Indiana University Press, 1995.

Klein, Herbert. *The Atlantic Slave Trade*. New York: Cambridge University Press, 1999.

Knox, Robert. *Races of Men: A Philosophical Enquiry into the Influence of Race over the Destinies of Nations* (1850), reprint. ed. London: H. Renshaw, 1862.

Kohn, Hans. *American Nationalism: An Interpretative Essay*. New York: Macmillan, 1957.

Krasner, James. *The Entangled Eye: Visual Perception and the Representation of Nature in Post-Darwinian Narrative*. New York: Oxford University Press, 1992.

Kuhn, Reinhard. *Corruption in Paradise: The Child in Western Literature*. Hanover, N.H.: University Press of New England, 1982.

Kusmer, Kenneth. "Toward a Comparative History of Racism and Xenophobia in the United States and Germany, 1865–1933." Pp. 145–81 in *Bridging the Atlantic: The Question of American Exceptionalism in Perspective*, eds. Elisabeth Glaser and Hermann Wellenreuther. New York: Cambridge University Press, 2002.

Ladd, Barbara. *Nationalism and the Color Line in George Cable, Mark Twain and William Faulkner*. Baton Rouge: Louisiana State University Press, 1996.

Lane, Christopher. *The Psychoanalysis of Race*. New York: Columbia University Press, 1998.

Lane, Lunsford. *The Narrative of Lunsford Lane*. Boston: J. C. Torrey, 1842.

Lang, Amy Schrager. *The Syntax of Class: Writing Inequality in Nineteenth-Century America*. Princeton: Princeton University Press, 2003.

Langdon, Mary. *Ida May: A Story of Things Actual and Possible*. Boston: Phillips, Sampson, 1854.

Langley, Lester. *America and the Americas: The United States in the Western Hemisphere.* Athens: University of Georgia Press, 1989.

———. *The Americas in the Modern Age.* New Haven, Conn.: Yale University Press, 2003.

Larcom, Lucy. *A New England Girlhood Outlined from Memory.* Boston: Houghton Mifflin, 1889.

Larson, Erik. *The Devil in the White City: Murder, Magic, and Madness at the Fair That Changed America.* New York: Crown, 2003.

Lazarre, Jane. *Beyond the Whiteness of Whiteness.* Durham: Duke University Press, 1995.

Lazo, Rodrigo. *Writing to Cuba: Filibustering and Cuban Exiles in the United States.* Chapel Hill: University of North Carolina Press, 2005.

Leclerc, Frédéric. *Texas and Its Revolution* (1838), trans. James Shepherd, reprint. ed. Houston: Anson Jones Press, 1950.

Lerman, Katharine. "Wilhelmine Germany." Pp. 163–85 in *Nineteenth-Century Germany: Politics, Culture, and Society 1780–1918*, ed. John Breuilly. New York: Oxford University Press, 2001.

Lerner, Laurence. *Angels and Absences: Child Deaths in the Nineteenth Century.* Nashville, Tenn.: Vanderbilt University Press, 1997.

Lesnik-Obersteined, Karín. *Children in Culture: Approaches to Childhood.* New York: St. Martin's Press, 1998.

Levin, Jerome. *Theories of the Self.* Washington, D.C.: Hemisphere, 1992.

Levine, Robert S. "Circulating the Nation: David Walker, the Missouri Compromise, and the Rise of the Black Press." Pp. 17–36 in *The Black Press: New Literary and Historical Essays*, ed. Todd Vogel. New Brunswick, N.J.: Rutgers University Press, 2001.

———. "Introduction." Pp. ix–xxxv in *Dred: A Tale of the Great Dismal Swamp.* New York: Penguin Classics, 2000.

———. "Road to Africa: Frederick Douglass's Rome." *African American Review* 34, no. 2 (Summer 2000): 217–31.

———. "Slavery, Race, and American Literary Genealogies." *Early American Literature* 36, no. 1 (2001): 89–114.

Levy, David M., and Sandra J. Peart, eds. *The Political Economy of Slavery*, vol. 4. Bristol: Thoemmes, 2004.

Levy, Leonard W., and Harlan B. Phillips. "The Roberts Case: Source of the 'Separate but Equal' Doctrine." *American Historical Review* 56, no. 3 (April 1951): 510–18.

Lewis, David Levering, ed. *W. E. B. Du Bois: A Reader.* New York: Henry Holt, 1995.

Lieber, Francis. *Essays on Property and Labour, as Connected with Natural Law and the Continuation of Society.* New York: Harper and Brothers, 1841.

Limón, José. *American Encounters: Greater Mexico, the United States, and the Erotics of Culture.* Boston: Beacon Press, 1998.

Lincoln, Abraham. "Notes for Political Speech." P. 291 in *Collected Works of Abraham*

Lincoln, vol. 6, ed. Roy Basler. New Brunswick, N.J.: Rutgers University Press, 1953.

Linke, Uli. *Blood and Nation: The European Aesthetics of Race*. Philadelphia: University of Pennsylvania Press, 1999.

Lipsitz, George. "The Possessive Investment in Whiteness: Racialized Social Democracy and the 'White' Problem in American Studies." *American Quarterly* 47 (September 1995): 369–87.

Livermore, George. *An Historical Research Respecting the Opinions of the Founders of the Republic in Negroes as Slaves, as Citizens, and as Soldiers*. Boston: A. Williams, 1862.

Locke, John. *Some Thoughts Concerning Education* (1693). Pp. 111–326 in *The Educational Writings of John Locke*, ed. James Axtell. Cambridge: Cambridge University Press, 1968.

Logan, Rayford. *Betrayal of the Negro: From Rutherford B. Hayes to Woodrow Wilson*. New York: Collier, 1965.

Love, Eric. *Race over Empire: Racism and U.S. Imperialism, 1865-1900*. Chapel Hill: University of North Carolina Press, 2004.

Lowell, James Russell. "Shall We Ever Be Republican?" Pp. 52–60 in *Anti-Slavery Papers*. New York: Houghton Mifflin, 1902.

Lyell, Sir Charles. *Travels in North America in the Years 1841-42*, 2 vols. New York: Wiley and Putnam, 1845.

Lynes, Russell. *The Domesticated Americans*. New York: Harper and Row, 1957.

Maceo, Antonio. *Antonio Maceo: Political Ideology, Letters and Other Documents*, vol. 1, ed. Cuban Society of Historical and International Study. Havana: SCEHI, 1950.

Macleod, David. *The Age of the Child: Children in America, 1890-1920*. New York: Twayne Publishers, 1998.

Mann, Arthur. *The One and the Many: Reflections on American Identity*. Chicago: University of Chicago Press, 1979.

Manners, Robert. "Cuba." Pp. 7–44 in *Cuba and Other Verse*. Chicago: Way and Williams, 1898.

Margolis, Diane Rothbard. *The Fabric of Self: A Theory of Ethics and Emotions*. New Haven, Conn.: Yale University Press, 1998.

Margolis, Joseph. *Selves and Other Texts: The Case for Cultural Realism*. University Park: Pennsylvania State University Press, 2001.

Martí, José. "My Race." Pp. 319–22 in *José Martí: Selected Writings*, ed. Esther Allen. New York: Penguin Classics, 2002.

———. "Our America" (1891). Pp. 289–96 in *José Martí: Selected Writings*, ed. Esther Allen. New York: Penguin, 2002.

Marx, Anthony. *Faith in Nation: Exclusionary Origins of Nationalism*. New York: Oxford University Press, 2003.

———. *Making Race and Nation: A Comparison of South Africa, the United States, and Brazil*. New York: Cambridge University Press, 1998.

Mason, Jennifer. *Civilized Creatures: Urban Animals, Sentimental Culture, and American Literature, 1850-1900*. Baltimore: Johns Hopkins University Press, 2005.

May, Robert E. *Manifest Destiny's Underworld: Filibustering in Antebellum America.* Chapel Hill: University of North Carolina Press, 2002.

Mayo, M. J. "The Mental Capacity of the American Negro." *Archive of Psychology* 28 (1913): 1–17, 59.

McCarthy, Tom. "The Real Little Lord Fauntleroy." *American Heritage* 21, no. 2 (1970): 50–55.

McClintock, Ann. "No Longer in a Future Heaven: Gender, Race and Nationalism." Pp. 89–112 in *Dangerous Liaisons: Gender, Nation, and Postcolonial Perspectives*, eds. Anne McClintock, Aamir Mufti, and Ella Shohat. Minneapolis: University of Minnesota Press, 1997.

McDaniel, H. F., and N. A. Taylor. *The Coming Empire; or, Two Thousand Miles in Texas on Horseback.* New York: A. S. Barnes, 1877.

McGavran, James Holt, ed. *Literature and the Child: Romantic Continuations, Postmodern Contestations.* Iowa City: University of Iowa Press, 1999.

McKee, Patricia. *Producing American Races: Henry James, William Faulkner, and Toni Morrison.* Durham: Duke University Press, 1999.

McKie, Thomas. "A Brief History of Insanity and Tuberculosis in the Southern Negro." *Journal of the American Medical Association* (March 20, 1888).

McMillan, James B. "Historical Notes on American Words." *American Speech* 21, no. 3 (1946): 180–81.

Meares, Russell. *Intimacy and Alienation: Memory, Trauma and Personal Being.* London: Routledge, 2000.

Mennel, Robert. *Thorns and Thistles: Juvenile Delinquents in the United States 1825–1940.* Hanover, N.H.: University Press of New England, 1973.

Michaels, Walter. "Jim Crow Henry James?" *Henry James Review* 16 (1995): 286–91.

———. *Our America: Nativism, Modernism, and Pluralism.* Durham: Duke University Press, 1995.

Mill, John Stuart. *The Contest in America.* Boston: Little, Brown, 1862.

———. "On Liberty." Pp. 185–321 in *The Philosophy of John Stuart Mill*, ed. Marshall Cohen. New York: Modern Library, 1961.

Mills, Charles. *Blackness Visible: Essays on Philosophy and Race.* Ithaca: Cornell University Press, 1989.

———. *From Class to Race: Essays in White Marxism and Black Radicalism.* New York: Rowman and Littlefield, 2003.

———. *The Racial Contract.* Ithaca: Cornell University Press, 1997.

Mintz, Steven. *Huck's Raft: A History of American Childhood.* Cambridge, Mass: Harvard University Press, 2004.

———. *A Prison of Expectations: The Family in Victorian Culture.* New York: New York University Press, 1983.

Mitchell, Katharyne, Sallie A. Marston, and Cindi Katz, eds. *Life's Work: Geographies of Social Reproduction.* Malden, Mass.: Blackwell, 2004.

Mommsen, Wolfgang. "The Renaissance of the Nation-State and the Historians." Pp. 283–301 in *German and American Nationalism: A Comparative Perspective*, eds. Hartmut Lehmann and Hermann Wellenreuther. Oxford: Berg, 1999.

Montejano, David. *Anglos and Mexicans in the Making of Texas, 1836–1986*. Austin: University of Texas Press, 1987.

Moon, Michael. " 'The Gentle Boy from the Dangerous Classes': Pederasty, Domesticity and Capitalism in Horatio Alger." *Representations* 19 (Summer 1987): 87–110.

———. *A Small Boy and Others: Imitation and Initiation in American Culture from Henry James to Andy Warhol*. Durham: Duke University Press, 1998.

Morgan, Edmund. *American Slavery, American Freedom: The Ordeal of Colonial Virginia*. New York: W. W. Norton, 1975.

Morrison, Toni. *Playing in the Dark: Whiteness and the Literary Imagination*. New York: Random House, 1992.

Morse, Jedediah. *The American Geography; or, A View of the Present Situation of the United States of America* (1789), reprint. ed. New York: Arno, 1970.

Morse, Josiah. "A Comparison of White and Colored Children," *Popular Science Monthly* (1914).

Morton, Oliver. *The Southern Empire, with Other Papers*. Boston: Houghton, Mifflin, 1892.

Moss, Elizabeth. *Domestic Novelists in the Old South: Defenders of Southern Culture*. Baton Rouge: Louisiana State University Press, 1992.

Murphy, Gretchen. *Hemispheric Imaginings: The Monroe Doctrine and Narratives of U.S. Empire*. Durham: Duke University Press, 2005.

Murray, Gail Schmunk. *American Children's Literature and the Construction of Childhood*. New York: Twayne Publishers, 1998.

Musgrave, George Clarke. *Under Three Flags in Cuba: A Personal Account of the Cuban Insurrection and Spanish-American War*. Boston: Little, Brown, 1899.

Nance, John M., ed. "A Letter Book of Joseph Eve." *Southwestern Historical Quarterly* 43 (1940): 493–94.

National Committee for Mental Hygiene, Inc. *Report of the Maryland Mental Hygiene Survey with Recommendations*. Baltimore, 1921.

Nealon, Christopher. *Foundlings: Lesbian and Gay Historical Emotion before Stonewall*. Durham: Duke University Press, 2001.

Newell, C. (Rev.). *History of the Revolution in Texas*. New York: Wiley and Putnam, 1838.

Newman, Judie. "Was Tom White? Stowe's *Dred* and Twain's *Pudd'nhead Wilson*." Pp. 67–81 in *Soft Canons: American Women Writers and the Masculine Tradition*, ed. Karen Kilcup. Iowa City: University of Iowa Press, 1999.

Nicholson, Philip. *Who Do We Think We Are? Race and Nation in the Modern World*. New York: Sharpe, 2001.

Nordeau, Max. *Degeneration*. New York: D. Appleton, 1895.

North, Thomas. *Five Years in Texas; or, What You Did Not Hear during the War*. Cincinnati: Elm Street Print Company, 1871.

Nourse, James D. *Remarks on the Past and Its Legacies to American Society*. Louisville: Morton and Griswold, 1847.

Nudelman, Franny. "Emblem and Product of Sin: The Poisoned Child in *The Scarlet*

Letter and Domestic Advice Literature." *Yale Journal of Criticism* 10, no. 1 (1997): 193–213.

Nussbaum, Martha. *Hiding from Humanity: Disgust, Shame and the Law*. Princeton: Princeton University Press, 2004.

Odum, Howard. *Social and Mental Traits of the Negro*. New York: AMS Press, 1910.

O'Gorman, Edmundo. *The Invention of America: An Inquiry into the Historical Nature of the New World and the Meaning of its History*. Bloomington: Indiana University Press, 1961.

Olmsted, Frederick Law. *The Cotton Kingdom* (1861), reprint. ed. New York: Modern Library, 1969.

———. *A Journey in the Seaboard Slave States in the Years 1853–1854 with Remarks on Their Economy* (1856), reprint. ed. New York: Knickerbocker Press, 1904.

———. *A Journey through Texas; or, A Saddle-Trip on the Southwestern Frontier*. New York: Dix, Edwards, 1857.

Omi, Michael, and Howard Winant, eds. *Racial Formation in the United States*. New York: Routledge, 1994.

Optic, Oliver. *Watch and Wait; or, The Young Fugitives*. Boston: Lee and Shepard.

Orsosz, Joel. *Curators and Culture: The Museum Movement in America, 1740–1870*. Tuscaloosa: University of Alabama Press, 1990.

Otis, James. *The Rights of the British Colonies Asserted and Proved*. Boston: Edes and Gill, 1765.

Otten, Thomas. "Pauline Hopkins and the Hidden Self of Race." *English Literary History* 59 (1992): 256–77.

Oviedo, Ricardo Batrell. *Para la Historia*. Havana: Seoane and Alvarez, 1912.

Paine, Thomas. *The Political Writings of Thomas Paine* (1837), reprint. ed. Middletown, N.J.: George Evans, 1837.

Parish, John Carl. *The Emergence of the Idea of Manifest Destiny*. Berkeley: University of California Press, 1932.

Parker, Theodore. *Collected Works*, vol. 5, ed. Francis P. Cobbe. London, 1863.

Paxton, Philip. *Stray Yankee in Texas*. New York: Redfield, 1853.

Pecora, Vincent, ed. *Nations and Identities: Classic Readings*. New York: Blackwell, 2001.

Perkins, Francis. "Opening Statement by the Chairman," General Session, 18 January 1940." In *Proceedings of the White House Conference on Children in a Democracy, Washington, D.C., January 18–20, 1940*, Bureau publication no. 266. Washington, D.C.: U.S. Government Printing Office, 1940.

Pernick, Martin. *The Black Stork: Eugenics and the Death of "Defective" Babies in American Medicine and Motion Pictures since 1915*. New York: Oxford University Press, 1996.

Perry, Thomas Sergeant, ed. *The Life and Letters of Francis Lieber*. Boston: J. R. Osgood, 1882.

Person, Stow, ed., *Evolutionary Thought in America*. New Haven, Conn.: Yale University Press, 1950.

Phillips, Adam. *The Beast in the Nursery: On Curiosity and Other Appetites*. New York: Vintage, 1998.

Pickens, Lucy Holcombe. *The Free Flag of Cuba* (1854), reprint. ed. Baton Rouge: Louisiana State University Press, 2002.

Pizer, Donald, ed. *The Cambridge Companion to American Realism and Naturalism*. New York: Cambridge University Press, 1995.

Plummer, Brenda Gayle. "Firmin and Martí at the Intersection of Pan-Americanism and Pan-Africanism." Pp. 210–28 in *José Martí's "Our America": From National to Hemispheric Cultural Studies*, eds. Jeffrey Belnap and Raul Fernandez. Durham: Duke University Press, 1998.

Pochmann, Henry. *German Culture in America: Philosophical and Literary Influences 1600–1900*. Madison: University of Wisconsin Press, 1957.

Poesche, Theodore, and Charles Goepp. *The New Rome; or, The United States in the World*. New York: G. P. Putnam, 1853.

Portuondo, Fernando, and Hortensia Picardo, eds. *Letters*, vol. 1. Havana: Social Science Editorial, 1982.

Posnock, Ross. *Color and Culture: Black Writers and the Making of the Modern Intellectual*. Boston: Harvard University Press, 1998.

Poulton, Edward, ed. *Charles Darwin and* The Origin of the Species: *Addresses, Etc., in America and England in the Year of the Two Anniversaries*. New York: Longman, Green, 1909.

Pratt, Julius. "The Origin of 'Manifest Destiny.'" *American Historical Review* 32 (1927): 795–98.

Preston, Samuel, and Michael Haines. *Fatal Years: Child Mortality in Late Nineteenth-Century America*. Princeton: Princeton University Press, 1991.

Pyne, Kathleen. *Art and the Higher Life: Painting and Evolutionary Though in Late Nineteenth-Century America*. Austin: University of Texas Press, 1996.

Quesada, Gonzalo de. *War in Cuba; or, the Great Struggle for Freedom*. Washington, D.C.: Liberty Publishing, 1896.

Rancière, Jacques. "Who Is the Subject of the Rights of Man?" *South Atlantic Quarterly* 103, no. 2 (2004): 297–310.

Randall, Elinor, trans. *On Education by José Martí: Articles on Educational Theory, Pedagogy, and Writings for Children from "The Age of Gold."* New York: Monthly Review Press, 1979.

Rawls, John. *Political Liberalism*. New York: Columbia University Press, 1993.

Ray, J. Morrison. "Observations upon Eye Diseases and Blindness in the Colored Race." *New York Medical Journal* (July 18, 1896): 88.

Raymond, R. H. "A Plea for Free Speech." Pp. 240–56 in *Autographs for Freedom*, ed. Julia Griffiths. Boston: Jewett, 1853.

Reed Jr., Adolph. *Class Notes: Posing as Politics and Other Thoughts on the American Scene*. New York: New Press, 2000.

———. *W. E. B. Du Bois and American Political Thought*. New York: Oxford University Press, 1997.

Reicher, Steve, and Nick Hopkins. *Self and Nation: Categorization, Contestation and Mobilization*. London: Sage Publications, 2001.

Reid, Captain Mayne. *The Boy Slaves*. Boston: Fields, Osgood, 1869.

Reinier, Jacqueline S. *From Virtue to Character: American Childhood 1775–1850*. New York: Twayne Publishers, 1996.

Renan, Ernest. "What Is a Nation?" (1882). Pp. 162–77 in *Nations and Identities: Classic Readings*, ed. Vincent Pecora. Malden, Mass.: Blackwell, 2001.

Renner, Stanley. " 'Red Hair, Very Red, Close-Curling': Sexual Hysteria, Physiognomical Bogeymen, and the 'Ghosts' in *The Turn of the Screw*." Pp. 223–42 in *Henry James: The Turn of the Screw*, ed. Peter Beidler. Boston: Bedford Books, 1995.

Report of the Decision of the Supreme Court of the United States and the Opinions of the Judges Thereof in the Case of Dred Scott v. John Sanford. December term 1856. New York: De Cap Press, 1970.

Richardson, Theresa. *The Century of the Child: The Mental Hygiene Movement and Social Policy in the United States and Canada*. New York: State University of New York Press, 1989.

Robinson, Cedric. *Black Marxism: The Making of the Black Radical Tradition*. Chapel Hill: University of North Carolina Press, 1983.

Rogin, Michael. *Fathers and Children: Andrew Jackson and the Subjugation of the American Indian*. New York: Knopf, 1975.

Romero, Rolando. "Border of Fear, Border of Desire." *Borderlines* 1, no. 1 (1993): 36–70.

Roosevelt, Theodore. *The Rough Riders*. New York: Scribner's, 1905.

Rose, Jacqueline. *The Case of Peter Pan: The Impossibility of Children's Fiction*. London: Macmillan, 1984.

Ross, Marlon. "Commentary: Pleasuring Identity, or the Delicious Politics of Belonging." *New Literary History* 31 (2000): 827–50.

Rothenberg, Paula, ed. *Race, Class and Gender in the United States: An Integrated Study*, 2d ed. New York: St. Martin's Press, 1992.

Rothfels, Nigel. "Aztecs, Aborigines, and Ape-People: Science and Freaks in Germany, 1850–1900." Pp. 158–73 in *Freakery: Cultural Spectacles of the Extraordinary Body*, ed. Rosemarie Garland Thomson. New York: New York University Press, 1996.

———. *Savages and Beasts: The Birth of the Modern Zoo*. Baltimore: Johns Hopkins University Press, 2002.

Rotker, Susan. *The American Chronicles of José Martí: Journalism and Modernity in Spanish America*, trans. Jennifer French and Katherine Semler. Hanover, N.H.: University Press of New England, 2000.

Rowe, John Carlos. *Literary Culture and U.S. Imperialism: From the Revolution to World War II*. New York: Oxford University Press, 2000.

———. *The New American Studies*. Minneapolis: University of Minnesota Press, 2002.

Rowe, John Carlos. *The Other Henry James*. Durham: Duke University Press, 1998.

Rush, Benjamin. *Of the Mode of Education Proper in a Republic* (1798). Pp. 87–97 in *Selected Writings of Benjamin Rush*, ed. Dagobert D. Runes. New York: Philosophical Library, 1947.

———. *Thoughts upon Female Education*. Philadelphia: Prichard and Hall, 1787.

Ryan, Mary. *The Cradle of the Middle Class: The Family in Oneida County New York, 1790–1865*. Cambridge, Mass.: Harvard University Press, 1981.

Ryan, Susan. "Charity Begins at Home: Stowe's Antislavery Novels and the Forms of Benevolent Citizenship." *American Literature* 72, no. 4 (December 2000): 751–82.

Saldaña-Portillo, María Josefina. " 'Wavering on the Horizon of Social Being': The Treaty of Guadalupe-Hidalgo and the Legacy of Its Racial Character in Americo Paredes's *George Washington Gómez*." *Radical History Review* 89 (Spring 2004): 135–64.

Saldívar, José David. *Border Matters: Remapping American Cultural Studies*. Berkeley: University of California Press, 1997.

Samuels, Shirley. *Romances of the Republic: Women, the Family, and Violence in the Literature of the Early American Nation*. New York: Oxford University Press, 1996.

Samuels, Shirley, ed. *The Culture of Sentiment: Race, Gender, and Sentimentality in Nineteenth-Century America*. New York: Oxford University Press, 1993.

Sánchez-Eppler, Karen. *Dependent States: Childhood, Autonomy, and Social Order in Nineteenth-Century America*. Chicago: University of Chicago Press, 2005.

Scheper-Hughes, Nancy, and Carolyn Sargent. *Small Wars: The Cultural Politics of Childhood*. Berkeley: University of California Press, 1998.

Schöllgen, Gregor, ed. *Escape into War: The Foreign Policy of Imperial Germany*. London: St. Martin's Press, 2000.

Schrager, Cynthia. "Pauline Hopkins and William James: The New Psychology and the Politics of Race." Pp. 307–30 in *Female Subjects in Black and White: Race, Psychoanalysis, Feminism*, eds. Elizabeth Abel, Barbara Christian, and Helen Moglen. Berkeley: University of California Press, 1997.

Scott, Joan. "Fantasy Echo: History and the Construction of Identity." *Critical Inquiry* 27 (2001): 285–304.

Scott, Rebecca. *Degrees of Freedom: Louisiana and Cuba after Slavery*. Cambridge, Mass.: Harvard University Press, 2005.

Searle-White, Joshua. *The Psychology of Nationalism*. New York: Palgrave, 2001.

Sedgwick, Catharine Maria. *Home*. Boston: James Munroe, 1835.

Sedgwick, Eve Kosofsky. *Epistemology of the Closet*. Berkeley: University of California Press, 1990.

Seguín, Juan. *A Revolution Remembered: The Memoirs and Selected Correspondence of Juan N. Seguín*, ed. Jesús de la Teja. Austin: State House Press, 1991.

Seiter, Ellen. *Sold Separately: Children and Parents in Consumer Cultures*. New Brunswick, N.J.: Rutgers University Press, 1993.

Semmel, Bernard. *The Liberal Ideal and the Demons of Empire: Theories of Imperialism from Adam Smith to Lenin*. Baltimore: Johns Hopkins University Press, 1993.

Sexton, Rebecca Grant. *A Southern Woman of Letters: The Correspondence of Augusta Jane Evans Wilson*. Charleston: University of South Carolina Press, 2002.

Shapiro, Ian. *Democratic Justice*. New Haven, Conn.: Yale University Press, 1999.

————. *The Evolution of Rights in Liberal Theory*. New York: Cambridge University Press, 1986.

Sharp, Granville. *Law of Liberty; or Royal Law*. London: White, 1776.

Shepherdson, Charles. *Vital Signs: Nature and Culture in Psychoanalysis*. New York: Routledge, 1998.

Shepp, James, and Daniel Shepp. *Shepp's World's Fair Photographed*. Chicago: Globe Bible Publishing, 1893.

Sherwood, Mrs. *The Recaptured Negro*. Boston: Samuel T. Armstrong, 1821.

Shi, David. *Facing Facts: Realism in American Thought and Culture, 1850–1920*. New York: Oxford University Press, 1995.

Shohat, Ella. "Columbus, Palestine and Arab-Jews: Toward a Relational Approach to Community Identity." Pp. 88–106 in *Cultural Readings of Imperialism: Edward Said and the Gravity of History*, eds. Keith Ansell-Pearson, Benita Parry, and Judith Squires. London: Lawrence and Wishart, 1997.

Sidaway, James. *Imagined Regional Communities: Integration and Sovereignty in the Global South*. New York: Routledge, 2002.

Silber, Nina. *Romance of Reunion: Northerners and the South, 1865–1900*. Chapel Hill: University of North Carolina Press, 1993.

Simms, William Gilmore. *Katharine Walton*. Chicago: Donohue, Henneberry, 1885.

————. "An Oration on the Sixty-Ninth Anniversary of American Independence." Speech presented before the Town Council, Aiken, S.C., 1844.

————. "Treatment of Slaves in the Southern States." *Southern Quarterly Review* 5, no. 9 (1852): 209–20.

Slotkin, Richard. *Regeneration through Violence: The Mythology of the American Frontier, 1600–1860*. Middletown, Conn.: Wesleyan University Press, 1973.

Smith, Anna Tolman. "A Study in Race Psychology," *Popular Science Monthly* (1897): 354–60.

Smith, Anthony. *The Ethnic Origins of Nations*. New York: Blackwell, 1986.

Smith, Ashbel. *Addresses, Etc*. Private printing, Stealing Library, Yale University, New Haven, Conn.

Smith, Felipe. *American Body Politics: Race, Gender, and Black Literary Renaissance*. Athens: University of Georgia Press, 1998.

Smith, Jon, and Deborah Cohn, eds. *Look Away! The U.S. South in New World Studies*. Durham: Duke University Press, 2004.

Smith, Shawn Michelle. *American Archives: Gender, Race, and Class in Visual Culture*. Princeton: Princeton University Press, 1999.

Smithwick, Noah. *The Evolution of a State; or, Recollections of Old Texas Days*, comp. Nanna Smithwick Donaldson. Austin: Gammel, 1900.

Sommer, Doris. *Proceed with Caution: When Engaged by Minority Writing in the Americas*. Cambridge, Mass.: Harvard University Press, 1999.

Sorby, Angela. *Schoolroom Poets: Childhood, Performance, and the Place of American Poetry, 1865–1917*. Durham: University of New Hampshire Press, 2005.

Speed, Jonathon. "The Hunt for Garza." *Harper's Weekly* (January 30, 1892).

Spencer, Herbert. *Education: Intellectual, Moral, and Physical* (1860), reprint. ed. New York: Appleton, 1898.

Spencer, Margaret, Geraldine Brookins, and Walter Allen, eds. *Beginnings: The Social and Affective Development of Black Children*. London: Lawrence Erlbaum Associates, 1985.

Stahl, J. D. "Mark Twain's 'Slovenly Peter' in the Context of Twain and German Culture." *Lion and the Unicorn* 20, no. 2. (1996): 166–80.

Steedman, Carolyn. *Strange Dislocations: Childhood and the Idea of Human Interiority, 1780–1930*. Cambridge, Mass.: Harvard University Press, 1995.

Stephens, Sharon, ed. *Children and the Politics of Culture*. Princeton: Princeton University Press, 1995.

Stimpson, Catharine. "Reading for Love: Canons, Paracanons, and Whistling Jo March." *New Literary History* 21, no. 4 (1990): 957–76.

Stoler, Ann Laura. *Carnal Knowledge and Imperial Power: Race and the Intimate in Colonial Rule*. Berkeley: University of California Press, 2002.

Stone Jr., Albert. *The Innocent Eye: Childhood in Mark Twain's Imagination*. New Haven, Conn.: Yale University Press, 1961.

Story, William. *A Treatise on the Law of Contracts Not under Seal* (1844), reprint. ed. New York: Arno Press, 1972.

Stowe, Harriet Beecher. *Household Papers and Stories*. Boston: Houghton Mifflin, 1896.

———. *Uncle Tom's Cabin; or, Life among the Lowly* (1852), reprint. ed. New York: Penguin Books, 1981.

Streeby, Shelley. *American Sensations: Class, Empire, and the Production of Popular Culture*. Berkeley: University of California Press, 2002.

Sulley, James. *Studies of Childhood* (1895), reprint. ed. New York: D. Appleton, 1914.

Sundquist, Eric. "Mark Twain and Homer Plessy." *Representations* 24 (1988): 102–28.

Tagg, John. "A Democracy of the Image: Photographic Portraiture and Commodity Production." Pp. 34–60 in *The Burden of Representation: Essays on Photographies and Histories*. Minneapolis: University of Minnesota Press, 1988.

Takaki, Ronald. *Iron Cages: Race and Culture in Nineteenth-Century America*. Seattle: University of Washington Press, 1979.

Tate, Claudia. *Psychoanalysis and Black Novels: Desire and the Protocols of Race*. New York: Oxford University Press, 1998.

Taylor, Charles. *Sources of the Self: The Making of the Modern Identity*. Cambridge, Mass.: Harvard University Press, 1989.

Thomas, Brook. "Tragedies of Race, Training, Birth and Communities of Competent Pudd'nheads." *American Literary History* 1998 1(4): 754–86.

Thomas, Emory. *The Confederate Nation, 1861–1865*. New York: Harper and Row, 1979.

Thoreau, Henry David. "A Plea for Captain John Brown." Pp. 385–433 in *Echoes of Harper's Ferry*, ed. James Redpath. Boston: Thayer and Eldridge, 1860.

Tomasi, John. *Liberalism beyond Justice: Citizens, Society, and the Boundaries of Political Theory*. Princeton: Princeton University Press, 2001.

Tompkins, Jane. *Sensational Designs: The Cultural Work of American Fiction, 1790–1860*. New York: Oxford University Press, 1985.

De Tocqueville, Alexis. *Democracy in America* (1835), reprint. ed. New York: Signet, 1956.

Toynton, Evelyn. *Growing Up in America, 1830–1860*. Brookfield, Conn: Millbrook Press, 1995.

Trilling, Lionel. *The Liberal Imagination: Essays on Literature and Society*. New York: Viking Press, 1950.

Tucker, St. George. *A Dissertation on Slavery: With a Proposal for the Gradual Abolition of It in the State of Virginia* (1796), reprint. ed. Westport, Conn.: Negro Universities Press, 1970.

Tutorow, Norman. *Texas Annexation and the Mexican War: A Political Study of the Old Northwest*. Palo Alto, Calif.: Chadwick House, 1987.

Twain, Mark. "The German Chicago." Pp. 244–62 in *The Complete Works of Mark Twain* (1891), reprint. ed. New York: Harper and Brothers, 1925.

———. *Pudd'nhead Wilson and Those Extraordinary Twins* (1894), reprint. ed. New York: Penguin, 1969.

———. *Slovenly Peter: or Happy Tales and Funny Pictures*. Druck: Appl, Wemding, 1985.

vom Bruch, Rüdiger. "Culture as an Expression of Nationalist Values in Germany." Pp. 165–85 in *German and American Nationalism: A Comparative Perspective*, eds. Harmut Lehmann and Hermann Wellenreuther. Oxford: Berg, 1999.

Wald, Priscilla. *Constituting Americans: Cultural Anxiety and Narrative Form*. Durham: Duke University Press, 1995.

Walker, Lennie. "South's First Woman Novelist Started Career Here." *San Antonio Express* (October 6, 1935).

Walsh, Kevin. *The Representation of the Past: Museums and Heritage in the Post-Modern World*. London: Routledge, 1992.

Ward, Forrest. "Pre-Revolutionary Activity in Brazoria County." *Southwestern Historical Quarterly* 65 (1960): 212–31.

Warner, Michael. "Zones of Privacy." Pp. 75–113 in *What's Left of Theory? New Work on the Politics of Literary Theory*. eds. Judith Butler, John Guillory, and Kendall Thomas. New York: Routledge, 2000.

Warren, James Perrin. *Culture of Eloquence: Oratory and Reform in Antebellum America*. University Park: Pennsylvania State University Press, 1999.

Warren, Kenneth. *Black and White Strangers: Race and American Literary Realism*. Chicago: University of Chicago Press, 1993.

Washington, Booker T. "Signs of Progress among the Negroes." *Century Magazine* 59 (1900): 472–78.

Webster, Noah. *A Grammatical Institute of the English Language*, part 1 (1783), reprint. ed. Menston, U.K.: Scolar Press, 1968.

Weinberg, Albert K. *Manifest Destiny: A Study of Nationalist Expansionism in American History*. Baltimore: Johns Hopkins University Press, 1935.

Weinstein, Cindy. *Family, Kinship, and Sympathy in Nineteenth-Century American Literature*. New York: Cambridge University Press, 2004.

————. "A Sort of Adopted Daughter: Family Relations in *The Lamplighter*." ELH 68, no. 4 (2001): 1023–47.

Welch, William L. "Lorenzo Sabine and the Assault on Sumner." *New England Quarterly* 65 (1992): 298–302.

Wertheimer, Eric. *Imagined Empires: Incas, Aztecs, and the New World of American Literature, 1771–1876*. New York: Cambridge University Press, 1999.

West, Cornel. "The Dilemma of the Black Intellectual." *Critical Quarterly* 29, no. 4 (Winter 1987): 39–52.

West, Elliot, and Paula Petrik. *Small Worlds: Children and Adolescents in America, 1850–1950*. Lawrence: University of Kansas Press, 1992.

Westfahl, Gary, and George Slusser, eds. *Nursery Realms: Children in the Worlds of Science Fiction, Fantasy, and Horror*. Athens: University of Georgia Press, 1999.

Wexler, Laura. *Tender Violence: Domestic Visions in an Age of U.S. Imperialism*. Chapel Hill: University of North Carolina Press, 2000.

————. "Tender Violence: Literary Eavesdropping, Domestic, Fiction, and Educational Reform." Pp. 12–32 in *The Culture of Sentiment: Race, Gender, and Sentimentality in Nineteenth-Century America*, ed. Shirley Samuels. New York: Oxford University Press, 1993.

Wheatley, Phillis. "To the Right Honorable William Earl of Dartmouth." Pp. 69 in *Poems on Various Subjects, Religious and Moral*. London: A. Bell, 1773.

Wheeler, Joseph (Gen.), Herschel V. Cashin, Charles Alexander, William Anderson, Arthur M. Brown, and Horace W. Bivins. *Under Fire with the 10th U.S. Cavalry: A Purely Military History of the Negro*. New York: F. Tennyson Neely, 1899.

Whitaker, Arthur. *The Western Hemisphere Idea: Its Rise and Decline*. Ithaca: Cornell University Press, 1954.

Whitman, Mark, ed. *Removing a Badge of Slavery: The Record of Brown v. Board of Education*. Princeton: Markus Wiener, 1993.

Whitman, Walt. "Democratic Vistas." Pp. 235–47 in *Selected Poems and Prose* (1892), ed. A. Norman Jeffares, reprint. ed. New York: Oxford University Press, 1966.

————. "There Was a Child Went Forth." Pp. 2117–18 in *Anthology of American Literature*, vol. 1, eds. George McMichael, J. C. Levenson, and Leo Marx. Upper Saddle River, N.J.: Prentice Hall, 2000.

Willard, Charles. *Liberalism and the Problem of Knowledge: A New Rhetoric for Modern Democracy*. Chicago: University of Chicago Press, 1996.

Williams, Susan S. " 'Promoting an Extensive Sale': The Production and Reception of *The Lamplighter*." *New England Quarterly* 69, no. 2 (1996): 179–200.

Wilson, Anna. "*Little Lord Fauntleroy*: The Darling of Mothers and the Abomination of a Generation." *American Literary History* 18 (1996): 232–58.

Wishy, Bernard. *The Child and the Republic: The Dawn of American Child Nurture.* Philadelphia: University of Pennsylvania Press, 1968.

Woolman, John. *Considerations on the Keeping of Negroes* (1754), reprint. ed. Northampton, Mass.: Gehenna Press, 1970.

Yelland, Nicola, ed. *Gender in Early Childhood.* London: Routledge, 1998.

Yellin, Jean Fagan. *Women and Sisters: The Antislavery Feminists in American Culture.* New Haven, Conn.: Yale University Press, 1989.

Young, Elizabeth. *Disarming the Nation: Women's Writing and the American Civil War.* Chicago: University of Chicago Press, 1999.

Zack, Naomi. *Philosophy of Science and Race.* New York: Routledge, 2002.

Zelizer, Viviana A. *Pricing the Priceless Child: The Changing Social Value of Children.* New York: Basic Books, 1985.

Žižek, Slavoj. "Enjoy Your Nation as Yourself!" Pp. 200–37 in *Tarrying with the Negative: Kant, Hegel, and the Critique of Ideology.* Durham: Duke University Press, 1993.

———. *The Plague of Fantasies: Kant, Hegel, and the Critique of Ideology.* London: Verso, 1997.

INDEX

Caroline Levander is a professor of English and director of the Humanities Research Center at Rice University. She is the author of *Voices of the Nation: Women and Public Speech in Nineteenth-Century American Literature and Culture* (Cambridge, 1998) and coeditor, with Carol J. Singley, of *The American Child: A Cultural Studies Reader* (Rutgers, 2003).

Library of Congress Cataloging-in-Publication Data

Levander, Caroline Field.
Cradle of liberty : race, the child, and national belonging from Thomas Jefferson to W. E. B. Du Bois / Caroline F. Levander.
p. cm.
Includes bibliographical references and index.
ISBN-13: 978-0-8223-3856-7 (cloth : alk. paper)
ISBN-10: 0-8223-3856-4 (cloth : alk. paper)
ISBN-13: 978-0-8223-3872-7 (pbk. : alk. paper)
ISBN-10: 0-8223-3872-6 (pbk. : alk. paper)
1. Children's rights—United States. 2. United States—Ethnic relations.
3. Children in literature. I. Title.
HQ789.L48 2006
305.23089'00973—dc22
2006012767